The Craft and Art of Scenic Design

The Craft and Art of Scenic Design: Strategies, Concepts, and Resources explores how to design stage scenery from a practical and conceptual perspective. Discussion of conceptualizing the design through script analysis and research is followed by a comprehensive overview of execution: collaboration with directors and other designers, working with spaces, developing an effective design process, and the aesthetics of stage design. This book features case studies, key words, tip boxes, definitions, and chapter exercises. Additionally, it provides advice on portfolio and career development, contracts, and working with a union.

Robert Klingelhoefer is Associate Professor of Scenic Design and Director of the Design and Technology Program in the School of Theatre and Dance at West Virginia University. Mr. Klingelhoefer has previously been Resident Designer for the Fulton Theatre in Lancaster, Pennsylvania; the Contemporary American Theatre Festival in Shepherdstown, West Virginia; and the Jean Cocteau Repertory Theatre and Pan Asian Repertory Theatre, both in New York City. His work has been seen nationwide for companies including the Walnut Street Theatre, Capital Repertory Theatre, the Asolo Theatre, Phoenix Theatre Ensemble, and the New York State Theatre Institute, among many others. Internationally he has had productions performed at the International Festival of Experimental Theatre in Cairo, Egypt, and the Market Theatre in Johannesburg, South Africa. He has been a member of United Scenic Artists, Local 829, since 1983.

The Craft and Art of Scenic Design

Strategies, Concepts, and Resources

Robert Klingelhoefer

NEW YORK AND LONDON

First published 2017
by Routledge
711 Third Avenue, New York, NY 10017

and by Routledge
2 Park Square, Milton Park, Abingdon, Oxon OX14 4RN

Routledge is an imprint of the Taylor & Francis Group, an informa business

Library of Congress Cataloging-in-Publication Data
Names: Klingelhoefer, Robert, author.
Title: The craft and art of scenic design : strategies, concepts, and resources / Robert Klingelhoefer.
Description: New York : Routledge, 2017. | Includes bibliographical references and index.
Identifiers: LCCN 2016023160 | ISBN 9781138183773 (hbk : alk. paper) |
    ISBN 9781138937642 (pbk : alk. paper) | ISBN 9781315676173 (ebk : alk. paper)
Subjects: LCSH: Theaters—Stage-setting and scenery.
Classification: LCC PN2091.S8 K485 2017 | DDC 792.02/5—dc23
LC record available at https://lccn.loc.gov/2016023160

ISBN: 978-1-138-93765-9 (hbk)
ISBN: 978-1-138-93764-2 (pbk)
ISBN: 978-1-315-67617-3 (ebk)

Typeset in Gill Sans Std & Avenir LT Std
by Apex CoVantage, LLC

CONTENTS

ACKNOWLEDGMENTS

In the midst of trying to create a book that aspires to teach a craft and art that I have practiced for 40 years and taught for 10, I think about how many people have been involved in my own education.

At 15, I fell down the rabbit hole to find myself working as a volunteer in a professional theatre. The first play I ever saw was one I had worked on: Shakespeare's *Julius Caesar*. I sat in the dark theatre and saw magic created with the lights I had hung and the scenery I had painted. With even more unbelievable luck, I fell under the tutelage of the company's resident set designers, who saw something in me that I didn't know existed. I thank them for their insight, their kindness, and those early lessons.

I was on fire. I inhaled every book on scene design I could get my hands on. When it was time to start an undergraduate program, I was so impatient to begin actually designing that I was a terrible student, full of myself and difficult to deal with, I'm sure. I did learn a lot from my design professor, Davy Davis, in spite of myself. We kept in touch over the years, and he has been one of my key sounding boards for this project, test-driving parts of it with his students and giving me feedback. I'm very grateful.

By my junior year I was getting design jobs at small professional theatres, dinner theatres, and an opera company and quit school to work. I couldn't make any other choice. I thank the producers who had the bravery to hire a very young, very raw designer. I learned a lot from realizing as I worked on those early projects how much I didn't know.

When I had worked a few years in this market, I used summer stock as a way to move on. That first summer of stock taught me an enormous amount as I designed seven shows between April and October and painted them as well. At the end of that season I moved to New York and was soon designing workshops and for small companies.

A designer's career is formed largely by his relationships with directors, and among the many I have been lucky enough to learn from, three stand out as requiring special thanks.

Paul Giovanni, Eve Adamson, and Michael Mitchell taught me so much about how to design but even more about how to live a life in the theatre with grace and passion. I am as proud to have had them as my friends as I am of the work we did together.

I would like to thank my colleagues at West Virginia University, who made my transition from the professional world to the academic one so easy and pleasant. I came to teaching late and could not have begun it as smoothly without them.

Most teachers soon realize how much they learn from their students, and I'd like to thank all of mine.

Next, I have to thank those who helped this book become what it is by contributing photos of their amazing work: Alexander Dodge, Robert Israel, Jaroslav Malina, Walt Spangler, Paul Steinberg, and George Tsypin. A big thank you, also, to Stacey Walker and Meredith Darnell at Taylor & Francis for their guidance.

And finally, to the most important people in my life: Debbie, the girl who moved to New York with me, all those years ago, my partner in life and art, and our son, Matt, who grew up around it all. Your love, and patience, have made it all worthwhile.

INTRODUCTION

CRAFT (AND ART)

The terms **craft** and **art** sometimes seem to be in opposition. Craft often sounds inferior to art, as in a "craft project" as opposed to a work of "fine art." Art often sounds full of mysterious, intangible qualities while craft seems to consist of definable goals and practice-able steps.

Most of any art form is craft. When work is of an extremely high level of craft, it can create a spark of connection with its viewer. When this spark occurs, all the sweat and worry, all the craft transcends into a moment of surprise, a flash of meaning.

All aspects of the scene designer's work can be approached as craft. The challenge is to recognize the importance of all the decisions that need to be made. A well-chosen chair placed in a useful position onstage is in many ways one of the most important decisions to be made, and that chair needs to be chosen and placed with craft.

Even the aspects of the work that seem the most intangible, can be approached with craft. The study of the text, research, and conceptual thinking are skills best practiced and mastered with planning, thoroughness, and purpose.

The scenic designer must have knowledge of, and abilities in, a daunting variety of areas.

In 1941, Robert Edmond Jones wrote:

A Stage Designer is, in a very real sense, a jack-of-all-trades. He can make blueprints and murals and patterns and light plots. He can design fireplaces and bodices and bridges and wigs. He understands architecture but is not an architect: can paint a portrait, but is not a painter; creates costumes but is not a couturier. Although he is able to call upon any or all of these varied gifts at will, he is not concerned with any one of them for its own sake. These talents are only the tools of his trade.[1]

It is hard to improve on Robert Edmond Jones, but we could add more to the list: strong management and interpersonal skills; a working knowledge of construction in wood, metal, and plastics; and today, 75 years later, skills using a dazzling, ever-changing array of digital tools.

The scope of these skills presents a challenge when approaching the training of students preparing to enter the field. A typical BFA program in Theatre Design and Technology spends the freshman year bringing the student to a foundation level in all aspects of theatre. In the sophomore year, the basic elements of design and drafting, by hand and CAD, are introduced as design students begin to specialize into general training in theatre design and technology. In the junior year they take a scene design course, their first stand-alone course in that craft. In their few remaining semesters their instructors hope to get them polished enough to join the profession at an entry-level position or go on to grad school. At the graduate level, the student designer is expected to be in command of his skills so he can develop his identity as an artist.

There is so much to learn, and teach, in so little time.

The scenic designer is a problem solver.

The problems he solves, and questions he must answer, are of many different types.

Some are about understanding the theatrical text that is at the core of his project. What does the play mean? What does the playwright intend it to mean, what does it mean to the designer and his collaborators, and what will it, or should it, mean to a contemporary audience?

For all answers to these questions, the designer must ask: What do I need to learn about the places, people, things, and ideas that are a part of this problem?

Some of the questions are more concrete. What is needed to present this play in the way we are considering? What should the space it is presented in be like? What is the theatre space we will actually be using like? If these two answers are different, how will we resolve that difference?

So many questions.

The answers arrived at will be unique to the individual designer, working with a particular director on a specific production.

The answers will make the set what it is and determine how well it works. The answers will make it the artistic expression of the designer and his collaborators.

This book is not about the answers; it is about the questions.

The answers cannot be taught; they cannot be told to you. The designer must find the answers for himself in both senses; he himself must find them, and the answers he seeks are answers for him only.

It is the goal of this book to help students of the craft examine these questions, understand them and their implications clearly, and develop strategies as to how to begin to answer them. It is conceived with the hope that a text that focuses on the design process, giving information on aspects of it that the designer might consider at each step of the way, some strategies that might help him make stronger decisions, and some resources that would help him execute those plans might be useful.

It is my hope that in using this text as a general resource to their training, students will find a guide to make their learning curve less steep.

To accomplish this, designs that deal with these questions will be shown, not as definitive answers but to help clarify the process. In looking at these case studies it strikes me how often the key to the design was a small thing, a connection. The way two images bump up against each other and make something that was not there before. The way an idea or an object that seemed to be from the past can, in the blink of an eye, seem as of the present as your next breath.

I am very aware that any designer's attempt to create such a work is doomed to be limited by his own range of knowledge and skill. The only solution to this seems to be to plow, humbly, forward with one's own, admittedly somewhat subjective, ideas and, like in the theatre, hope your audience will suspend its disbelief and go along for the ride.

NOTE

1. Robert Edmond Jones, *The Dramatic Imagination* (New York: Theatre Arts Books, 1941), 69.

CHAPTER I

THE NATURE OF THE CRAFT

Design for the theatre is a very special field. In the chapters that follow we will attempt to look at it through the prism of its individual aspects: work with the director and with the text, research, the design idea, and using theatrical space. In this first chapter, however, it seems necessary to look at the craft and art as a whole and attempt to define what is at its core: **the nature of the craft**.

This is not easy.

Each project the scenic designer undertakes has its own demands, ranging wildly in style, period, and intent. His work is in collaboration with others whose work he affects and who's in turn affects his. He may go from a large stage to a tiny one in a variety of architectural forms. The style of his designs may vary from realism to abstraction to poetic to industrial in four successive, or even concurrent, projects. And no two designers will approach the same play in the same way.

A single statement that attempts to define the goals of the scenic designer is therefore difficult to make, but a good place to start might be:

The scenic designer's task is to imagine and plan the visual and physical aspects of how a particular performance-event will be presented in a particular space.

Imagine and **plan** speak to the two sides of the designer's work. Imagine implies the creation of something new, of something that does not yet exist. Plan implies the process of executing these creative thoughts. It can be said that the designer's work is 10 percent inspiration and 90 percent organization and communication, but the creative phase is, of course, crucial to creating a good design, and organization and communication are critical to shepherding that creation through the process of its construction until it arrives onstage and the actors and the audience make it complete. The designer may create beautiful renderings and models and meticulous drafting as part of this process, but the designer's true "product" is a performance environment in which the play takes place.

Visual and **physical** speak to how this environment will look and how it will work. The designer does not simply make pictures. He is, in fact, more concerned with problem solving; the problems he solves involve not just the practical but the aesthetic and the emotional. What does the play need to work in the space? This includes the tangible objects required like a chair, a window, and a spinning wheel, but also a certain quality of space and a certain mood.

Particular speaks to the fact that the designer's work is always one-of-a-kind, a particular play, in a particular space, with a particular team of collaborators, at a particular moment in their lives and in history.

ASSESSING DESIGN

Work in the field of scenic design has an obligation to serve the play for which it is created. This means that the breadth of design work being done at any given time will be as wide-ranging in style and intent as the plays being produced at that time. Because design serves the play, its assessment must include its appropriateness for that play. This is very subjective.

Another handicap to evaluating stage design is that we must acknowledge that it is very difficult to fully assess a design without seeing it in production, in real time, with all the other elements that are a part of the production in place to contribute to the overall impact of the performance. From photographs alone so much is lost, but theatre is a temporal art; it is here and then gone. If we are to learn from it, we must make do with what evidence we have.

In a field made so diverse by the range of theatre literature, and the immeasurable differences in designers' and directors' approaches to that work, can we say what good design is objectively? Not completely. But, again, to begin the work we need to try.

After filtering out as many of the variables and as much of my personal taste as I can, the following is a list of three things that might serve to define a successful design:

- **The scenic design supports and extends ideas in the play.**

- **The scenic design effectively and creatively solves problems of presenting the play in the given space and production circumstances.**

- **The scenic design seems of the present, a contemporary view of the play, valid and interesting for a contemporary audience**.

To supply more detail let's examine each of these items individually:

The scenic design supports and extends ideas in the play. Support of the ideas in the play would seem obvious but for the many ways it can go wrong. The designer cannot support the ideas of the play if he has not put enough work into understanding those ideas. Designers are visual artists, and sometimes their visual skills take them too quickly past reading, researching, and talking about the play, to the creation of visually strong designs, which on closer examination do not fully fit the play. While what "fits the play" is very subjective, aspiring to this, in his own way, must be considered one of the designer's chief goals.

Extending ideas in the play concerns taking the playwright's ideas past how they are presented in the play or in a different direction than the playwright imagined. This may at first sound like an imposition on the play,

and it indeed can be. But when the playwright lets his manuscript, written in solitude, out into the world to be produced the play is forever changed. A director, several designers, and a cast of actors will bring out ideas in the text that the playwright may only have given cursory thought to. Think of the different colors and textures different actors of great skill have brought to the same role: Lee J. Cobb and Phillip Seymour Hoffman as Willie Loman or Laurence Olivier and Kevin Spacey as Richard III. Different designers' approaches will lead to colors and textures that can add just as much to the production.

Sometimes a play written in the past has different meanings in the present than the playwright could have imagined, and the production team will be responsible for explaining this meaning to a modern audience by either putting it in a context that makes the premise more understandable or simply by addressing its meaning in the present. The First Folio lists *The Merchant of Venice* as a comedy, and one of the shocks of producing the play is that most of the text is indeed a delightful romantic comedy. This comes as a shock because in the contemporary world we are so aware of the anti-Semitism in the play. This element changes how we feel about the play in a post-Holocaust world. While racism has never been right, and should be called out wherever it appears, in Shakespeare's time it did not present the ethical dilemma it does today. Do we let this aspect of the play change profoundly how the play is perceived?

The scenic design effectively and creatively solves problems of presenting the play in the given space and production circumstances. The second key part of the scenic designer's task is his challenge to make the ideas and required elements in the text work in the finite space in which the play will be performed and solving problems presented by this initial coming together of potential and reality. Often ideas and requirements in the play will be at odds with the space or budget parameters. The space may be too small for some element in the play or too large for its budget. The director and the scenic designer are charged with making these challenges work. The solutions may range from simple nips and tucks to more severe changes. Big, complex plays and musicals may require a profound re-imagining of the work.

Most productions have to make hard decisions about what to do and how to do it within a budget made months before the design work began, sometimes without much consideration of the design and technical needs of the piece. The designer's goal should always be to use conceptual ideas to reconceive the production in ways that make the space and budget work. This is a fundamental part of his mission, and not doing so will only force cuts late in the process that can only weaken the design.

The scenic design seems of the present, a contemporary view of the play, valid and interesting for contemporary audiences. It can be said that all theatre is contemporary because it is always a live performance event. Regardless of the period in which the play was written or is set, the performance is now. While not every play may want an aggressively contemporary-looking design, the designer's work acts as a bridge between the history of the play and today's audience.

Production: *Oklahoma!*

The designs for this production of *Oklahoma!* may serve to illustrate some of these ideas. One reason to choose it for this purpose is that *Oklahoma!* is, on the face of it, a pretty straightforward musical from the era of great musicals. It is well known. It is safe.

In planning any production, the designer and director look at the text of the play from many different viewpoints. Much of this book is an examination of that work. The decisions made in the design process shape what is put on the stage. In planning this production of *Oklahoma!* it was decided that while the story is essentially realistic, its tone, especially in the music and lyrics, becomes something of a fantasy, a dream of life in a better time in a golden, open place. Oscar Hammerstein II was determined to turn the description at the beginning of Lynn Riggs's play *Green Grow the Lilacs*, on which Oklahoma is based, into lyrics his audience would hear:

> It is a radiant summer morning several years ago, the kind of morning which, enveloping the shapes of earth—men, cattle in a meadow, blades of young corn, streams—makes them seem to exist now for the first time, their images giving off a golden emanation that is partly true and partly a trick of the imagination, focusing to keep alive a loveliness that may pass away.[1]

It was decided for this production that the character at the center of the play was Laurey. This was her dream; the summer of a young woman on the edge of growing up, and falling in love.

The first photo (**Figure 1.1**) is a preshow look.[2] The production used no front curtain and this is what the audience saw when it entered the theatre. A large window frame hung in the space with long trailing gauzy curtains that an unseen fan blew lazily. It was an image of summer breezes that might trigger an emotional response in audience members. The window image

FIGURE 1.1   *Preshow*

would repeat in the Dream Ballet (**Figure 1.4**) and the wedding scene where it would be made clear for the first time that this was Laurey's bedroom window.

The window hangs at a skewed angle. The portals also are skewed.

> **Skew**—an oblique or slanting movement, position, or direction.

This simple change of angle sends a message to the audience that this production will have a feeling of fantasy. To counter that, most elements of the set appear to be made of rough wood, which would be a realistic material for the time and place in which the play is set. However, this material choice extends to elements that, in realism, would not be made of these materials, like the slatted cloud unit up center. This intentionally mixed message suggests that this world is both real and a fantasy and has,

FIGURE 1.2   *Laurey's farm house*

FIGURE 1.3   *The Smokehouse*

FIGURE 1.4 *Dream Ballet*

hopefully, a charming and unexpected feeling. It is also inherently theatrical, suggesting that this is not an attempt at reproducing reality.

The slatted cloud unit was in almost every scene. It rose into view during the overture. The use of the **element of design: line** in the designs was very intentional, with horizontal lines used in calmer moments, and angled chaotic lines used in more disturbing moments like Jud's Smokehouse (**Figure 1.3**) and the Dream Ballet where a cut-drop flew in combining with the motion of the cloud unit to give the feeling of a forming tornado.

> **The elements of design** (line, shape, form, texture, color, etc.) are the building blocks of all art forms and basic descriptors used in their analysis.

For all its strong visuals, the set was actually relatively simple, allowing it to move quickly and smoothly. It tried to create a fresh look that would let the audience experience Laurie's summer fantasy in a new way even if they had seen *Oklahoma!* many times.

Production Credits

Oklahoma! Fulton Theatre, 2008
Director: Michael Mitchell
Set Design: Robert Klingelhoefer
Costume Design: Beth Dunkleberger
Light Design: Paul Black

A LANGUAGE OF CLUES

The designer works with elements and materials that communicate to the audience. These messages are sent individually and in combinations. The color may communicate one thing and the shapes of the architectural elements used another, or they may work together in harmony. There is no right or wrong in this.

What matters is that the designer controls the message. His work can be thought of as a **language of clues**. He chooses the elements he uses to communicate a feeling about the play to the audience.

Because he works in a finite space with limited means, the designer seeks shapes and materials that can stand in for elements he cannot, or chooses not to, use.

FIGURE 1.5 *Scenic trees*

What he is doing by making these choices is creating clues that serve as signposts for audience members, signposts that tell them a bit of necessary information.

Perhaps only God can make a tree, but the scenic designer will make a wide variety of stand-in trees (**Figure 1.5**). A realistic tree is seldom attempted onstage, first, because it is difficult and expensive to create a tree that seems realistic, with hundreds of branches and thousands of leaves. Second, and more important, the theatre is inherently unrealistic. It can suggest realism, when it chooses to, but is, on a very basic level, a heightened artificial art form that depends on its audience's ability to suspend disbelief, accept the artifice of the form, and go along with the story presented. This artifice makes a real tree seem wrong onstage, somehow, like words spoken in a lost language.

Arnold Aronson in his *Looking Into the Abyss: Essays on Scenography* writes, "Yet in the contemporary world it is virtually impossible to fool anyone through scenography; even the most cleverly done trees are perceived as signs of trees."[3]

Therefore, for both practical and aesthetic reasons, the designer will imagine tree stand-ins for a wide variety of show-specific designs. In the theatre things are always subjective, always seen through the filter of the project at hand. A tree in a comedy is not the same as a tree in a tragedy. A tree in *Macbeth* is not the same as one in *Love's Labour's Lost*.

It is the nature of the craft that a stick of wood, some paint, and a piece of fabric can, as if by alchemy, create an image in the audience's imagination, an image that is more than the sum of its parts.

Comparing film and theatre, Aronson writes,

The cinematic image transforms even the most blatant fantasy into reality. The theater, on the other hand, though composed of real objects—wood, canvas, paint, papier-mache, and the like—transforms a concrete reality into a kind of fantasy. Everything on the stage becomes a sign.[4]

The designer's clues combine to evoke in the audience a feeling, an emotion, a somewhat undefined memory, like a dream you can't quite remember. His work should be curiously unfinished and provoke interest in the audience to know more.

The designer's work is not complete until it is part of the performance. The clues he gives suggest meaning without delivering complete information. The set does not tell the story. It provides a space that allows the story to be told within it. There is a sense in a good design of incompleteness, a waiting for the performers to tell the story that will bring the entire event together. This requires boldness and restraint; an acknowledgement of how your work is a part of the whole.

SUMMARY

Scenic design is a complex craft, which uses a special language of space and image to communicate ideas to the audience in an often subliminal way that will complement and support the story and help give it life.

NOTES

1. Lynn Rigs, *Green Grow the Lilacs* quoted in Richard Rodgers and Oscar Hammerstein II, *Six Plays by Rodgers and Hammerstein* (New York: Random House, 1942), 7.
2. Unless otherwise credited, all photos and illustrations are the work of the author.
3. Arnold Aronson, *Looking Into the Abyss: Essays on Scenography* (Ann Arbor: University of Michigan Press, 2003), 20.
4. Aronson, *Looking Into the Abyss: Essays on Scenography*, 91.

CHAPTER 2

SCENIC DESIGN IN THE PAST AND TODAY

To work seriously in any field, it is necessary to understand both something of its history and the characteristics of the work being done today. The theatre has a long and distinguished history. The role of scenic design in it has changed quite a bit over the centuries but never so much as in the last 100 years.

A (VERY) BRIEF HISTORY OF STAGE DESIGN

The Greek and Roman Theatre

To start at the beginning, the theatre of ancient Greece and Rome was a fixed architectural form that placed the audience in an arc around a performance space, providing a focused playing area and an architectural background that contained some permanent entrances (**Figure 2.1**). For the most part this background was not scenic. It did not give specific information as to location or mood. There may have been the use some scenic treatments and of stage machinery—the crane of deus ex machina fame, and *periaktoi*, three-sided rotating panels—but this is uncertain. Much of what Greek and Roman performances were like is lost to us.

What remains is a relationship, in architecture, between storyteller and audience.

The Elizabethan Stage

This open stage form is also very much the Elizabethan model (**Figure 2.2**). Shakespeare's Globe

FIGURE 2.1 *The theatre at Epidarus*
© Ekaterina Pokrovsky / Shutterstock.com

was a performance space that did not change scenically very much from palace to heath. Scenes were played in front of an architectural facade that provided doors for entrances and exits, and a raised balcony. Shakespeare wrote most of his scenes with characters entering at the beginning of the scene and exiting at the end because there was no scenic or lighting solution to how they could appear or disappear. Ever practical, the playwright solved the problem, often having the players announce the location they were entering. Again, stage machinery may have been used in a modest way, and there may have been scenic treatments involved, such as the painted "heavens" on the ceiling above the stage.

Revival of the Elizabethan stage form in the mid-twentieth century brought the term **open stage** into common use. It is generally used for a thrust stage form in which the performance space pushes into the audience, and scenic components are generally more sculptural and less complete than in the proscenium form.

Asian Theatre

This fixed architectural "non-scenic" approach is cross-cultural, with Asian theatre examples such as Japanese Noh and Kabuki, and Chinese Opera having very strict, "non-scenic" solutions to staging. The Noh stage, shown in **Figure 2.3**, codified the actor's movement and positions onstage, and even the building materials of the stage, the traditional choice being unfinished hinoki wood. Painted on the back wall of the stage is the *kagami-ita*, a tree symbolic as the manner of entrance of spirits onto the stage. It is a metaphor for the act of theatre, not a scenic element representing a location.

The Seventeenth and Eighteenth Centuries

The Baroque Theatre, following Renaissance developments in perspective, saw the rise of the Proscenium stage form, which is still the most common today. This form of theatre architecture placed the audience so that it looked at the stage through a frame that tightened the viewing angle so perspective effects of the painted scenery, most often of elaborate architecture, would work. This form of production stayed in practice throughout the seventeenth and eighteenth centuries. Cesky Krumholz Castle in the Czech Republic, shown in **Figure 2.4**, was built in 1680–1682 and renovated with modern stage machinery in 1765. It is one of very few

FIGURE 2.2   *The new Globe Theatre*
Julia Fikse | Dreamstime.com

FIGURE 2.3   *Noh theatre*

© Hayakato / Shutterstock.com

FIGURE 2.4   *Castle Cesky Krumholz Theatre, Czech Republic*

Alexwardle at Wikipedia.en.org (public domain)

Baroque theatres that have survived still containing some of its original scenery.

The Nineteenth Century

In the nineteenth century the dramatic style in fashion became Naturalism but basically continued this pictorial scenic form (see **Figure 2.5**), but with its subject matter changing from gods and kings to more ordinary people and locations. Another facet of the theatre of the nineteenth century was that because its scenery was often ordered from a stock list of generic locales made by a Scenic Studio (#7B Moonlit Lake or #32 Fancy Castle) and costumes were often chosen by the individual actor, there was a lack of unity, of cohesiveness, in the look of productions. As more and more theatre artists thought this should change, the job of designer was born.

Modern Stage Design

The changes in the late nineteenth and early twentieth centuries that ushered in the modern period of stage design roughly paralleled the changes that were occurring in the birth of modern art. The arts changed for many reasons, but two important factors were the advent of photography and psychology. Photography took away from art what had been its principal function, recording visual reality. Psychology initiated the study of the inner self, and writers in all media began to look inside. Art was free to follow. The art movements of symbolism, expressionism, and many others became important.

In stage design, the realistic two-dimensional painting previously in vogue began to seem busy, dated, and false. Many theatre artists began to work toward a simplified, less literal look. Two designers of note at this time, Edward Gordon Craig and Adolphe Appia, wrote articles and books on these new ideas that became very influential. Both advocated a clean architectural space on stage in which detail would be replaced by mood and the actor would move through a spare three-dimensional space (see **Figure 2.6**). Integral to their ideas was a new technology. Electric lighting had become technically feasible onstage, and this made possible the use of lighting as a design element.

The period of Modern Stage Design was born.

FIGURE 2.5   *Production still,* If I Were King, *New York, 1901*
Courtesy of the Museum of the City of New York

FIGURE 2.6 *Edward Gordon Craig's model for* Hamlet, *Moscow Art Theatre, 1911*
Wikimedia.org (public domain)

Modern Stage Design

Modern Stage Design would be characterized by:

Simplification: In revolting against strict naturalism, designers would eliminate detail that was visually unnecessary so it would not distract from the story and the performer. With this simplification would come more use of symbolic and metaphoric imagery.

Unification: A major part of the new design was the realization that all elements of a production should be unified and therefore designed. This period gives rise to the profession of stage designer as we understand it today.

Lighting as a design element: Electrical stage lighting was just becoming possible in this period and designers were first seeing how important designed light would be to the new ideas. Changeable lighting would go hand-in-hand with the new simplified architectural use of space.

Three-dimensionality: Scenery would become less flat painting and more 3D and sculptural. With this would come more emphasis on texture and on the treatment of the stage as a real, finite space with less dependence on the illusion of painted space.

Robert Edmond Jones traveled to Europe in 1913 with the goal of seeing the new theatrical forms begun by Craig and Appia and brought into the mainstream of German theatre by director Max Reinhart. Jones came back to America with this Continental Stagecraft and launched a career that would make him the most important designer of his generation. His 1922 *Macbeth* for director Arthur Hopkins (**Figure 2.7**) was panned in the press when it opened but was clearly ahead of its time with its progressively more distorted arches and giant masks of the witches hung above the stage.

Jo Mielziner worked as an assistant to Robert Edmond Jones and then followed Jones as the preeminent designer of the next generation, designing a list of the great plays and musicals of the postwar years that is unmatched in the American theatre, until his death in 1976. His design for *Death of a Salesman* is one of the most iconic designs in modern theatre history (**Figure 2.8**), so respected that director Mike Nichols chose to use it for the 2014 Broadway revival starring Phillip Seymour Hoffman, 65 years after the premiere production.

Mielziner's design for Arthur Miller's *After the Fall* is interesting in that in many ways it is a clear continuation of elements of the Continental Stagecraft

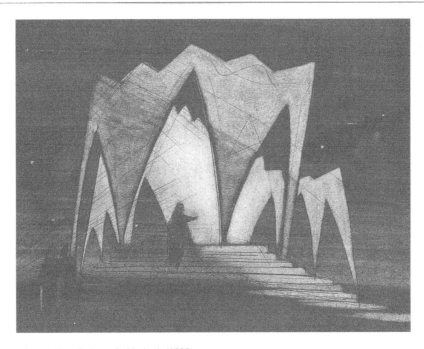

FIGURE 2.7   *Robert Edmond Jones's design for* Macbeth *(1922)*
From *The Theatre of Robert Edmond* Jones © 1958 by Ralph Pendleton. Reprinted by permission of Wesleyan University Press

FIGURE 2.8   *Jo Mielziner's design for* Death of a Salesman, *1949*
Courtesy of the Mielziner Estate—Bud H. Gibbs

FIGURE 2.9 *Jo Mielziner's design for* After the Fall, *1964*
Courtesy of the Mielziner Estate—Bud H. Gibbs

of 50 years before, its multiple levels capable of being used as individual locations or furniture pieces with lighting to lead the eye and provide mood (**Figure 2.9**).

A wonderful tradition continued when, after assisting Jo Mielziner, Ming Cho Lee would become the most important American designer of our time through the strength of his elegant work and the influence of his teaching upon many generations of designers at Yale School of Drama. His design for Tennessee Williams's *The Gnadiges Fraulein* is clear and simple yet deeply evocative (**Figure 2.10**).

Lee's *Electra* (**Figure 2.11**) is a landmark production because it embodies the direction he began in the early 1960s as resident designer at the New York Shakespeare Festival to bring the influence of Brecht to American design. (See "Brecht and His Designers" following).

FIGURE 2.10   *Ming Cho Lee's 1/2-inch model for* The Gnadiges Fraulein, *Broadway, 1966*
From *Ming Cho Lee: A Life in Design* ©2014 by Arnold Aronson. Reprinted by permission of Theatre Communications Group

FIGURE 2.11   *Ming Cho Lee's ½-inch model for* Electra, *New York Shakespeare Festival, 1964*
From *Ming Cho Lee: A Life in Design* ©2014 by Arnold Aronson. Reprinted by permission of Theatre Communications Group

FIGURE 2.12 *Jo Mielziner's design for* Cat on a Hot Tin Roof, *1955*
Courtesy of the Mielziner Estate—Bud H. Gibbs

A Closer Look: An Example of Modern Stage Design

Cat on a Hot Tin Roof

Designer: Jo Mielziner
Broadway 1955

Mielziner's evocative design is an example of modern stage design for its use of:

Simplification: The bedroom of the Mississippi plantation house is reduced to simple space-defining shapes and the essential pieces of furniture. A ceiling piece and the raked platform define the room with the suggestion of columns upstage (US).

Unification: The simplification and limited number of pieces create unity.

Lighting as a design element: The lighting is an important designed element. In this scene a projection of louvered shutters fills the US area.

Three-dimensionality: The objects in space and powerful sense of lighting create a strong three-dimensional quality even with such simplification.

Positions Onstage

Throughout this work, abbreviations are used to note positions onstage:

US is upstage or farther away from the audience.

DS is downstage or closer to the audience.

MS is midstage.

SR and SL are the actor's right and left looking toward the audience.

Combining the preceding will give DSR, DSC, and DSL for downstage right, center, and left, respectively; MR, MC, and ML for midstage right, center, and left, respectively; and USR, USC, and USL for upstage right, center, and left, respectively.

Resources: Some Important Designers of the Modern Era

As this chapter is intended only as a very brief history of the craft of scenic design, a thorough list of all the meaningful designers in the field is impossible. In the spirit of brevity, the following list is only a skeleton to put some of the biggest names in chronological order and encourage further investigation.

The aspiring designer should take very seriously the study of the multitude of talented artists who preceded him and those at the top of their game today. Only by doing this will he open his mind's eye to the great range of work that is possible.

Designer	Their dates	Books by or about them
Pioneers		
Edward Gordon Craig	1872–1966	*On the Art of the Theatre* (1911)
Adolphe Appia	1868–1928	*The Living Work of Art* (1921)
America		
Robert Edmond Jones	1887–1954	*The Dramatic Imagination* (1941)
Donald Oenslager	1902–1975	*Stage Design* (1975)
Lee Simonson	1888–1967	*The Stage Is Set* (1932)
Jo Mielziner	1901–1976	*Designing for the Theatre* (1965) *Mielziner* (2001) by Mary Henderson
Boris Aronson	1898–1980	*Boris Aronson* (1987) by Frank Rich and Lisa Aronson
Howard Bay	1912–1986	*Stage Design* (1974)
Ming Cho Lee	b.1930	*Ming Cho Lee* (2006) by Delbert Unruh *Ming Cho Lee: A Life in Design* (2014) by Arnold Aronson

THREE STRONG INFLUENCES ON DESIGN TODAY

Three movements within the modern period are worth looking at individually because their influence on late modern and postmodern design is so strong.

Constructivism

Russia in the early twentieth century was a hotbed of political and artistic change. Modernist ideas led to a style called Constructivism, which among other tenets favored **form** over **content**. This means that the artist places more importance on how the design **looks** or is **made** than what it **represents**.

Scene design responded to these ideas by becoming nonrepresentational and abstract. The set became a machine for acting, a space that involved the actor physically.

The influence of this on contemporary design is that we expect today that the stage will not necessarily be a picture or appear to be a place, but can be a purely theatrical/functional environment that the performer will very actively use. Constructivist designs typically used stairs, ladders, ramps, and mechanical elements with no realistic visual representation of location at all (**Figure 2.13**). Some noted constructivist designers included Lyubov Popova, Alexandra Exter, and the Stenberg brothers.

FIGURE 2.13   *Lyubov Popova's preliminary sketch for* The Magnanimous Cuckold, *ca. 1922*
© McNay Art Museum/Art Resource, NY

Constructivism's lasting influence is largely due to Boris Aronson's incorporation of its philosophies into many of his productions, Ming Cho Lee's merging of a constructivist sensibility with Brechtian ideas, and George Tsypin's constructivist Postmodernism.

Brecht and His Designers

The work of Bertolt Brecht and his designers, principally Caspar Neher, is in many ways the most far-reaching influence on scene design to this day. Brecht was influenced by some of the new art theories from Russia, especially the concept of **estrangement**, which became better known in his work, largely because of mistranslations of two related German words, as **alienation**. Brecht used the word *verfremdung*, which means estrangement. This has been mistaken for the word *entfremdung*, which means alienation as in Marx's theory of the alienation of the worker in the modern world.

Estrangement in art was written about in Russia, notably by art theorist Victor Shklovsky. It means to intentionally make something different than it is customarily expected; to make it "strange" so it will be regarded with greater care than something familiar and accepted without question. All of Brecht's well-known techniques, such as projected text, a white half-curtain, exposed lighting, and all the rest, were used to create this estrangement. Estrangement in stage design as a concept, beyond the specific techniques Brecht used, is perhaps his most widely influential legacy.

> This is neither naturalism nor any of the departures from naturalism that we know about" students say who have examined the stage created by Brecht's designers (chiefly Caspar Neher and Teo Otto). These designers usually started from a bare stage and placed on it whatever objects the action of the play required. Art? The art is in (a) the design of each object and (b) the placing of the objects. Spectators were often surprised how drastic the logic was. For example: if the action, though set in a room, makes no use of walls, you present a room without walls. Not Naturalism but Brecht called it realism.[1]

In this early Brecht/Neher production (**Figure 2.14**) several key design elements are used. Text on the side

FIGURE 2.14 *Caspar Neher's design for* The Threepenny Opera, *1928*
Arts Resource/NY

panels either identifies the location of the scene while there is no pictorial representation of it onstage or conveys an idea that Brecht wants his audience to think about in the context of the scene. The low horizontal line crossing the stage is the track for a white half-curtain that could be closed to cover the change of scenic elements US of it, or simply as way to signal changes of location, or transitions in the text. These staging devices create a theatre in which audience members are always aware that they are in a theatre. They are regarding the act of watching the play, not simply watching it. These ideas will affect all theatre that follows.

This **drastic logic** has become a fundamental approach to designing today. The starting from a bare stage and placing on it whatever objects the action of the play requires is much more important than it sounds, because it mandates that the designer start with a volume of finite space and a reasoned understanding of the play and what objects it requires. It puts the designer's focus on creating a useful space not a picture.

> *Caspar Neher never cared for the common German word "Buhnenbild" (or stage picture). "The words 'picture' and 'stage,'" he said, "don't go together." Nor did he like to be regarded as a "Buhnenbildner," though he was frequently called one; since the very idea of such a person seemed a hangover from the nineteenth century—not so bad as the stage painter or "Buhnenmaler" perhaps but still nevertheless a man who makes pictures. For the actor's theatre, with its need of an articulated stage and a modicum of illusion, the notion of "stage pictures" was no more acceptable than the French term "décor."[2]*

Brechtian design is a combination of the real and the theatrical. The props the actor uses were typically designed and made in a way that reflected a sense of use and the history of the object. The treatment of the stage space, however, was theatrical. This was a theatricalism in that it represented direct communication to the audience, not any sense of fancy or illusion. A montage of diverse elements— like maps, charts, and text—were combined onstage to comment on the action in the play. Painted drops, when used, had no obligation to be literal; they could use a bold, rough, sometimes primitive style. Primitivism was a style of painting in the fine arts at the time that advocated a very direct, unsophisticated approach.

Brecht and Neher were childhood friends. Brecht pursued poetry and Neher art. After World War II they both turned to theatre. In their early work, economics drove their working style to some degree, but it was firmly allied with theories of primitivism and estrangement. As their work developed, their process grew more integrated. In rehearsals Neher would sketch ideas for how the actors could play individual moments spatially and then he and Brecht would use these sketches to evolve the set design.

Their work was postponed by World War II but flourished after the war upon Brecht's founding of the Berliner Ensemble. When this group, still one of the world's great companies, toured to Great Britain immediately after the war, its work was tremendously influential on British design and would contribute a great deal to the very influential Royal Shakespeare Company "look." By the late 1960s the effect of Brechtian work had been profoundly assimilated into stage design worldwide.

Action Design

A rich tradition of scene design in Czechoslovakia grew even richer following World War II, beginning with the work of Frantisek Troester, also an influential teacher. Josef Svoboda developed worldwide fame for his spare, technologically rich productions, during a period in which the National Theatre in Prague was very highly funded, allowing resident designer Svoboda the otherwise unheard of ability to do research and development on a wide range of new ideas and materials.

But it is in the work and theories of a group of younger designers working primarily in smaller theatres that a methodology of scene design was developed that serves as a bridge from the modern to the postmodern. They called it **Action Design**.

> *Action Design, a scenographic methodology with its formative roots in the former Czechoslovakia, is, in fact, an approach to all aspects of theatre production. A highly metaphorical approach, it eschews decoration for its own sake. The term Action Design designates an approach to scenography that is physically and psychologically functional, and intimately interactive with the actor.[3]*

Scenography is a term used for the theory that one designer should, ideally, be responsible for creating all the aspects of stage design. This is more a European model than in America, where it has always been the practice for separate designers to create the scenic design, costume design, and lighting design. Scenography also suggests that if the visual elements of a design are fully integrated, as is the ideal, then the term *set designer* is less accurate.

Dennis Christilles and Delbert Unruh write in their article "The Semiotics of Action Design" that this methodology has four main principles:

The first is functionality: everything placed onstage must be either physically or psychologically functional. Mere decoration or interior design tends to dull and obscure direct and effective theatrical communication.

A second principle of Action Design is its emphasis on collaboration. The scenic environment must be created after a rigorous examination of the text in close collaboration with the director.

A third principle of Action Design is its pursuit of a complex, ever-shifting metaphorical structure.

A fourth principle of Action Design is an intense irony, manifesting itself in the realization that, no matter how many meanings might be attached to the setting as it interacts with the text, director, and actors, the objects onstage never deny their reality—as both concrete objects and purposefully theatrical materials used in the fictive construction.[4]

These theories clearly come down the path that modern design began and especially reflect the ideas Brecht and Neher worked with 30 years before. The intense irony expressed in the fourth principle is a key concept

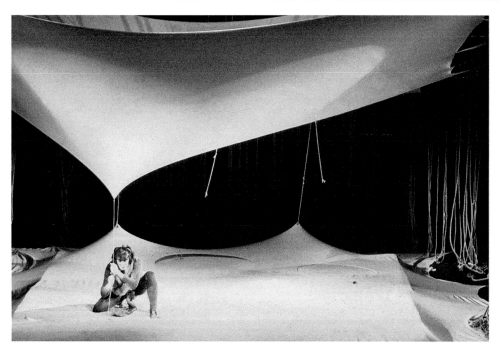

FIGURE 2.15 *Jaroslav Malina's design for* A Midsummer Night's Dream, *ABC Theatre, Prague, 1984*
Malina designed the scenery, lighting, and costumes for this production, which featured layers of stretch fabric that allowed interaction with the performers and metaphorically physicalized the overlapping worlds of the human characters and the fairies.
Courtesy of Jaroslav Malina
Photograph by Dusan Simanek

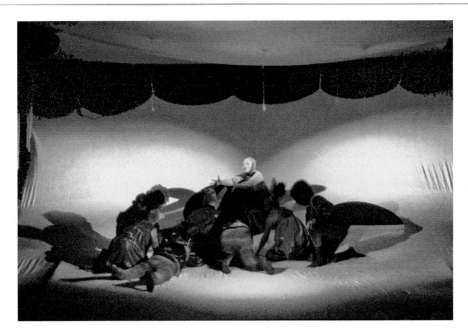

FIGURE 2.16   *Jaroslav Malina's design for* A Midsummer Night's Dream
This design shows another function, the lifted floor top layer of the stretch fabric with holes for the appearance of Titania and the fairies.
Courtesy of Jaroslav Malina
Photograph by Dusan Simanek

of postmodern design today. Some of the designers associated with Action Design are Jaroslav Malina, Miroslav Melena, Jan Dusek, and Joseph Ciller.

CONTEMPORARY PRACTICE: POSTMODERN STAGE DESIGN

By the mid-1970s art and stage design had changed enough that scholars and critics began to use a new term to describe the present and therefore still-evolving type of work: **Postmodernism**.

> *If modern design moved the stage away from the specific, tangible, illusionistic world of romanticism and realism into a generalized, theatrical, and poetic realm in which the pictorial image functioned as an extension of the playwright's themes and structures (a metanarrative), then postmodern design is a dissonant reminder that no single point of view is possible, even within a single image.*
>
> *Through the use of discordance, ugliness, and juxtaposition—what postmodernists call rupture,*

> *discontinuity, disjuncture—the spectator of postmodern design is constantly made aware of the experience of viewing, at the same time, in the most successful examples, made aware of the whole history, context, and reverberations of an image in the contemporary world.*[5]

Before we look at stage design today, it would be useful to look at an art-based definition of Postmodernism.

> **Postmodern art** *is a term used to describe an art movement which was thought to be in contradiction to some aspect of Modernism, or to have emerged or developed in its aftermath. In general, movements such as Intermedia, Installation art, Conceptual Art and Multimedia, particularly involving video are described as postmodern.*
>
> *There are several characteristics which define the term "postmodern" in art; these include . . . appropriation, performance art, the recycling of past styles and themes in a modern-day context, as well as the break-up of the barrier between fine and high arts and low art and popular culture.*[6]

Characteristics of Postmodern Design

Some of the characteristics listed in the preceding quote are important in assessing contemporary stage design:

Appropriation is the taking of an existing image and incorporating it into the stage design. It is most commonly taking an image from the past and using it consciously and without apology with its past meaning seen at the same time as its new one. Postmodernism also maintains that there is no single image that can be used in art today because, as so many images exist, artistic truth is in the echoes and reverberations created between them.

Recycling of past styles and themes in a modern-day context is related to appropriation but speaks to something else as well. Many definitions note of Postmodernism a degree of yearning for the past that modern "cool" makes ironic.

The breaking of barriers between fine art and popular culture includes the use of pop culture imagery as well as ideas. It can also be seen in the setting of classic works in an aggressively contemporary setting.

One of the strongest changes in stage design theory was a reexamination of the importance of unity.

For half a century at least, it has been accepted that the theatre is a unity and that all the elements should try to blend—this has led to the emergence of the director. But it has largely become a matter of external unity, a fairly external blending of styles so that contradictory styles do not jar. When we consider how the inner unity of a complex work can be expressed we may find quite the reverse—that a jarring of externals is quite essential.[7]

The desire for unity, so much a part of the forming of modern design, now seems not to be as important. Design can use diverse, even contradictory elements if the overall effect brought meaning to the production.

Richard Peduzzi, working with frequent collaborator director Patrice Chereau, created a Ring cycle in 1976 for composer Richard Wagner's theatre at Bayreuth that abandoned the fairy-tale past of most previous approaches to the great work in favor of a politicized context of the nineteenth century, the period of the work's creation (**Figure 2.17**). Rhine maidens populated a hydro-electric dam, and the gods were robber barons in this early-postmodern landmark production.

Working in another legendary collaboration, John Conklin and director Mark Lamos essentially created a

FIGURE 2.17   *Richard Peduzzi's design for* The Ring Cycle (Das Rheingold), Bayreuth, 1976
©LeBrecht Images

new American design idiom in a series of productions at Hartford Stage in the 1980s (**Figure 2.18**), combining contemporary elements with appropriated images and strongly sub-conscious choices like the suspended rocking chair in this adaptation of *Pericles*.

An American Ring Cycle as much a landmark as Peduzzi's before it, Robert Israel's 1985 Ring for Seattle Opera (**Figure 2.19**) created a look that used nineteenth-century design styles in startlingly modern ways by turning them on their ear. In discussing the

FIGURE 2.18   *John Conklin's design for* Pericles, *Hartford Stage, 1983*
Photograph by Jennifer W. Lester

FIGURE 2.19   *Robert Israel's design for* The Ring Cycle (Gotterdammerung), *Seattle Opera, 1986*
Courtesy of Robert Israel

FIGURE 2.20   *George Tsypin's design for the* Magic Flute, *Metropolitan Opera*
Courtesy of George Tsypin

production, Arnold Aronson, today's preeminent historian of theatre design, said the set "becomes postmodern in its blend of illusion with the destruction of illusion."[8]

George Tsypin has created designs for theatre and opera that blend Russian Constructivism with his early training in architecture and a passion for the use of strikingly contemporary materials, especially clear glass and plastic. His *Magic Flute* for director Julie Taymor at the Metropolitan Opera (**Figure 2.20**) creates enigmatic symbols and architecture that are extremely bold and dream-like. Arnold Aronson writes of Tsypin's work that he "ransacks history, draws freely from wide-ranging styles and periods, and bluntly mixes the stunningly beautiful with the harsh and ugly."[9]

A Closer Look: A Postmodern Example

Un Ballo in Maschera is an 1859 opera by Guiseppe Verdi and was designed by Paul Steinberg in a recent Metropolitan Opera production directed by David Alden. He used the appropriated image of a classical-style ceiling mural of Icarus falling to earth in strong contrast to severe modern spaces, and used reflective surfaces as both a way to extend and distort them.

Being a theatre designer is to be part of a continuum of interpretation, always remaining fluid and changing in the attempt to communicate ideas to a contemporary audience through the lens of contemporary society. The unique aspect of being a theatre designer is being able to reinvent one's aesthetic approach to suit the needs of each new project. Research is primary; grounding a design in the details of real cultural issues, no matter how abstract it may become, creates a visual language that can be intuited by an audience.

I put enormous trust in the power of metaphor; the right substitution of one image for another can

FIGURES 2.21–4   *Paul Steinberg's design for* Un Ballo in Maschera, *Metropolitan Opera, 2012*
Courtesy of Paul Steinberg/Photo by George Mott

FIGURES 2.21–4 *Continued*

illuminate the truth of a text in ways that a more literal telling cannot. The happy discovery made by juxtaposing two images creates a third resonating visual idea that gives me a lot of pleasure.

I am intrigued by the possible uses of contemporary eclecticism for the theatre. In the course of a career a stage designer learns the design vocabularies of almost every period and place. The usual practice is to employ one stylistic vocabulary in each solution. The Post-Modernist use of eclecticism poses the challenge of combining ideas from various styles to form a new expression.[10]

Postmodernism Wrap-Up

Postmodern stage design has a bold dream-like quality often referred to as imagistic. As in dreams the images used tend to come from the extremes of beauty or ugliness and exist in relationships with each other that seem to exhibit a kind of logic but one that is hard to define. The dreams often include images from a past remembered with fondness, but which we are too sophisticated to still accept.

DESIRE UNDER THE ELMS: EXAMPLES OF CHANGE

As one last example of how stage design has changed in less than 100 years, look at these productions for Eugene O'Neill's *Desire under the Elms*.

Figure 2.25 shows the original production in 1924 designed by Robert Edmond Jones. It appears quite straightforward and realistic, but exemplifies early Modernism in that it is *simplified realism* as opposed to naturalism. The elements have been chosen by

FIGURE 2.25   *Robert Edmond Jones's design for* Desire under the Elms, *1924*
From *The Theatre of Robert Edmond* Jones © 1958 by Ralph Pendleton. Reprinted by permission of Wesleyan University Press

FIGURE 2.26 *Walt Spangler's design for* Desire under the Elms, *2011*
Courtesy of Walt Spangler

the designer to convey a simple, stark New England setting. This production was prepared very much to the playwright's descriptions.

Eighty-five years later styles have changed. In his postmodern design for a 2011 Broadway production, Walt Spangler in some ways reverts to an almost naturalistic look, with very gritty elements (**Figure 2.26**). Rocks are real and seem heavy. The house is dilapidated rough wood.

But the house is suspended surrealistically above the stage and the rocks fill the stage space to a dream-like degree. The ideas that led to this design are supported by the text. Spangler has said that he wanted the rocks to represent life on the brutal New England farms that required the farmers to constantly move heavy stones to clear new fields. While no elms are onstage, the hanging stones, which seem to be counterweights to the house, are also metaphors for the trees. The juxtaposition of naturalism and surrealism make this a very different production from the original.

RESOURCES: SOME CONTEMPORARY AMERICAN DESIGNERS AND HOW TO FIND OUT MORE

The following list is by no means complete but features some notable designers at work today. Their websites will give an excellent snapshot of contemporary American design.

Designer	Website or web reference
Alexander Dodge	http://www.alexanderdodgedesign.com
Riccardo Hernandez	https://vimeo.com/13044130
Adrienne Lobel	http://www.adriannelobel.com
Derek McLane	http://derekmclane.org/home.html
Scott Pask	http://www.scottpaskstudio.com
Todd Rosenthal	http://www.toddar.com
Walt Spangler	http://www.waltspangler.com
Paul Steinberg	http://www.paulsteinberg.com
George Tsypin	http://www.georgetsypin.com
David Zinn	http://www.mrdavidzinn.work/

A FINAL NOTE

The discussion of stage design in this chapter, and indeed in this entire work, is somewhat skewed toward the most contemporary aspects of design. In any period there is art that is deemed cutting edge and other work that, while solid and beautiful, is not so edgy. Scene design has an obligation to serve the plays for which it is created, and this means many plays produced today will have designs that are realistic, or more decorative than conceptual, because that is what the play asks for. In no way do I intend to exclude or diminish these designs, or the designers who created them, but I think addressing what is strongest and most contemporary better serves the purposes of teaching how to design today.

READING LIST

Looking into the Abyss: Essays on Scenography, by Arnold Aronson
Theatre and Performance Design: A Reader in Scenography, edited by Jane Collins and Andrew Nesbit

SUMMARY

- Starting at the dawn of the twentieth-century, Modern Stage Design pioneered simplicity, unity, three-dimensionality, and the use of lighting as a design element.

- The job of designer originated in this modern period

- Russian Constructivism, the work of Bertolt Brecht and Caspar Neher, and Action Design were three influences on the transition to Postmodernism in the mid-1970s.

- Postmodernism is characterized by intensely visual dream-like designs that feature appropriated images, the use of popular art forms, and the often ironic use of images and themes from the past.

A NOTE ON THE PROJECTS

Following are the first two of several projects that appear at the ends of chapters in this book that can be used in a class setting or by an individual to provide some hands-on learning in addition to the general text and illustrations of this book.

I include these with some trepidation, because I appreciate that many instructors will have their own projects that have been successful for them and not need these. There is no reason the teacher must use all or any of these projects; the instructor can pick and choose or use his own. In this last case, I suggest he consider arranging his own projects to follow the most appropriate chapter.

Project: Research a Designer

The first goal of this project is to familiarize you with several contemporary American designers who are working at the top of their craft today.

The second goal is that by looking at their work carefully and being forced to present your thoughts about it, you will develop your critical eye and the vocabulary used to talk about design.

Go to the websites listed on page 29, and explore the portfolios of these contemporary American designers. Look at all their work and see what excites your eye and your imagination. When you've looked at all of them, pick one you are particularly interested in.

For the designer you chose, make a PowerPoint presentation that features at least eight of their designs. The PowerPoint should be mostly images of their work not text. Your class presentation of this PowerPoint will be verbal, but the PowerPoint itself may contain some text as talking points.

Your class presentation may cover a little designer bio: "Alexander Dodge has worked on Broadway, at the Shaw Festival . . . ," and so on, but it should focus on what characteristics of their work most strike you.

Think About

How does this designer use space?

What materials, colors, textures, and so on does this person favor?

To what relative degree does he or she design sculpturally, or depend on surface treatments?

Are his or her designs generally historical research based or more abstract?

Look at the work and decide what general characteristics this designer has. There will be work he or she has done that varies significantly from what you see as his or her "style." Make your image choices support your thoughts.

The following are some terms used in contemporary design to describe ideas or techniques.

Skewed	Abstract, abstracted	Use of color	Line quality	
Texture	Mass	Form	Selected realism	Disunity
Appropriation	Metaphor	Irony		

Project: Sketch and Plan

Much of the design process is drawing in 2D while thinking in 3D.

A designer's quick thumbnail sketch is destined to be a three-dimensional construction on a stage. The more you can relate the 2D exploration to the 3D reality, the better. Stage designs are not pretty pictures; they are architectural creations in space.

This project is designed to start you thinking in 3D terms. It is common practice for a designer to switch from drawing an audience view sketch to drawing a sketchy groundplan view. In doing this he explores the connection between plan and elevation, and thinks of his design in 3D.

The example in **Figure 2.27** is a thumbnail sketch directly above a rough groundplan. Note the light vertical construction lines used to carry the position of elements up from one to the other. This technique will work equally well from sketch to plan, or plan to sketch.

The Project

Pick five varied set designs that you like from the designers listed in the Research a Designer project. Try to choose different types of sets so you have a variety of challenges to work with. Be prepared to explain your choices.

Using the example as your model, draw a thumbnail sketch of each design with a groundplan below it on separate pieces of 8.5 x 11 paper. You will probably need to do each one several times to produce good work. Draw lightly at first so you can overdraw your initial lines.

This is sketching, not drafting. You should use a straightedge, but keep your drawing loose.

You may not know much about the theatre from the photo of the set design. Draw what you know and leave out the rest.

Include a human figure for scale whether there was one in the photo of the design or not.

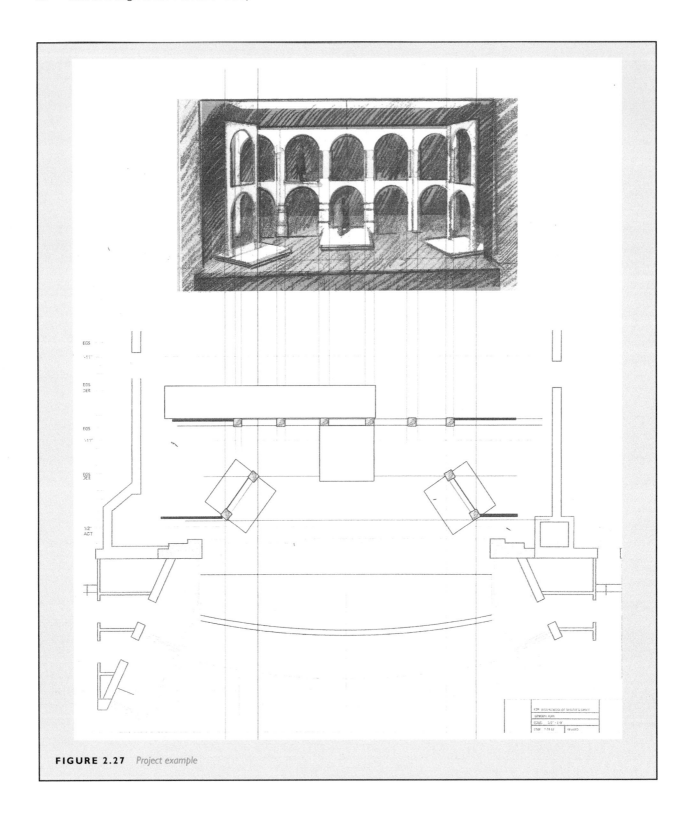

FIGURE 2.27 *Project example*

NOTES

1. Eric Bentley, *The Brecht Commentaries* (London: Eyre Methuen, 1981), 255.
2. John Willet, *Caspar Neher: Brecht's Designer* (London: Methuen, 1986), 13.
3. Dennis Christilles and Delbert Unruh, *The Semiotics of Action Design*, Project Muse, Volume 6, Number 2, September 1996, https://muse.jhu.edu/article/35164
4. Christilles and Unruh, *The Semiotics of Action Design.*
5. Arnold Aronson, *Looking Into the Abyss: Essays on Scenography* (Ann Arbor: University of Michigan Press, 2003), 14.
6. Marilyn Stokstad and Michael Cothren, e-Study Guide for *Art History Portables Book 6: 18th-21st Century*, https://books.google.com/books?id=wrYIAgAAQBAJ&pg=PT138&lpg=PT138&dq
7. Peter Brook, *The Empty Space* (New York: Touchstone, 1968), 39
8. Aronson, *Looking Into the Abyss: Essays on Scenography*, 20.
9. Aronson, *Looking Into the Abyss: Essays on Scenography*, 207.
10. Paul Steinberg, Personal Website: http://www.paulsteinberg.com, used by permission.

CHAPTER 3

WORKING WITH
DIRECTORS

COLLABORATION

Collaboration is at the core of the theatre. It is one of the things that makes designing in the theatre unique. Unlike other art forms where the artist creates his work alone, in the theatre the designer works from the very beginning with others.

As important as all the collaborators involved in the long process of realizing a design on the stage are, the first and most important is the director.

The most vital part of the designer's responsibility concerns determining the size, shape, and rules of the **world of the play**. The director's mission is exactly the same. Though their paths will diverge, the designer to oversee the construction of the set and the director to oversee the actor's rehearsals, the work the set designer and the director do together is the single most important part of the process affecting what the performance will be.

The scenic design sets the parameters and the ground rules of this fictive "world." It defines the overall world visually and physically.

There are several reasons that the director deserves to be covered in this, the first chapter that begins a look at the designer's process. The first is the importance of the work he and the scenic designer will do. Their decisions

> The expression **the world of the play** refers to the play, its characters and context, as a living thing; a world with its own visual and physical qualities and rules as to how things work. These looks and rules may have little to do with the real world, the realism outside the theatre, but they must have an integrity and specificity as true, in their way, as that of the real world. It is the mission of the director and designers to discover the details of the world of the play at hand. Their discoveries may be intuitive or obvious, hazy or crystal clear, but the goal is to find, and then present onstage, a world whose characteristics seem right, inevitable, and true.

will determine the fundamentals of how the space in which the play is presented will work for the performer and what the audience will think and feel about the play.

The second reason to begin with the director is that, in the professional theatre, the director is usually the reason you, the designer, got the job. In most cases a director you have worked with before or who has seen your work, or has had you recommended to him by someone who has seen your work, will contact you, or request the theatre company do so.

Additionally, in professional practice, the set designer and the director begin their process the earliest. The set will have to begin construction earlier than work on the costumes or lighting, so the scenic designer and the director often meet first. In the professional world the members of the design team may be in separate states or countries until late in the process. Unless all the designers are available from the beginning of design talks, as in a university setting, the initial design talks may be just the director and the scenic designer.

The sooner you, as a young designer, realize that the most important part of your work is an effective, enlightening, and exciting collaboration with the director, the better for your designing *and* your career.

Considerations in Working with a Director

- You and the director have **exactly the same concerns**. Your eventual responsibilities will differ, but your goals together should be exactly the same. Your collaboration is vitally important to the resulting production.

- Your primary job together is to shape the spatial, visual, and physical rules of a performance. In your early talks with the director **focus on the play, the story and its themes, and its characters**. Do not focus on "scenery" until you have to. These initial decisions are about what makes the play work.

- A scenic designer's work involves a lot of different skills. He must work with color, texture, form, and space and understand paint, fabrics, furniture and a hundred other things. **His single most important skill must be as a collaborator.** Your career in the business is affected by your success in working with directors.

STRATEGIES: TALKING ABOUT THE PLAY

The designer begins his work, after he is hired for a production, by reading the script. Working with that text will be covered in Chapter 4, but while we are looking at the director-designer relationship, let's look at strategies

---

Note: Because each chapter looks at a different aspect of the designer's work, there may seem to be some duplication. In **Chapter 4, "Working with Text,"** aspects of text analysis will be discussed that may seem similar to some of the following questions that a designer and director should discuss. The difference is one of focus. Here the focus is on how the discussion between designer and director can lead to common ground in approaching the play. In Chapter 4 the focus is on the designer's own study of the text.

---

for talking with the director about the play. Every designer has a different approach to every play and with every director.

Here Are Some Things to Consider

- **First, talk about the play, *not* the scenery.** There will be much to say about the play as a whole before you need to ask how many doors the director wants. By talking about the play first, you present yourself as a collaborator not just a technician ready to get started with providing "things." It is an important lesson to learn that just because the playwright says in the play's set description that the set has doors to the garden SR and a staircase USL, it does not necessarily mean your design needs to. At the beginning of every process, the stage is a blank canvas where no element should go unexamined as to its necessity. Before you can address how many doors are needed, you may need to ask, "Why a door?"

- **Ask what the play is about.** This is not what happens in the play; you know that from your reading of the script. That is plot. What the play is about speaks more to theme, and this is an area of great importance to the designer. We could say, "*Macbeth* is about ambition and murder leading to madness." For the designer this provides a clear, strong overview of the play that can be used to design that world.

- **Talk about the characters**, their interactions, and their effect on their environment, or its effect on them. Who are these people? Why do they do what they do? Why should we care? In most cases, the design will be seen through the characters' eyes. It is their world and therefore specific to their story, emotions, and context. By talking about their relationship to their environment you are also talking about the relationship between performer and space. This is at the core of what the designer and director need to determine. Establishing who the key characters are and whether we see the play though their eyes lets the designer work on creating a specific world from viewpoints inside the play not outside it. We will address this concept of inside and outside again in later sections. The more the physical world expresses the outlook of key characters, the more specific it becomes and this **specificity is the designer's goal**.

- **Is there a progression in the play?** Does the play begin with one idea, feeling, or emotion and gradually change to another? If it does, what does this progression tell the audience? How can the designer make this progression clear? Is it a seamless, almost imperceptible change, or are there dramatic moments when the audience should be aware of the change?

- **Talk about what you find interesting about the play.** Why are we doing this play? Why here and now? What does the play say to a contemporary audience? By thinking about the play's relevance to the audience you can find ways to make that relevance clearer.

- **Listen.** It is tremendously important that you listen at these early meetings. If you get locked into an idea too early in the process it can blind you to other choices and lead you to hear other people's ideas only in relation to your own. This can cause you to miss a lot of possibilities.

Directors are all different, as are designers, in regard to how fluent they are in describing what they think about design ideas. These earliest discussions, especially,

Robert Edmond Jones's 1921 production of *Macbeth* was controversial at its opening and was much maligned in the press (**Figure 3.1**). One of its design ideas that was clearly ahead of its time was a distortion of the scenic elements as the play progressed.

FIGURE 3.1   *Robert Edmond Jones's design for* Macbeth *(Banquet Scene), 1921*

From *The Theatre of Robert Edmond Jones* © 1958 by Ralph Pendleton. Reprinted by permission of Wesleyan University Press

can be about finding a common language. Sometimes the director may not feel ready to talk to you with confidence about the design and may need to be drawn out. It is important not to waste time even in this early phase of the process. Some directors are especially visually oriented and may come to a first meeting with their own visual research. It is important that you react positively to both extremes. Both may bring frustrations—the one not giving you enough information and the other bringing too much. With the first, you have the chance to discover, in your discussions, the direction to go together. In the second case you have the chance to start a little further down the path by having images that the director has already found interesting.

COLLABORATING THROUGH IMAGES

An activity that can help the director and designers come together in their work on the play is the **charrette**. To do a charrette all participants bring in images they have found that they feel say something about the world of the play. Some can be more scenery related and others more concerned with other areas. Some may be specific research but, in general, a process such as this may best use more nonspecific, emotional images. Generally, each participant brings the same number of images, which need not all be references to their own area. Each image is discussed by the group. Gradually images are selected by the group that all feel are useful and a collage is made of them that can act as a reference tool throughout the remaining parts of the design process. **Figure 3.2** shows a collage for *Hamlet*.

STRATEGIES: AS MEETINGS PROGRESS

What to Show the Director and When

In a perfect world I don't like to bring sketches or even research to a first meeting. That being said, I have done so in many cases. I have also brought sketches and research, and then chosen not to show them after some initial conversation has taken place. I like to do some

FIGURE 3.2 *Charrette collage for* Hamlet
Courtesy of Davy Davis, University of Denver

FIGURE 3.3   *Sketch*

research after the first meeting and then bring that to a second one before I do or show sketches. Sometimes the calendar will not permit this. I frequently do a Photoshop mash-up of some key research images as the first thing I show.

Whatever the media, some visual representation of what the play might look like is created and shown. I said "what the *play* might look like" not the set, because I feel that at this early stage there is so much you do not yet know that trying to create a sketch that looks too much like a complete design is impossible and limiting. It can be misleading to all involved and seem like you have arrived at a finished design too soon. Once this first visualization has been discussed, the next priority is to begin to deal with the space in which the performance will take place. The place to start on that front is with a rough groundplan.

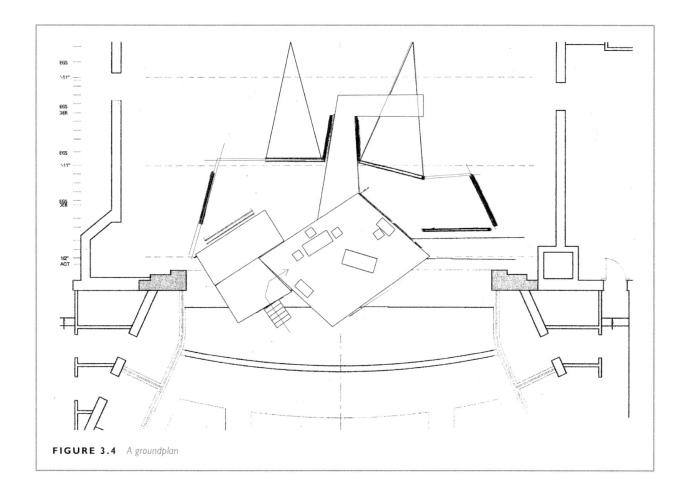

FIGURE 3.4   *A groundplan*

The Groundplan

The groundplan is a drawing that is a view of the stage looking down from above. It shows the size and position of all the elements of the set. Early groundplans may be sketched over printed plans of the theatre. Later versions will be drafted in scale. Later sections of this book will look at the groundplan in more detail and from different perspectives. For the director and the designer in their collaboration to give shape and meaning to the play, the groundplan is both a road map and a contract.

As a road map it presents destinations and routes to travel between them. Every destination has its particular purposes and possibilities. This chair is a destination for one character to go to at one moment of the play, to become small and give up focus, and in another moment for another character to bring the audience's focus to himself for an intense scene with a co-conspirator. This landing at the base of the stairs is a stage within a stage for the telling of news to an assembled group, and later the launch of a dramatic exit as another character climbs the stairs, exhausted, to meet his fate.

Think of the groundplan as what drives the characters to move, to cross, to take action.

As a contract, it is the promise of the director to the designer and the designer to the director that this is where they will start. This is the map to the journey they will ask their audience to take. It is the first and most important concrete commitment as to where the production will go.

> I have worked with joy with many marvelous designers—but at times been caught in strange traps, as when a designer reaches a compelling solution too fast—so that I have found myself having to accept or refuse shapes before I had sensed what shapes seemed to be imminent in the text. When I accepted the wrong shape, because I could find no compelling reason for opposing the designer's conviction, I locked myself in a trap out of which the production could never evolve.[1]
>
> —Peter Brook, *The Empty Space*

No pressure!

THINKING LIKE A DIRECTOR

Designing Moments

It is important to understand that a designer does not simply design a set. With the director and the rest of the production team, the designer devises a production idea. This, to me, is

FIGURE 3.5   *Sketches for a sequence of moments in Love's Labour's Lost*
For the play within the play, a curtain is raised covering the set seen so far, a combination of foliage and mirrored panels that reflected it.

FIGURE 3.6   *Sketches for a sequence of moments in* Love's Labour's Lost
The play, The Masque of the Nine Worthies, *takes place before this curtain.*

FIGURE 3.7   *Sketches for a sequence of moments in* Love's Labour's Lost
As the play progresses, an ominous shadow appears on the curtain. It is the messenger bearing news to the princess and her retinue of the king, her father's, death. The curtain is dropped, the play over.

the most interesting aspect of design. Think of the work as designing theatrical moments, not scenery. Looked at in this light, scenery is just stuff. If your concern is designing moments, you start work by trying to find ways to do the play in the given space with elements that support what happens in the play and give the audience a way to understand them. If this means there are walls and doors, fine, but approaching your work in this way will help you design things from a text and performer-driven perspective and not begin by designing a picture that the actors merely inhabit.

FIGURE 3.8 *Sketches for a Sequence of moments in* Love's Labour's Lost
While the curtain is raised, the mirror panels are turned to a black side. The previous glittering, artificial court is now a real, empty forest. Leaves fall as all the characters say their goodbyes and exit.

Blocking

The director's challenge is to plan the movements of the actors to aid the audience's understanding of the play, and simply to keep the actor who is the focus of a particular moment in an advantageous position, one in which he will be the focus of the other actors and clearly seen by the audience. This is **blocking**. This positioning of the actors is largely determined by the design of the set. Different types of movement have different qualities, such as a strong diagonal entrance or the meandering curves of a waltz. The design of the set in terms of the shaping of actor movement makes some movements possible and others impossible. I have many times seen a director describing how he sees the production in his mind make hand gestures of short, choppy motions, or graceful, smooth ones that told me a lot about what the design should be like.

When the designer and director use fixed elements such as furniture, they create a spot where an actor may remain stationary for a while. The angles at which these elements are placed determine the angles at which the actor will be seen by the audience. It is important that the actor be angled in such a way as to be **open** to the audience—to have his face clearly visible. It is

also desirable that the placement of furniture have some logic to the architecture of the set and other elements of furniture. Keeping a balance between what is open to the audience and what feels natural in regard to spatial relationships with other actors and the architectural sense of the setting can be very challenging. Placing furniture in a stage set is very different than placing furniture in your living room. The differences in different theatre types make for different problems for the designer. These will be covered in more detail in Chapter 7, "Space."

Stage Pictures

Moments in the blocking are sometimes referred to as stage pictures. These are most often iconic moments in the play for which the director has crafted an overall tableau—a visual arrangement of the stage and the actors as a picture. These are the moments an audience is most likely to remember. A moment will pass, and this picture will evolve into the next of hundreds more in a single production. It is worth discussing the physical elements the stage needs for these key pictures to be made. It is impossible for the director and designer to know, in this early phase in the process, all the things they will need, all the ways the set will need to be used. They should, however, know they are creating a space for meaningful moments.

Production Case Studies

Following are two production case studies, the first of many that will be featured in each following chapter. They are from actual productions I have designed. I use my own work, not because I hold the work up as a

definitive approach, but because I can explain more fully what each attempted conceptually and what production decisions were made in the process of creation. The points I hope the examples illustrate are specific to the chapter in which they appear. The two included here are both designs that were approached with the goal of creating moments first, not an overall cohesive set. The "sets" for each are extremely simple; the ideas behind the moments created, I hope, are not. As you will see they are very different plays.

Production: *Hamlet*

The most important part of the designer's work involves his getting "inside the play." This has been addressed in this chapter, and aspects of it will reappear in Chapter 4, "Working with Text"; Chapter 5, "Research, Period, and Visual History"; and Chapter 6, "The Designable Idea" as well as elsewhere throughout the book.

Getting inside the play involves making specific choices of what to put onstage and how these things will be used based on study of the world of the play and its characters. If the choices are too general or nonspecific, then we design a set that could serve any play with a similar location. If, in designing *Hamlet*, we assume we must design a castle, because we know the play takes place in Elsinore Castle, we make a surface choice; we look at the play from the outside. We pick a type of castle from our research that best fits our feeling for the play, the best color of stone for our ideas about the mood of the play, and all the appropriate detail that will make the set seem real and complete (**Figure 3.9**). We may design a very beautiful set, but is it *Hamlet*?

If we get more specific and put ourselves in the mind of the characters, we find different choices. What if we think of the setting as Hamlet's beloved boyhood home, which, on being summoned back from college, he finds a place of dark intrigue and corruption? His father is dead and his mother is married to his uncle, the murderer. Hamlet feels lost, isolated. Now we have a much deeper, more specific way to create a design, and the possibility that our audience will see in our choices a deeper emotional connection to the character and the play. This gives us much more to work with, but still would allow for different paths. Is the set light or dark? Is it composed of oppressive, twisted corridors or open, empty spaces?

Whichever path we take here, our design now comes from more inside the play. It is for specific characters. It is not just a set. It is an idea about the play.

The production of Hamlet shown here was the result of a great deal of thought and discussion about the play. The director saw different moments in the play as suggesting references to different film styles, from film noir to German expressionism to slapstick comedy.

I began to think about how much of our experience is filtered and understood via filmic images. It struck me that Hamlet was a man trapped in various kinds of films that he doesn't want to have a role in. The visitation of the ghost plunges him into a horror film. From his perspective, the machinations of King Claudius and the incestuous relationship between his uncle and his mother could be translated into a film-noir experience. Ophelia's love is part of a romantic Hollywood movie in which he is not able to play the hero. Finally, unable to act within these film worlds, he decides to stop watching his life as a film and accepts instead the unmediated role in which fate has cast him.[2]

—Director, Karen Lordi-Kirkham

This led to discussion that the set should be somewhat neutral so it would serve as a blank canvas for moments of different styles. To physicalize this blank canvas, a white scrim was considered for the scrim effects it could create and as a surface for

FIGURE 3.9   *Castle research*
© conrado/Shutterstock.com

projections. To connect the film idea to the character's actions, different ways of incorporating video were explored, both ways in which the characters could interface with the video and how the video could be used as scenery.

The play began with an unscripted moment of Hamlet sitting DC with an old movie projector watching home movies of his family. These were prerecorded with the cast.

In some soliloquies, Hamlet played to a live video camera, looking inside himself. The audience saw him with the camera, and his face in extreme close-up projected behind him (**Figure 3.10**).

We chose to put very little in this blank canvas of a stage, but one item came from discussion of how to stage the iconic Ghost scene. In the space, throughout the play, was a small castle, meant to seem a childhood toy. Hamlet interacted with this castle in various moments and set up a video camera on a tripod that caused the castle to be projected on the US scrim, as a scenic image of Elsinore in many scenes. It served, therefore, as a real object, as a metaphorical one, and as a practical element in the storytelling.

The ghost's appearance was created by the actor portraying the Ghost rising from a trap within the toy castle, seen simulta-neously by the audience, with the ethereal horror movie image projected on the scrim (**Figure 3.11**). Horatio and the soldiers, standing US of the scrim, reacted to the ghostly projected image. Hamlet sat apart and saw both images, the toy castle of his childhood, the idea of his father's murder, and the reactions of Horatio and the guards to the illusion of that image.

This duality supported Hamlet's isolation from the actions around him. The set was kept very spare so that these specific moments would take focus.

FIGURE 3.10   Hamlet: *A soliloquy*

Design Process Recap

- Ideas about the play were translated into moments of staging and visuals that supported and brought the ideas to life.
- These ideas were not so much considered as ideas of the design team as they were ideas of and about the characters in the situation in which the playwright placed them.
- Some of the major moments were planned ahead of time, but the process was regarded as fluid and the set kept simple and open enough to allow, not restrict, the creation of moments later in the process.

Production Credits

HAMLET, Dickinson College, 2001
Director: Karen Lordi-Kirkham
Set Design: Robert Klingelhoefer
Costume Design: Sherry Harper-McCombs
Lighting Design: Jim Drake

FIGURE 3.11   Hamlet: *Swordplay*

FIGURE 3.12   Hamlet: *The ghost appearance*

Production: *Charlotte's Web*

There can hardly be two more different plays than *Hamlet* and *Charlotte's Web*, and the latter would most often be thought of as a relatively simple, straightforward thing: a pig, a spider, and a barn. This production attempted to be a richer experience than that. The text was looked at in terms of being about growing up, about the cycles of nature, about life as a big, beautiful, triumphant, sad, ever-changing thing. There seemed to be many layers. The telling of a simple tale within the context of watching the change of seasons, of a child's growing up, and the passage of time. The audience should see and feel all those things.

> Early conversations for Charlotte's Web focused as much on the style of writing as the actual story. E.B. White was known for his simple, sparse prose and the seriousness in which he treated very simple ideas, characters, and settings. Before a single design was put on paper we relished in the images and words of the novel.
>
> At first these seemed to pull in two contrasting directions, the play featured interactions between humans and animals and required great shifts in scale as well as a medium that could present the passage of time and the changes that came with that reality.
>
> By focusing on simple elements that integrated scenic ideas we were able to build complex images by layering these ideas on top of each other. Ladders became fences, the animals in the model barn could become gigantic through video or tiny toys that Fern observed. Often the audience saw the actors manipulating the images as they played with the set and props, and whenever possible the essential dramatic action was performed only with the detail needed to display a given moment. Just as E.B. White was picking his words carefully we picked our key images and tools and created a grammar for the production.[3]
>
> —Director Eric Johnson

This led to the idea of trying to create a multiplicity of views, views of the microcosm and the macrocosm at the same time. Views of the child watching the animals grow and the adults watching the child grow, and the animals watching it all.

Throughout this book there will be discussion of the concept that the "production idea" is more important than "scenery." This production is an example of that idea. The set was very simple; the budget quite small. But with a big, clear idea, that could be implemented by all departments, the production was rich and multidimensional.

It was decided very early in the design process that video would be a major tool involved in the storytelling. In fact, this was a given part of the production from the assembly of the design team. In large part, the team that designed this *Charlotte's Web* was the same team responsible for *The Christmas Carol* presented in Chapter 6. This production followed *Christmas Carol* by six months. The director and video designer had worked together previously, and the set designer, video designer, and director would work together on several later productions at other theatres.

A good way to approach a design such as this is to consider how ideas discussed will be part of a **vocabulary** of how the story will be told. In this case, the desire for multiple viewpoints led to the idea of layering the live action with prerecorded video shot on outside locations with the actors as a way of providing elements that could not be shown onstage, such as the crowds at the state fair or the actions of a human character seen in a moment in the animal world. Projections could be used to create scale changes that would help the storytelling.

In addition, to make the video intimately connected to the live event it was decided to use, in a high percentage of the show, live video from a tiny camera that would be manipulated by the actors. This required its own scenery and props. A miniature barn was designed to look like a child's toy based on the illustrations of the Little Golden Books, and a miniature Ferris wheel was created to be used at the fair. **Figure 3.13** shows the "video table" with the barn, animal figures, and toy farm truck.

Figure 3.14 shows an example of the kinds of moments this vocabulary made possible. The scene was between children sledding. The actors involved in the scene were lit US of the scrim. Scenic images projected from the tiny live camera onto the scrim were of the barn and truck having flour "snow" sifted on them by the actors playing the sheep and the goose. The audience was aware of all of the different realities creating the magic of the moment.

FIGURE 3.13 Charlotte's Web: *The barn*

FIGURE 3.14 Charlotte's Web: *Snow*

FIGURE 3.15   Charlotte's Web: *The fair*

FIGURE 3.16   Charlotte's Web: *Climbing*

FIGURE 3.17   Charlotte's Web: *The web*

In designing scenery for video the choice of screen material and how the video will be integrated into the total look are the earliest and most important decisions. The screen choice here was white sharks-tooth scrim, a scrim that was a stock item in the theatre's soft goods inventory. The use of scrim would allow action behind the scrim to be lit and be visible creating another layer. The video was from a single projector hung front of house so it would play over the entire space. These decisions created the layers of a big, master image, and multiple ways other viewing layers could be added to it.

Scenically, a raised platform behind the scrim would place actors in a position to be seen above actors DS at stage level. Two platforms of different heights were designed on either side of the scrim, accessible by ladders. These ladders and platforms were painted as whitewashed rough wood like that used in a barn or animal pens at a fair, or farm fences.

Design Process Recap

- Ideas of ways to create multiple viewpoints informed the plans for the set and the use of video.
- What should be scenery, what should be video, and what should be live were determined by what would most effectively tell the story.
- Individual ideas were allowed to create the overall style of the piece rather than an overall style being allowed to affect the individual moments.
- The process was more a discovery of a vocabulary that could be used to tell the story than scenery.

Production Credits

Charlotte's Web, Fulton Theatre 2001
Director: Eric Johnson
Set Design: Robert Klingelhoefer
Video Design: Adam Larsen
Costume Design: Beth Dunkleberger
Light Design: Michael Wyant

SOME FINAL THOUGHTS ON COLLABORATION

Trust

The collaborative process is difficult enough at any time. It involves balancing the egos and very subjective thoughts and emotions of all involved, and requires the exchange of information that can be very difficult to express in words. When you are working with a new director, this can be especially stressful. The only solution is to try to pay extra attention to the personal relationship part of the process when you're working with someone new.

It is no surprise that directors and designers tend to forge long-term relationships. The communication, which comes with practice, between them makes the process faster and smoother. They communicate in shortcuts based on previous shared experience. Once you have developed trust in a relationship with a director, the collaborative process can be less stressful.

Openness and Change

Perhaps the most significant skill a designer in the theatre can possess is openness. The process of collaboration has many twists and turns. During the process ideas may come from any participant and will not necessarily come at the most opportune time. The designer needs to constantly guard against being rigid in his reactions to new ideas. This can be very hard. We all latch on to ideas and sometimes find it hard to give them up. This can be because we naturally like our own ideas, at least initially, more than someone else's. It can also occur because we have put a lot of work into an idea and don't want it "wasted" by a change of plan. But we need to see that a good idea is a good idea whenever it appears and be ready to accept it if it will make the work better. The scenic designer, because his shop deadlines come the earliest, is sometimes in the position of having a suggestion come up from the director or another designer that he recognizes as good, but that he cannot fully implement because work on the actual set has been done, money and other people's time spent. It may, however, be possible to make minor tweaks in this new direction, and the designer should explain why it is not fully possible and what he can do to at least partially implement the new idea.

The responsible designer should always try to be open to change but respectful of the commitments of manpower and money that have been spent to date or that the change will require.

Possibilities for change can sometimes be built into the design. This is to some degree a function of how interlocked the elements are to each other. If the set is a single architecturally complete structure, there may not be much that can be done, but if it is designed in a way that is a bit more open, with architectural elements that are not interconnected but make up a collective impression of the whole structure, those elements may be able to have their positions tweaked. A musical that might typically be designed with floating pieces within a system of moving panels can create a toy box that the designer and director can play in during technical rehearsals and take advantage of what they have learned in the rehearsal process.

When Things Don't Go Your Way

There will be times in the collaborative process when decisions will be made that you are not happy with. This is a given in a collaborative process. It is important that these moments don't throw you. In a perfect collaboration the participants may lose track of what was whose idea, but you must remember that the director is ultimately the person who calls the shots and makes the final decision among the ideas being considered. When a decision doesn't go your way, it is important that you find a way to make it work. Sometimes this can be by finding a way to shift the new idea toward something you like better, but sometimes you cannot. If you take the new request as a challenge to your creative abilities, you may find that you will surprise yourself with your solution and that you have stretched yourself a bit as an artist.

SUMMARY

- Work hard to be an equal collaborator with your director.

- Think about the production more than the scenery.

- Design moments not pictures.

- Stay open to change and keep trying to make the production better.

Project: The Project Play

In the following project and those through Chapter 7 you will work through a process of studying the most important aspects of creating a design. To do this you will need to pick a play to use. This play can be any one you like, but I have found that certain types of plays work best. I think the play chosen should be relatively short so it doesn't present too huge a list of problems to solve. It should have a basis in reality so its elements can be researched, but have aspects, too, that are conceptual or poetic enough to be interesting. I generally use *Riders to the Sea* by John Millington Synge. Tennessee Williams's *27 Wagons Full of Cotton* works well also. Williams in general is very good for early design projects, *Glass Menagerie* and *Streetcar Named Desire* particularly.

Project: Stage Pictures

In this project, you are to imagine three stage pictures for moments in your project play that capture the essence of the play. Examples of stage pictures from other well-known plays would include Lady Macbeth's sleepwalking scene, Medea at the palace door after she has killed her children, Willie Loman walking toward his house exhausted, and the two tramps waiting for Godot at the tree.

   Don't imagine the entire set, just the key elements in your stage picture and how the actor is placed in them and what he is doing. Write a brief description of each and then do a quick thumbnail sketch.

   When you are done, see if you can combine your three sketches in a way that might lead to a design that allows all three moments to take place.

NOTES

1. Peter Brook, *The Empty Space* (New York: Touchstone, 1968), 101.

2. Director's statement from the production program. Used by permission.

3. Director's statement, April 8, 2016, via email.

CHAPTER 4

WORKING WITH TEXT

In most cases, the designer's work begins with the text. There are exceptions to this, of course, such as designing dance in which the music and/or the choreographer's ideas take the place of text, or works that are developed in rehearsal and no preexisting text is used. Typically, however, after being hired to design a production, the designer will sit down with a play script that will be the spine for all his work on the project.

The study of the script is not easy. It takes time and care. The first part of the actor's rehearsal process is usually a period of "table work" in which the cast and director study the script in detail before the actors get on their feet. A similar period must be a part of the designer's work with their director.

Some people think that experienced professionals can sight-read a play the way some musicians sight-read a score, but this skill is as rare in the theatre as it is in music. A professional's analysis of a play is a long and painstaking process. In fact, a major characteristic of professionals is their recognition of the value of slow methodical table work.

Another mental power consists of the ability to understand the many meanings of words and the dramatic force that may be expressed by them. Art

students pay attention to shape and color; music students listen for pitch and timbre. Those who wish to make a living in the theatre should develop a sense of the expressiveness and emotion inherent in words.[1]

GENRE AND STYLE

These two terms refer to the play as a whole and help clarify its form and manner. In a play which is new to you, these may not be immediately clear. Conversely, in a play you do have some prior knowledge of, this knowledge may, without using fresh eyes, steer you in a clichéd direction.

Genre is a way to refer to the literary form of the play. Tragedy and Comedy are the two most basic genres and come originally from the Greek theatre. Drama is a genre that features conflict between characters we can regard as ordinary people. Farce is a subcategory of Comedy that features exaggerated characters, extreme situations, and broad comic elements. Opera and Musical Theatre are genres. The genre of the play is most often pretty obvious. There are some design responses to genre that are so common that they are ingrained into our sensibilities. Tragedy is often dark and monumental.

Comedy is usually bright and colorful. These responses for the designer can become clichés. Like any cliché they are founded on truth, but the designer's best practice is to avoid clichés wherever he can. Design for comedy should usually show some restraint. The set should not be funnier than the script. Likewise for Tragedy, a set that is heavy-handed can make a scene of light comic relief in the play impossible. The designer's best response is to design the moments he sees in the play, whatever their tone, and not force the play into an externally designed genre.

Style is a way to classify the overall visual qualities of the way a play was originally conceived and/or produced. This has much to do with the theatrical style of the period in which the play was originally presented. Realism is by far the most common style, meaning simply that the world of the play seems to be a believable place inhabited by believable characters. Expressionism is a style in which reality is presented in a subjective manner that exaggerates elements to express the emotional qualities of the characters. The Brechtian style, Constructivism, and Symbolism are styles whose origins are in different theatrical periods of the twentieth century.

*Dramatic styles may be broadly divided into two categories: **theatrical** (non-realistic or presentational) and **illusionistic** (realistic or representational). In **theatrical** styles, creating an impression of everyday life on stage is of little importance. The main purpose is to express the content with as little as possible coming between the play and the audience. . . . In contrast, **illusionistic** plays aim at being non-theatrical. Plot, characters, and dialogue are selected and arranged to give the closest approximation to actual life.*[2]

Style can help you understand why the play is as it is. It can be somewhat helpful in putting the play into a historical context, but to accept that a given play should be, or must be, designed in a certain style can be a huge trap. Most plays have elements of several styles within them that could be designed in different ways. To assume that a play is of a certain style and should be designed in just that way can abort the designer's obligation to study and understand the play and limit the meanings that can be expressed in its production. Whatever style the designer ultimately creates should come from inside the text, not as a pre-existing style applied to it.

THE TWO TYPES OF TEXT

The script will contain the dialogue that the audience will hear, and descriptions of how the playwright has envisioned the visual elements involved and a basic sense of how the characters might move about. These are called the **primary** and **secondary** text. It is important to understand the difference between these two types of text.

Primary Text

The story is in the words the actors speak and the audience hears. This is the **primary** text. The world the designer creates will always be seen in reference to these words. It may clearly support them, matching them in all particulars, or it may create dissonance between some details of the visual decisions and the actor's words. This difference can add to or distract from the production. Audience members will follow the dialogue, and their minds will look for meaning in what they see onstage. In most cases their reactions should be that the world they see supports the words they hear. When it does not they will look for reasons why. Many design decisions may create a heightened world that may be different from what the audience expects, but may still be easy for them to understand and accept. An audience brings to the theatre a willingness to suspend disbelief. People are willing to go with what they are presented as long as they can find meaning in it. Pushed too far, they will lose this willingness.

Secondary Text

The playwright's descriptions of how he envisions the world of the play and the stage directions are **secondary** text. These are important, in that they help the designer understand how the play was originally imagined, but the fact that the audience will never hear these words means that they do not carry the same weight as the dialogue. Outside of a few cases in which certain playwrights have insisted, legally, that designs for their plays stay close to what they envisioned, the design team is free to be flexible with their interpretation of these elements.

It is important and often helpful for the designer to consider why the playwright gives the information he does. In what ways might it be important? How could it help you understand what he was thinking? Why did he choose to describe the visual elements of the play in the way he does? By understanding this you may find a way to use these ideas in new and exciting ways.

You are then free to use, ignore, or adapt this information.

READING THE PLAY

First Read

It is generally good advice on your first reading of the play to try to simply let the story unfold in your mind, as much like the audience will eventually perceive it as possible. This is really the only time you will have this purity of response.

In subsequent readings make notes of specific needs, questions, or problems you see. It is very helpful to make a document that formalizes the needs and details in the script for easy reference later.

Consider Not Reading the Set Description

If the play has a lengthy or very detailed set description, consider skipping this information in the first read. Your audience will not hear it, and it will let you see what images are created in your imagination rather than what was in the playwright's.

Read Like a Director

Read the play as if you were directing it. If you read it only as a visual artist, you may miss information that affects your design but is hidden in the dialogue. Read dialogue for its meaning and its implied meaning. Is there a physical relationship between characters implied in what they say? Does the dialogue between two characters only work if they do not know a third character is onstage listening? How is this third character hidden from their view? There are many ways in which the relationship between characters or between characters and the physical space will affect the meaning in the words. Finding these in the early part of your process will help you imagine spaces that will support and enlighten them.

In the "letter scene" in *Love's Labour's Lost,* Act IV/Scene 3, Berowne is writing a love letter, something he has sworn not to do. When he hears his friend coming he must hide to avoid discovery. The friend is also writing a love letter, and he also hides when a third friend enters. Their hiding places need to be concealed enough to be believable, but they also all need to be seen by the audience. This is crucial information for the designer but the text is not helpful, with stage directions in various editions ranging from the nonexistent to merely that each character "steps aside" as he finishes his letter.

Read the text while paying attention to the movements of the actors. Who enters and from where? What geography will the design you create set up? When you place a door upstage left, and a character enters there with dialogue that she has come from town, the audience will assume that the town is in that direction. Will later entrances from the other side of the stage confuse the audience when dialogue there also refers to coming from town?

If a scene takes place at dawn, what side of the stage is east, and will all other references to time of day and direction of the sun be consistent? The lighting equipment that will create the rising and setting sun and the full moon will be the lighting designer's domain, but the windows the set designer places will determine where that light can come from.

In real life, conversations are held while people do things. Onstage it can sometimes seem that characters come onstage only to talk to each other. The director and the designer should look for things for the actors to do as they talk that are believable choices and contribute to character development and a clear, rich world of the play.

French Scenes

A way in which the designer might get a closer focus on understanding the needs of the play is through a study of its French scenes.

The term *French scenes* refers to a traditional way to break up a scene as written into smaller, more easily examined and rehearsed moments. Each time a new speech changes the focus of the action, it can be considered a new French scene. For instance, Actor A and Actor B have a conversation; then Actor C joins them and the three of them talk. These are two French scenes. Actor A and Actor B is one, and Actors A, B, and C is another.

Studying the play in this way can be helpful for the designer because it makes him slow down and see the mechanics of the play more clearly. Actor C made an entrance. Where did he come from? Is the answer to this in the dialogue? Were Actors A and B seated? Does Actor C need a seat as well? Is there a relationship between these characters as regards age, class, or gender that would cause Actor A or B to give up their seat to Actor C? Examining the play at this level of detail can tell you a lot about what your design needs to make possible.

THE BREAKDOWN

A written breakdown is an outline that can bring all the needs of the play together into one document and can keep you from spending 20 minutes leafing through the script every time you need to find a particular moment or element in the play.

It can also help you see the structure of the play, especially if it is a multiple scene play.

The breakdown needs to contain the following:

- Act and scene numbers and the location of each scene in outline form.

- The page number in the script (in a musical, always include the music number, such as "Music #11 'Why Are We Here—Reprise'" as cueing and scene shifts will fall at the beginning and end of musical numbers). It is important, if possible, for all members of the production team to work from the same version of the script so page numbers will be the same.

- Any information on time of day, season, or year.

- A brief description of the action in the scene.

- Physical things needed in the scene. (It is helpful to list anything the characters say about their world, because the audience will expect to see them that way.)

- Any details about the scene changes that the script suggests, like a blackout or an á vista change.

- Anything that seems to be a problem or question you will need to discuss.

Example

Dracula: Lord of the Undead

Act I

Prologue

Pg.2	**A Ship on the English Channel**—1807—Storm	DS—Bk Drop / Bk Scrim?
	Rigging	Lg. Ship Unit (splits?)
	Ship's wheel (US with Cabin behind)	
	Exit to Hold (Fire effect in the Hold)	
		Massive, quick shift
Pg.4	**Scene 1: Garden of Cook House**, Whitby—Afternoon	DS Open
	Mina and Lucy	
	Bench	
Pg.7	**Transition**: Newspaper Vendor	Tight SR or SL (Up?)
Pg. 8	**Scene 2: Athenaeum Club London**, the next morning	DS Open
	Arthur and Seward fencing	
	Need place to change clothes & store fencing equipment	
Pg.11	**Scene 3: Purfleet Asylum**—Renfield's Cell	Full Set
Pg.14	**Transition**: Newspaper Vendor	Tight SR or SL (Up?)
Pg.15	**Scene 4: Drawing Room at Hillingham**	Wagon from US?
	Evening entertainment: reading	
	Seating: 2 chairs	
Pg.21	**Scene 5: Gardens at Hillingham**	DS Open
	Arthur and Lord G in wheelchair	

FIGURE 4.1   *Sketches and a production photo for* Dracula, Lord of the Undead

In very complex multiple set productions the breakdown will get more complicated.

In a show with recurring scenes, sometimes it is helpful to assign a letter to each location to see that the play develops, for example, an A-B-C-A-D-A structure. This can help determine how and when shifts happen and how quickly they need to happen.

The repeats of Scene A, in this example, might make you consider whether this set should stay onstage and the other sets play in front of it or if the length or spatial demands of one of the other scenes make this impossible?

To assist in ease of reading, sometimes different colors are helpful.

Example

Around the World in Eighty Days Scenic Breakdown

Act One

Scene 1—Page 3

Location: Phileas Fogg's Home on Saville Row in London

Physical Needs:	Front Door (Mr. Forester opens)
Shift Notes:	"Cross fades" to Scene Two
Musical Numbers:	"Members of the Serving Class"

Scene 2—Page 9 Multiple Scenes / Fast Moving Location

#1. Drawing Room Reform Club in Pall Mall

Four seated playing cards
A Globe

#2. House at Saville Row (pg. 13)

Preparations

#3. Taxi Cab

Travel: Pulls away
Driver (above)

#4. Charing Cross Station

Train
Musical Number: "In Only Eighty Days"

Scene 3—Page 17 Single Location

Location: Paris, France. Le Maison Bleu Royale Hotel and Dance Hall

(Described as being pulled from a Toulouse-Lautrec painting).

Time:	Night
Physical Needs:	Food, place for cancan girls to dance
Implied Needs:	Table and chair
Musical Number:	"The World You Love"

Scene 4—Page 24 Multiple Simultaneous Locations

Location

The London Exchange (short, one side of stage)
Suez, Egypt (other side of stage)
Fogg's ship The Mongolia (docks during scene)
    Practical upper deck
    Practical lower deck porthole
Musical Number: "Detective Inspector Fix"

FIGURE 4.2 *Sketches for* Around the World in 80 Days

In the preceding *Around the World in 80 Days* example, the color-coding was helpful in clarifying locations and encouraged the idea of color-coding the sets for easy audience identification as well.

REVIEWING THE FACTS

In studying the script carefully, we can borrow some process and terminology from the acting side of the business. The influence of Konstantin Stanislavski is well known as it affects the actor's craft. Within this work is an organized manner for studying text, much of which is equally useful to designers.

Stanislavski referred to the study of the basic elements of the play as **reviewing the facts**. Like the process of a detective's investigation this means asking Who, What, Where, When, How, and Why.

Who and What = Character and Action

The Character's World

The best way to get inside the play and find ways to make strong, detailed decisions about how to design it is to try to understand the characters and why they do what they do. This will give insight into actions in the play and the ways in which the character see their world. Remember that it is **their** world not yours. The more your design seems to come from their view of the world, the better.

What Is the Principal Character's Relationship to Their World?

Annie, in the musical of the same name, is an orphan in a big city. A scene at Daddy Warbucks's mansion is at Christmas time, so it is winter. To be an orphan in the winter in a big city must be lonely and cold. This alone gives

you a lot to work with. The scenes in the orphanage and on the streets of New York could be in strongly cool colors with snow on the ground and the buildings. By contrast, her life changes when she goes to live with Daddy Warbucks, so the sets there could be warm, perhaps golden to reflect his wealth. Now you have very strong visual choices that follow the character's view of the world and change when her situation changes. These choices would make Annie's world elicit a strong emotional reaction. These contrasts are warm and cold, soft and hard. These are adjectives describing the world of the play.

Design for theatre is never objective. The worlds the scenic designer creates are one of a kind. They represent a world seen through the subjective filters of the playwright, the characters, the context, and the director and designer's own responses.

Protagonist and Antagonist

The conflict in the play, and there is almost always a conflict in the Aristotelian sense, can tell you a lot about the play. Who is the protagonist and who is the antagonist? The protagonist, from the Greek for "lead actor," is the main character in a story. The antagonist creates challenges for the protagonist, creating conflict. Sometimes the antagonist might be a force or an issue, not a person.

When and Where = Time and Place

Time

Time figures into the world of the play in three basic ways: the time the play was written, the time in which the play is set, and the time that passes in the play.

The realities of the time the play is set in, its period, is important because the forces at play in a particular period are what shape the pressures on, and actions of, the characters.

The passage of time in the play is important as it affects the condition of the set. A drawing room seen in two different scenes set several years apart may age much like its inhabitants. Even if the passage of time is not drastic, it will be important to track the changes in the props, and the condition of the room; in later scenes is the room disheveled by the action?

The season affects the set designer because it affects the characters; should there be a fire in the fireplace in winter or gauzy curtains to blow at the open windows in summer? The time of day if the set is seen only in night or day may strongly affect the designer's color choices.

Place

Whatever the degree to which the set expresses the location of the play realistically or metaphorically, it always affects the characters and understanding of the play.

How and Why = Plot, Theme, and Mood

Plot

The plot is what happens in the play, the actions and reactions. These are, of course, very important.

Plot is usually pretty clear:

• The witches present Macbeth with an image of himself as king.

• Lady Macbeth pushes Macbeth to kill King Duncan.

• To consolidate his power and prevent the witches' prophecy that Banquo's heirs will inherit the throne, Macbeth has Banquo killed.

• Banquo's son Malcolm brings an army to Birnham Wood to fight Macbeth.

Theme

The theme is the "greater truth" of what is going on in the play. Behind the plot there are ideas at work. In *Macbeth*, it could be said that "ambition and murder lead to madness." This is theme. Theme is extremely important to the designer because it lets him deal with the feeling of the greater visual world. This is what will unify the various

locations and elements in the play. In Chapter 6 we will look at creating a concise written statement of the greater world of the play in order to find a **designable idea**. (More on this in Chapter 6, "The Designable Idea.")

While the Theme is a satisfactory summary statement of the play's ideology, it remains just that—a fixed summary, a definitive final statement of the play's action. But in performance, the Theme is revealed through events that happen in real time.[3]

But to be effective for actors, directors, and designers, these concepts need to be translated from the abstract to the concrete, from the realm of ideas back to the realm of human behavior shown in the play itself.[4]

Mood

The given circumstances of time, location, season, and social conditions can be effective sources of mood. Plot can elicit mood through tension, suspense, climax, and release. Moods can be activated by the mental states and emotions of the characters and the things they do.[5]

The scenic designer must be a master of mood because his work is particular to this play, this moment, this mood. The visual aspect of scenic design can express a lot about mood before a line of dialogue is spoken.

WORKING WITH WORDS

Sometimes the playwright helps us with his use of certain words that may give us insight into the play. Adjectives he uses in the stage directions to describe the set or that characters use to describe things can be very helpful in forming ideas about the visual world. Go through the script and write down all the adjectives and visual terms the playwright uses to describe things. Is there a common thread among them? Can you group them by what they describe and begin to see how the playwright thinks the characters see their world?

The Style of the Playwright's Language

Sometimes the style of the playwright's language may give clues to the designer. If he uses ornate, flowery language it might be useful to design the set with similar qualities. Shakespeare's language in *Love's Labour's Lost* is full of word play and banter between characters. The set could be designed with a playful, complex feeling to reflect this.

David Mamet's *Glengarry Glen Ross* gives no set description or information about the actor's positions or movement at all. The designer is left to find what he can from the text and the style of the writing. We know the play was written in 1984 and the language sounds contemporary. We find, from a reference to taking a character to O'Hare Airport, that the play takes place in Chicago. That is about all we have to go on. Mamet's use of language is sparse and clipped, often in short, incomplete sentences. Could this staccato style translate into a visually spare look with isolated architectural elements that don't connect to each other to convey the sense of emptiness and unease that the play creates?

Words as Images

Sometimes the images the playwright uses can give us information. Shakespeare uses allusions to nature in many of his plays. In *Macbeth*, for instance, there are a great number of references to birds. This is not to say that birds are important to the understanding of the play or that Shakespeare was trying to say something important by using bird allusions, but where choices need to be made about the image on a shield or the design of a tapestry the use of bird imagery might connect the visual world to the language of the play.

In *Romeo and Juliet* there are many uses of words relating to light and dark.

> But all so soon as the **all-cheering sun**
> Should in the furthest east begin to draw
> The **shady curtains** from Aurora's bed,
> Away from the **light** steals home my heavy son,
> And private in his chamber pens himself,
> Shuts up his windows, **locks far daylight out**
> And makes himself **an artificial night**:
> **Black and portentous** must this humour prove,
> Unless good counsel may the cause remove.
>
> Act I, Scene I

> O, she doth teach the **torches to burn bright**!
>
> Act I, Scene 5

> But, soft! What **light** through yonder window breaks?
> It is the east, and **Juliet is the sun**.
> Arise, **fair sun**, and kill the **envious moon**,
> Who is already sick and pale with grief,
> That thou her maid art far more fair than she:
> The **brightness** of her cheek would shame those
>   **stars**,
> As **daylight** doth a lamp
>
> Act II, Scene 2

> The grey-eyed morn smiles on the **frowning night**,
> Chequering the eastern clouds with **streaks of**
>   **light**,
> And **flecked darkness** like a drunkard reels
> From forth day's path and Titan's fiery wheels:
> Now, ere the **sun** advance his burning eye,
> The **day** to cheer and **night's** dank dew to dry,
>
> Act II, Scene 3

> O, she is lame! love's heralds should be thoughts,
> Which ten times faster glide than the **sun's beams**,
> Driving back **shadows** over louring hills:
>
> Act II, Scene 5

> Come, **night**; come, Romeo; come, **thou day in**
>   **night**;
> For thou wilt lie upon the **wings of night**
> Whiter than new snow on a raven's back.
>
> Act III, Scene 2

> Yon light is not **day-light**, I know it, I:
> It is some meteor that the **sun** exhales,
> To be to thee this **night** a **torch-bearer**,
> And **light thee** on thy way to Mantua:
>
> Act III, Scene 5

> A grave? O no! **a lantern**, slaughter'd youth,
> For here lies Juliet, and her beauty makes
> This vault a feasting presence **full of light**
>
> Act V, Scene 3

Could a design make connections between Romeo and Juliet's love being about light (sunlight or moonlight) and the moments when their love is threatened be about darkness? Could transitions in the play be about scenic units shifting in ways that block the light and create shadows that plunge the play into tragic darkness?

FIGURE 4.3   *Ricardo Hernandez's design for* Romeo and Juliet, *ART, 2006 Lighting by D. M. Wood*
© T. Charles Erickson Photography

FIGURE 4.4   *Ricardo Hernandez's design for* Romeo and Juliet, *ART, 2006 Lighting by D. M. Wood*
© T. Charles Erickson Photography

Music as Text

When designing musicals and opera the music becomes as important in helping find the mood, and emotional feel of the piece, as the text. Remember that the lyrics to a song are text that advances the story. It is common for a designer to play the music to a show he is working on, and other music by, or in the style of, the project's composer to set the mood as he works.

Production: *The Glass Menagerie*

An interesting aspect of *The Glass Menagerie* is that in the original script, Tennessee Williams indicated the use of projected text and images at various times during the play. This Brechtian-sounding device was not implemented in the original production, but has been explored by designers since, both in literal ways and in variations that attempt to satisfy Williams's desire for additional imagery.

This design attempted to provide some of this extra imagery in several different ways. It used projections on two large rear projection panels that were hidden among the suggestion of floating tenement windows that surrounded the set. When Amanda relived her girlhood, an image of the plantation world transformed the space. When the conversation continually returned to the need for gentleman callers, images of Arrow collar advertisements were projected.

The design also included a forced-perspective apartment house facade that disappeared into the orchestra pit, as did the fire escape, and a neighboring apartment fire escape on which a "neighbor" musician played St. Louis blues guitar. The windows could be lit up or projected on, and in one case, could be streaked with real rain. A large, shadowy male figure loomed above the set. This was, literally, a billboard for the Continental Shoe Company where Tom works and, metaphorically, both an image of the wished-for gentleman caller so dominant in the play and the absent male figure of the father. Williams's desired extra imagery was incorporated in different ways than those he described, but was made a strong part of the production.

FIGURE 4.5   *1/2-inch model for The Glass Menagerie*

FIGURE 4.6   *1/2-inch model for* The Glass Menagerie

FIGURE 4.7   *1/2-inch model for* The Glass Menagerie

FIGURE 4.8 Glass Menagerie *production photos*

FIGURE 4.9 Glass Menagerie *production photos*

Production Credits

THE GLASS MENAGERIE, Fulton Theatre, 1999
Director: Michael Mitchell
Set Design & Projections: Robert Klingelhoefer
Costume Design: Beth Dunkleberger
Light Design: Bill Simmons

READING LIST

Script Analysis for Directors, Designers and Actors, by James Thomas

SUMMARY

- The text is the most important source of information for the designer

- Text work that will give you a detailed understanding of characters, actions, and mood is critical to the success of your design.

- Your work with the text must go much further than just a study of the visual.

Project: Text

Do the following text steps with your project play.

A. The Breakdown

Using the examples given previously as your form, create a scenic breakdown of your project play. Remember to record all possible information you can get from the script. Include a brief description of what happens in the scene, what objects it requires, the time of day, and the page number in the script.

B. The Characters

Now make a list of the characters in the play. For each one give the character's age, his or her relationship with other characters, a physical description, and a personality description. Give as much of their lives previous to the play as you can find in the script.

C. Word Images

The words the playwright has the characters use reflects a great deal on how he sees them and how they see their world. Go through the script and make a list of all the visually oriented words the characters say or the playwright uses in the secondary text. As you make the list, categorize the words by which character says them. When you have completed your list, separate the words by groups reflecting what they describe, for example: Words describing the set, words describing the greater world of the play, or words describing the characters.

D. French Scenes

Do a French scene breakdown of your project play. Break it into French scenes and create a list of them, numbering the French scenes, describing the moment, and listing any thoughts you have about how the scene might play or what it might need.

NOTES

1. James Thomas, *Script Analysis for Directors, Designers and Actors* (London: Elsevier/Focal Press, 2005), xxxiii.

2. Thomas, *Script Analysis for Directors, Designers and Actors*, 307.
3. Thomas, *Script Analysis for Directors, Designers and Actors*, 19.
4. Thomas, *Script Analysis for Directors, Designers and Actors*, 21.
5. Thomas, *Script Analysis for Directors, Designers and Actors*, 260.

CHAPTER 5

RESEARCH, PERIOD, AND VISUAL HISTORY

RESEARCH AND HISTORY

Research is a huge part of the design process. Many designers enjoy this phase of the work the most, because in doing research on the play they are exploring options and learning many things that might be useful. It is also early in the process when anything is possible and deadline pressures have yet to hit.

Research can be about ideas as much as about things. Research about the play and playwright may provide key information on the interpretation of the play. Reading criticism of the play can help you understand it more quickly. Playwrights write plays for a reason, either from something in their lives, or to express something they feel strongly about in the world. Knowing what these inspirations are can explain much.

Research is what gives the designer the details of periods, places, and things from which to build his designs. Even the most abstract designs require research because you must have something to abstract from. The designer's imagination, however fertile, is helped enormously by details he can use to provide richness and authority to his work.

Because the approaches to different projects set in the same period can be so varied, even many experiences with a period will not be preparation for all projects. Scenic design, as we have noted, is about creating one-of-a-kind work every time. No matter how many times you

design using the vocabulary of a certain period, you will need to do additional research for details you have never come across before.

Additionally, the designer must have a broad awareness of the visual look of all periods of world history because production-based research is no substitute for a core understanding of the whole subject. Only with this larger understanding will he be able to be initially conversant on period, before detailed research is done, and also be able to make connections between periods based on their visual similarities or contexts.

MAKING THE PAST REAL

Some theatre-goers are put off by period plays. They feel that plays from a distant time period can't connect to them today. It is the responsibility of the director and designers to make their work compelling to their audience. We can do this in different ways in different plays—sometimes by bringing a degree of the contemporary into the past, and sometimes by making sure we bring the past to life. To do this for our audience, we have to do it, first, for ourselves.

Think of historical periods as real places, not old pictures in a dusty book; as places with very specific looks, colors, tastes, and smells instead of dead places in the past. The characters in the play you are designing live

FIGURE 5.1   *Research images from online texture sites*
www.textures.com

in this place at this time. Take a walk with them, whether it is down a foggy, gas-lit street in Dickens's London, ripe with the smell of the Thames, or a crowded, colorful alley in Calcutta redolent of cardamom and cumin. Make these places real to yourself, and your heightened appreciation of them can help you adapt them to work onstage.

After years in the business, a scenic designer accumulates an enormous amount of knowledge of wide-ranging subjects. It is not so much the dates and places of history he will focus on but the history of how people lived, what they ate, what they wore, what kinds of chairs they sat on, and what kinds of beds they slept in. For the designer this is practical knowledge. He looks at human history with a sense of acquisitiveness, on the lookout for the details that will best serve him in creating the **world of the play** for his current project.

In truth, this acquisitiveness is stronger than his desire for total accuracy. While it may be important to keep everything onstage believably within one period, audiences are not historians and the theatre is not realistic. Decisions about the world of the play are stronger than truth.

The designer should use period detail as he does everything else: to advance the audience's understanding of the play and to help the director and actor articulate character. It is often the oddness of a period's artifacts to modern eyes that can be useful in making a period seem specific and fresh.

Pre-photographic Research

Time periods since the invention of photography are much easier for the designer to research. In looking at previous periods, you have to look more carefully. Much of what we have from earlier times are art works commissioned by the wealthy that strongly skew to only the high end of society. There is very little art that depicts everyday people of most time periods before, say, the Italian Renaissance of the fifteenth century, or even until the explosion of printing technology in the eighteenth century. In using the artwork of early periods you have to look for background elements and objects, not the people in the foreground. In medieval art there are occasionally poor people or craftsmen in the background of religious works. Works of a calendar nature like *Les Très Riches Heures du Duc de Berry*, a book of hours, containing prayers to be said at certain times of day and month and season, show farmers at work in their fields and homes using tools of the period (**Figure 5.2**).

FIGURE 5.2   *February from* Les Très Riches Heures du Duc de Berry
Wikimedia.org (Public Domain)

In the eighteenth century, advances in the technology of printing made images much more available to the common man, and so subjects shifted to things that the common man was interested in. By far the most useful artist of the eighteenth century in England, for designers researching that period, is William Hogarth. The advances in printing made it possible for artists like Hogarth to create paintings and then engravings of those paintings that would be affordable to all. He also pioneered sequential art, a series of prints that told a story, the grandfather of today's graphic novel. His work is full of humor and detail. In the print **Beer Street** in **Figure 5.3**, Hogarth celebrates beer's contribution to man's happiness and a thriving society; businesses flourish with the exception of the Pawn Shop. This print has a companion piece, **Gin Lane**, which warns of gin's dangers; families fall apart and businesses close. Look at *Beer Street* and see all the potential for research.

FIGURE 5.3   *William Hogarth,* Beer Street

Wikimedia.org (Public Domain)

Photographic Research

Photographed periods have several advantages. Because they are more recent there is less lost over time. Because photography was economical enough to be used by a greater number of people than had access to art, there are more existing images, and they tend to include a wider range of economic levels.

Early photography has a sepia hue. The time period when photography began was, ironically, also when a wide range of very bright, strong aniline dyes were invented, making it a very colorful time quite different from the monochromatic world we see in the photographs. In looking at artifacts from the past, always remember that they were once used by people living in the present, who regarded them as new, exciting, and modern. The past was not lived in sepia tones.

Economic Style

It may be necessary to research a period 10, 20, or even 50 years earlier than the date of your play's period to find elements that are right for lower economic level characters. It is important to remember that most of us today live in architecture that is 25 years old or older. Most of your clothing is not this year's fashions. These facts have always been true. A poor farmer's home in rural France changed very little between 1200 and the French Revolution.

ACQUISITIVE RESEARCH

For the designer historical periods are rich shopping marts of useful elements and ideas. What you find you filter through the play and transform into something different.

Look at **Figure 5.4**. *Dining at Mayor Rockox's House*. It is a Dutch painting ca. 1630–1635 by Frans Francken the Elder. Northern Renaissance painters from about 1500 tend to show a lot of detail in their work, and a surprising amount of middle-class subjects. Widespread trade all over the world led to an explosion of the middle class in about 1600 especially in Holland.

Mayor Rockox's house is the home of a wealthy, educated man. This is clear because the room is well appointed and quite detailed. He has acquired a lot of art, some classical and some of his own time. These are the first things we see, but there is much more.

For all the richness of the room, the floor is made of bare, wide wooden planks with large, visible nail heads. In some ways this is unexpected. We might have expected a polished floor and rich carpets. Whatever the historical reason for this floor we only need to think about what it would mean to the design we are working on.

We could use its roughness as a contrast to the more finished aspects of the room that could suggest a rough or unfinished quality to the world of the play. If this didn't seem right for our project, we could look at the painting again and see the red and black checkered tiles in the hearth area. We could use this as the room's floor for a more polished look.

The windows on the left side are made of lots of small panes of glass held in place by leading. This is typical of the period because glass could not yet be manufactured in large panes. The lower half of the window has solid wooden shutters on it. These shutters are evidently there for privacy and possibly to make the window more secure from robbers. A hundred years earlier the shutters might have been heavier and over the entire window as protection against attack in war. Again, to the designer, this detail could be made even more important, the shutters heavier over the entire window to support a more threatening outside world in the play, or a more isolated, paranoid aspect of a character's personality.

There is so much a designer could use in this painting. By keeping his focus on the characters and themes of the play, and varying what he takes from the research, there are many different ways to go (see **Figures 5.5** and **5.6** for examples).

FIGURE 5.4 *Franz Franken II (1581–1642)*, Dining at Mayor Rockox's House
©Blauel/Gnamm/ARTOTHEK

FIGURE 5.5   *A design based on* Dining at Mayor Rockox's House

FIGURE 5.6   *A design based on* Dining at Mayor Rockox's House

FIGURE 5.7 *Alexander Dodge's design for* Dog in the Manger
Courtesy of Alexander Dodge

Making the Past Fresh

Making connections between a historical period and today is an important way to make a play seem fresh. We noticed that some of Mayor Rockox's art works were of his own time period. They were to him, therefore, modern art. Making these paintings seem more modern to our eyes in some way would make the play seem more contemporary to a modern audience.

The designer looks for ways to give a period work a sense of the contemporary. In his design for *Dog in the Manger* at the Shakespeare Theatre, Alexander Dodge did this in several ways.

> We were exploring the idea of being spied on and not having any privacy within the imperial court. The perforated walls suggested a confessional and were ideal for eavesdropping. The large portraits were of the Queen who was always watching even when she wasn't present.[1]
>
> —Alexander Dodge

These portraits were much larger in scale than they would have been in the actual period. In fact they had the feeling of the miniatures of artists of the period like Nicholas Hillyard but scaled up and were often cropped in a contemporary manner. In one scene their repetition brought to mind Andy Warhol's multiple portraits

(**Figures 5.7** and **5.9** show Dodge's portaits and **Figure 5.8** shows Warhol's).

FIGURE 5.8 *Andy Warhol's* Multiple Portrait of Marilyn Monroe

FIGURE 5.9   *Alexander Dodge's design for* Dog in the Manger
Courtesy of Alexander Dodge

PERIOD

Playwrights will generally state, in secondary-text opening statements, in what year the play takes place. If there is no period stated, it is generally because the play takes place in the time it was written. Some plays are about such specific events that the period will be easy to determine. It would be hard to set the musical *Titanic* in any other year than when that famous ship actually sank. If, however, the period of the play is not stated or inherent in the material, the production team may decide to set it in a period other than the one in which it was written. The text then needs to be examined for specific references or important context that may make it fit more comfortably in one period than another. The style of the language, specific words or terms, or social structures may be important considerations. Social structures like the importance of a religious reference or a monarchic government may be very specific to certain periods, and shifting the play to a period with a very different context may create more problems than it solves.

The playwright may set the play in one period but refer, directly or obliquely, to another. *The Crucible* is a more interesting play if we know that Arthur Miller was writing about the witch trials of the House Un-American Activities Commission in his contemporary Washington of 1950 in the guise of the witch trials in Salem in 1690. *The Crucible* is a play that wants to stay, visually, in its seventeenth-century setting and not be updated because Miller has already shifted its period.

Other plays take comfortably to modernization and may make stronger connections to a modern audience when shifted. Shakespeare's *Julius Caesar* works very well in modern dress and a visual world of contemporary politics (**Figure 5.10**). Shakespeare is generally strong enough to make the move to a variety of periods.

The choice to move the period of a play, like most design decisions, is best made in reaction to themes, ideas, or elements inside the play, not as a surface decision of "Wouldn't it be cool if . . . ?" Consider as your goal that any shift in period should be made to enhance the audience's understanding of the play. Setting *Volpone* in gold rush California might, however, bring some energy to the play's theme of greed, and a great deal of humor. *Henry V* has been set during the Vietnam War where its themes of patriotism and honor resonate, but the conflict

FIGURE 5.10   *Alexander Dodge's design for* Julius Caesar
Courtesy of Alexander Dodge

between medieval and modern warfare can be potentially distracting when the language is more bows and arrows and the props are more M-16s.

Anachronisms

An anachronism is a thing that belongs to a period other than the one in which it is presented. This can be either something conspicuously old-fashioned in a modern setting or something from the contemporary world in a past period, like a telephone in the eighteenth century.

In most cases, the designer will try to avoid using an element that is "wrong" for the period. This is part of the same rule that says there should be unity among all the elements of the design. As we have previously noted, however, sometimes breaking that unity can be good thing, with the "wrong" thing bringing a disunity that communicates a great deal. Peter Brook writes of a production of *Love's Labour's Lost* that was set in early eighteenth-century costume except for the bumbling character Constable Dull, who was dressed as a Victorian bobby, and that this anachronism contributed to the

humor of the character and was so "right" that it was almost unnoticeable.

In most productions, however, the designer's research will be finding furniture, and objects, that are correct for the period. The designer is responsible for making sure that unwanted anachronisms do not appear. Sometimes practical decisions of what will work onstage will require a problem to be solved in a nonperiod manner. Lanterns are regularly wired with battery-powered "candles," and a quill pen may be rigged with a black marker so there is no need for a spillable bottle of ink onstage. But generally, in addition to making insightful artistic choices, the designer will do much research just to determine what is right for the period.

Period Costumes

Because a set can often be somewhat abstract, the strongest sense of period in a production may come from the costumes. The set designer and director may talk about the degree to which the period is important in the costumes as a part of determining how far the look of the set may go from period reality.

WHAT TO RESEARCH

The script will generate many diverse subjects to research, including the period of the play and the art, architecture, and décor that might be used in the design.

Play and Playwright

Initially it is useful to research the play itself. There is much to learn about the play and the playwright, his work, and his world. Learning about the playwright will let you understand how this play fits into the context of his other works and whether his work shows common concerns or themes. The social history of when the play was written can be helpful in understanding the play's context, themes, and ideas. Understanding what the playwright was trying to accomplish with his play will help you understand what is important in its production. All this serves to help the designer develop ideas about the play.

- The *specific location:* Where does the story of the play take place? What is the actual room, or other spaces that is represented by the set onstage? (a ballroom, a tenement kitchen)
- The *general location:* What is the city or country around the specific location? (Vienna, Chicago)
- The *time period:* What are the conditions and styles that make up the context of the world of the play? (architecture, art, history, social concerns)
- *Actions* in the play: What do the characters onstage do, and how do the things they use work? (How was laundry done in 1897 Chicago?)
- *Specific props* and *details:* Many plays need a great deal of detail in the set itself and the props. (What did a 1910 Carpet Sweeper look like?)

Other Productions

Researching previous productions of the play at hand can be very helpful in understanding how the play works. Learning from the printed script how a play functions on a stage is not easy. (If it was, it would not be necessary to study and practice the craft to the degree to which it is). Seeing how others have solved the same problems can be very helpful.

> It must be a point of pride to the designer that he is not copying other designs.
>
> **"Immature artists copy; great artists steal."** This quote has been credited to Pablo Picasso, William Faulkner, and others. The lesson is that in "stealing" an idea from a previous source, you make it your own, and in so doing transform it. In copying you just recreate the original with the implication of plagiarism. Every artist and designer has been deeply influenced by the work of others. Most will freely admit the debt they owe to their teachers, mentors, and preceding generations. In a sense, nothing is truly original, and we are all part of an artistic continuum—the advancement of our chosen craft.

Previous productions may also serve as a source of things not to do. Your disagreement with another production's choices may push you in an opposite, new direction.

Also, certain productions are so iconic that knowledge of them is crucial to the discussion of how to design them now. Being unaware of an important previous production is not just a lack of knowledge; it shows your ignorance of the history of your field.

Nonspecific Research

Once ideas in the play have been identified, and specific research strings have been followed, there is often the need to explore less objective research. This can be anything that you feel will be of value to the design: cocoons and Venus flytraps for *Midsummer Night's Dream,* photomicrography of insects, stormy skies, or abandoned asylums. Search strings for nonspecific research are sometimes difficult. Be specific. Avoid searching for vague or general terms like *fear.* Sometimes adding a period reference to the search terms is helpful, like "a Victorian asylum" or "an eighteenth century slaughterhouse".

How Much Research Is Enough?

There is really no answer to this, because sometimes you find a very useful image quickly, but in general you should find enough images for a particular subject that you can make choices between them and consider combining details from several sources in what you create. Also, when you begin your research you don't really know where it will lead, and if you save only an image or two of a particular subject, you may find you need more later and can't find that great site you were on.

Doing more research than you think you will need will help you later on this or a future project.

The Right Stuff

While the designer may sometimes play fast and loose with historical accuracy to create a desired effect, it is important to be sure you are getting what you think you are. The Internet provides an amazing amount of information but sometimes doesn't make it easy to authenticate. The best advice is to do some of your research from sites you can trust, for instance, those of major museums and universities. This can give you a bottom line you can trust and use to compare research that you can't confirm. When you do image searches, don't automatically believe all you see. Go to the source site and see what it says about the image or if it cites the origin. Remember there have been many revival styles in furniture and architecture that may look like the original but have may have differences in details, materials, or manufacture.

A RESEARCH AGENDA

Researching a play can be a very convoluted process. Often search strings may take you to places you didn't expect. This can be very exciting and tremendously helpful. But there is always the danger that the path you chose to follow distracted you from another direction that might have been even better. Sometimes research feels like you are waiting for the one magic image that will give you what you need. It can be helpful to write out a research agenda to avoid letting a random search

cause you to miss something important. This is just a simple list of the things you are going to search for, and the search paths you plan to follow for each. Before you run to the studio to use what you have found, revisit the agenda and make sure you've covered all your bases.

Production Bible and Dropbox

Keeping a production bible with all your research in it has been a traditional way to stay organized. A Dropbox folder can do the same thing and make it possible for other members of the team to see and share work and ideas. Create folders that clearly identify the material, and date different images in the file name so the most current work can easily be identified.

COMBINING KEY IMAGES

After your research has reached a certain level, a few key images will often prove to be very important to the final design. Three or four diverse images will often create relationships between them that will resonate as if each says something true about the world of the play individually, but together they resolve into more than the sum of their parts.

It can be very helpful to see your research images together. Very often a breakthrough will come when you see your three best research images in close proximity. This can be accomplished traditionally by printing your images and laying them out on a table or pinning them to a bulletin board. Digitally you can combine images on the same page. Consider doing some quick color modification if it will help you see how the different images can work together or keep an image whose content is perfect but whose color palette is not what you want from distracting your eye.

Production: *Summer and Smoke*

An arena production of *Summer and Smoke* created a challenge for how to design and place the Angel statue, *Eternity*, that is an important feature of the play. Statues of angels were an obvious research item. Tennessee Williams originally titled the play *The Anatomy Chart*, and medical imagery could be useful to research, also. Scenes take place in the home/office of Dr. Buchannan. His son, John, also a doctor, is the love interest of repressed preacher's daughter Alma Winemiller. John spends his nights at Moon Lake Casino, and this shocks Alma. It would be interesting to research a casino look as well.

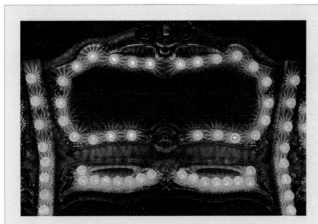

FIGURE 5.11 *Summer and Smoke research: casino sign*
© Puwadol Jaturawutthichai / Shutterstock.com

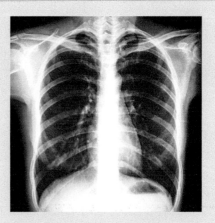

FIGURE 5.12 Summer and Smoke
research: X-ray
© JOAT / Shutterstock.com

FIGURE 5.13 Summer and Smoke *research: Angel statue*
© pio3 / Shutterstock.com

The research images in **Figures 5.11, 5.12,** and **5.13** and the sketch for the Angel statue in **Figure 5.14** show how research for all three of these ideas from the play was combined in the final design. The Angel was made of steel reinforcing bar shaped to give the statue form and suggest an internal structure like an x-ray. Before this armature was covered with pieces of linen-scrim, a string of lights was attached to its steel bones and another fixture was placed in the head where it could be aimed straight down. The linen-scrim gave the statue solidity at the top but "faded away" as the statue got closer to the base, which lessened sightline issues. The fixture in the head accented the ribcage, and the string of lights gave a casino sign feel.

Many times images seen in proximity to each other will create great energy and meaning by their similarities or differences. This combination can be made into a smash-up that strongly informs the design. It is often good to not over intellectualize

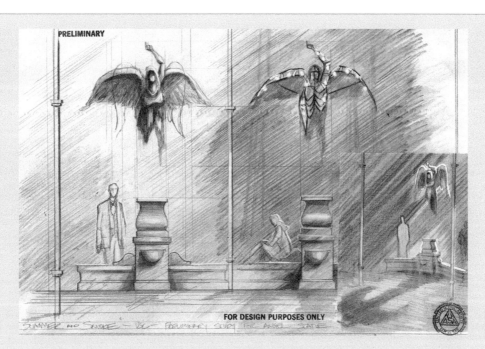

PRELIMINARY

FOR DESIGN PURPOSES ONLY

FIGURE 5.14   *Sketch of Angel statue for* Summer and Smoke

what seems to work. This can lead to taming what was initially bold and dynamic. Remember, if you have images that represent different parts or aspects of the play, leaving them to create some tension with each other may be what best expresses diverse aspects of the play.

MAKING CONNECTIONS

Sometimes the solution to a design problem may be solved by an unexpected connection to a period or culture very different from that of the play. This is only possible if you have a far-reaching knowledge of all periods.

Production: *The Grapes of Wrath*

For this production of *The Grapes of Wrath*, the director and I agreed right away that we wanted to emphasize a sense of great space, of distance, and the loneliness that goes with it. We agreed to keep set pieces minimal and to strip the three-quarters thrust space of all masking, opening it up wall to wall. It is very easy in a large multiple location play to create a lot of "stuff" that then needs room offstage to store, which means masking to hide it in this offstage position. If your initial goal is to maintain a large uncluttered space, you must make sure you are extremely economical with the pieces you use.

Research began and many useful images of the Dust Bowl were found. Particularly striking were images of the dust itself furrowed into rows to try to check its drift (**see Figure 5.15**). The line quality of the furrows would make an interesting floor pattern; its sinews would create long lines that would emphasize distance as well as be visually striking and at the same time "real" (**Figure 5.16**). There was also something about these patterns that suggested something else, and in realizing what that was, it was again apparent how important a well-rounded knowledge of art history is to the designer.

FIGURE 5.15 Grapes of Wrath *research*

Photograph by Dorothea Lange, 1938

FIGURE 5.16 Grapes of Wrath *photo*

The famous Zen garden at Ryoanji, near Kyoto, Japan, is a masterpiece (**Figure 5.17**). It features 15 stones set, in groups, onto a field of raked gravel. It is in the *karesansui* (dry landscape) style. The gravel is raked into patterns that are straight in open areas and echo the rock groupings' shapes as the patterns get closer to the groupings.

FIGURE 5.17 *Ryoanji research*
© Chuong Vu/Shutterstock.com

The viewer is to contemplate the garden as a microcosm in which rocks can be seen as islands, and the gravel patterns, the sea.

The effect of distance in microcosm was exactly what the *Grapes* design wanted to be about.

So I'd found something unexpected that promised to be useful. It supported the literal Dust Bowl images and gave some hints as to how they might be successfully used in new ways in a finite stage space.

What else was there to discover in these research images of Ryoanji?

Containing the rocks and gravel are low walls with a decaying surface that was interesting in texture and color. It was objectively a decaying wall, but with some more Zen contemplation, these walls easily evoked a slightly abstracted vista of additional space (**Figure 5.18**). This could be a way of creating a sense of greater depth in a way that was at once "real" and nonliteral. In many productions this extra distance would be accomplished with a literally depicted view painted on a drop, but that would seem false amid the simplicity of the *Grapes* design.

These walls evoked a sense of lonely distance without being in any way literal or pictorial. In the *Grapes* design they became a row of panels that looked like steel plates leaning up against the theatre's back wall. They could **evoke** distance without being a literal painted view. In a design so stripped down, anything "scenic" would have seemed artificial and wrong. The panels were left low so their shape would accentuate a wide perspective instead of a high one.

The posts used in many locations, as fences or to support a bit of a screen door, needed sockets to support them. These needed to be "above ground." They could not be set into the stage floor itself and a show deck, which would have to have been wall-to-wall in the space to keep the openness desired, would have been too expensive. The sockets, with or without posts, took the place of the 15 rocks at Ryoanji.

The completed set seemed real, yet artistic. It conveyed a feeling that was appropriate for the world of the play and was a strong use of the stage's finite space.

FIGURE 5.18   *Ryoanji research*

© cowardlion/Shutterstock.com

FIGURE 5.19   Grapes of Wrath *photo*

It is unlikely that any audience member who saw this production of *The Grapes of Wrath* realized the Ryoanji influence, though many of them probably had seen images of the garden at some point in their lives.

It was not the intention that the connection was important for the audience to understand, in fact it was better that they did not.

But the visual connection made between literal research of the 1930s' American Dust Bowl and the fifteenth-century Japanese garden led to decisions that were very helpful in creating an effective design.

FIGURE 5.20   Grapes of Wrath *photo*

FIGURE 5.21   Grapes of Wrath *photo*

FIGURE 5.22 Grapes of Wrath *photo*

Design Process Recap

- A desire for a great, open space led to making very simple choices as to what pieces to use.
- Research images from the dust bowl gave ideas about how the basic space should look
- Intuitive research from an unrelated period found ways to make the sense of space become an aesthetic choice

Production Credits

The Grapes of Wrath, WVU School of Theatre and Dance, 2008
Director: Jerry McGonigle
Set Design: Robert Klingelhoefer
Costume Design: Hannah Wold
Lighting Design: Alan McEwen

CREATING A RESEARCH FILE

In the not too distant past, most designers had lots of magazine subscriptions and clipped images they would use for a project they were working on or wanted to save for future projects. These usually filled cardboard boxes to which order was only occasionally brought in the designer's downtime. They were typically moved into folders organized by category and/or period.

The digital age has changed this somewhat, but it is still important to create and maintain a personal image file of research from all periods of history. You can add images you like that come from your show research as

that production wraps up and any other images you want to keep for the future.

Categories for historical periods included might be Egypt/Mesopotamia, Greece/Rome, the Middle Ages, Italian Renaissance, Northern Renaissance, Seventeenth Century, Eighteenth Century, Nineteenth Century, and Twentieth Century, though subcategories in some of these might be helpful. Include images in at least the following categories: Architecture, Interiors, Furniture, Art, and Color Palette.

Using the slideshow function can let you scroll through a category either in a specific search for something or to familiarize yourself with a period you haven't used in a while.

With the advent of digital rendering techniques, online research images can very quickly be put to use. Remember there are still books and magazines available that contain things not available online.

READING LIST

Essentials of Period Style, by Hal Tine
Period Styles for the Theatre, by Douglas A. Russell
The Styles of Ornament, by Alexander Speltz (online)

SUMMARY

- Research is vital to the success of every design.

- Don't make stuff up. Your imagination needs to be fed with real things you can adapt into what you want.

- Make a serious effort to learn as much as you can while researching a project. It'll make you a better designer.

- Start and keep up a file of period images for your personal collection

---

Project: Researching the Project Play

Do research in the following areas for your project play. Specifics given are for a production of *Riders to the Sea* (Synge), and these instructions are an example of a research agenda. By making a list of the things you need to investigate, you will avoid missing information if your research leads you far afield.

Play and Playwright

John Millington Synge (1871–1909)
The Irish Literary Revival
The Abbey Theatre
Other plays: *Playboy of the Western World, The Shadow of the Glen, The Well of the Saints*

The Specific Location

A cottage kitchen (a fishing family's home) on an island off the Irish coast, 1904
Architecture/construction: Stone? Thatch roof?
Interior treatments: walls, floor

The General Location

The Aran Islands
The west coast of Ireland

The Time Period

1904 Ireland
Politics
Religion

Actions in the Play

Turf stove
Spinning wool
Pot oven
Fishing

Specific Props and Details

"Nets, oil-skins, spinning wheel, some new boards"
Burial customs

Other Productions

Nonspecific Research

The sea
Storms at sea
Shipwrecks
Fishing boats

Textures

Stone
Turf
Thatch

Research Collage

When you have found images and information for the topics listed, pick those which you find strongest and arrange them on the table. Now think about the mood of the play. How well is the mood represented in your research? Do other of your images have a better sense of mood? Can you manipulate the images you have to better reflect the mood? When you have done what you can to improve the mood of your images, arrange them on a piece of black board and make a research collage. You can manipulate the size of your images and let the positions in which you place them begin to express an idea, if possible.

NOTE

1. Statement by the designer via email.

CHAPTER 6

THE DESIGNABLE IDEA

CHOICES

Making choices of what elements to put onstage and deciding what they will communicate to the audience is the core of the designer's work. To make these choices he needs to clearly define for himself the qualities he finds in the play.

Your work with the text and your research will provide much information to ponder. You must now come up with a fairly concise idea as to how you will approach your design.

There are several terms that can be used for this idea.

The term **concept** brings with it some baggage, having often been used to describe an idea of a director or designer that can seem to be laid on the play like a great weight. It forces the play into a mold that restricts it. This is, of course, unfair. *Concept* is just a word, but let's look at other choices.

The term **metaphor** can be helpful in making connections between things and ideas. As we will see throughout this book, connections are the lifeblood of the craft. Metaphor as a part of speech is a way to compare two unlike objects or ideas to provide a clearer description. A metaphor can also be said to be a thing regarded as representative or symbolic of something else, especially something abstract. Both meanings are useful to the designer. Both speak to his work of making one thing standing in for another.

The metaphor "The world is a prison" might lead to a design reminiscent of Piranesi with heavy staircases and stark shadows. The metaphor "Business is a game" might lead to a set for *How to Succeed . . .* that resembles a Monopoly board. The use of metaphor does not need to be literal. Texture is often used for its metaphorical meaning, where the medieval world of war in Shakespeare might be metallic, heavy, sharp, and brutal.

The term **designable idea** gives, perhaps, the most room for a range of ideas on which a design could be based. In looking at the themes and the characters in the text, we try to find insights on which to base our decisions. Some ideas are not easily designable because they are not inherently visual. Jealousy, for instance, might be a theme in the play, but it does not lend itself to visual elements we can use. The symbolic use of the color green alone will not make a good design, and *designable idea* implies a **visual** *and* **practical idea**.

What are needed are ideas about the play's themes, meaning, and context that are useful in the visual, practical work of the designer. How can we arrive at ideas about the play that can be translated into designable elements?

LOOKING FOR ADJECTIVES

Making a list of adjectives that describe, to you, the moods, ideas, and places in the play can be a good exercise. Adjectives such as *dark*, *hard*, and *gloomy* are perhaps useful, but more specificity in the choice of adjectives might lead to better examples. Adjectives such as *fragile*, *brutal*, *labyrinthine*, or *fractured* conjure up stronger visual ideas. Use, as well, adjectives in the text itself or that the playwright use to describe things in the play. Making a written list will both record your choices and make them easier to review.

Keep It Positive

When you look for descriptive words to help you describe the play, and when you talk about your design ideas to others, be aware how the words you use will be perceived. The play may be set in a very **rough**, **dark**, and **coarse** world, but in the theatre it should never be described as **drab**, **boring**, or **ugly**. In the same way, in talking about a past project, you should always refer to its **challenges** not its **problems**.

THE WRITTEN STATEMENT

It is helpful to create a simple, visually based, written statement about the play as a way to make your feelings about it clearer. This should ideally be quite short and very concise. If your first attempts are long and rambling, work on condensing and refining it until it contains no unnecessary element.

"Hamlet is called home after the murder of his father to find his boyhood home a place of intrigue and corruption."

"*Ragtime* plays out across a broad American canvas as the dawning of a new century sees its own uncertain future".

For this production of *Ragtime*, an American flag was superimposed on a dramatically lit cloud image (**Figure 6.1**; see the original cloud image in **Figure 6.2**) that could suggest the sunrise or sunset of the America century.

For the arena production of the play *Lidless* by Frances Ya-Chu Cowhig in **Figure 6.3**, the written statement "The memories of Guantanamo hang over the characters' heads, more real than their present daily life" led to a design that became just that—a Guantanamo-of-the-mind chain-link fence unit suspended over the space.

In his book *Script Analysis for Directors, Actors, and Designers*, James Thomas advises,

First, develop a concise literary statement that describes the important conditions in the play. Then present all the information in the play so that it is understood in a manner that relates to that description.[1]

Developing a statement of the main idea tests artistic awareness because it forces the artistic team to determine at the beginning of the process just what it is they want to say. It will stimulate thoughts about acting, directing, and design. Often it takes considerable practice to acquire the skills needed to define the main idea accurately. The growth of the skill can be nurtured by making it a habit to describe the main idea for any plays read or seen.[2]

FIGURE 6.1   *Ragtime sketch*

FIGURE 6.2   *Cloud research*
Mayang's Free Texture Library

FIGURE 6.3   *Design for the play* Lidless

The **designable idea** does not have to be complicated or profound. Think of it as simply a way to decide what to use and what not to use. For a recent production of *Kiss Me Kate*, the designable idea was something anyone who has worked in the theatre for long will understand. Sometimes you are trying to make something beautiful and perfect onstage as your real-life offstage is falling into chaos and disorder. This is a simple way to look at what happens to the characters in *Kiss Me Kate*, and make the decision that the onstage sets should be colorful, elegant, and spare, while the backstage sets should be cluttered, messy, and more monochromatic.

Kiss Me Kate needs no more complicated concept.

OBJECTS HAVE MEANING

Objects placed on a stage become more than the things they were in real life. They take on meaning because they were selected for a reason, and the audience is asked to interpret meaning from what they are, why they were chosen, and how they are placed and used.

This transference from a simple, real object to something meaningful is central to our concept of art. At least since the modern period in art began in the early twentieth century, objects brought from the real world into an art gallery and exhibited, sometimes with little or no transformation, have been regarded as art.

Think of Marcel Duchamp's "Fountain," a porcelain urinal. Because it is placed in a context that makes its viewer look at it with different eyes, it is art. This is tied to the concept of estrangement, mentioned in the discussion of Brecht in Chapter 2. Making the everyday "strange," that is, special, makes the viewer ask, "What does it mean?" "Why is this object here?"

Because the audience will look for meaning in what is placed onstage, the designer must explore what the objects he selects will, or can, mean.

The meaning objects bring can be an important way to find a designable idea.

Many objects the designer will choose create references to ideas that are fairly easy to understand:

Doors: Possibilities, options, different paths to take, escape, entrapment
Mirrors: Introspection, vanity, duplicity, elegance
Windows: Watching, being watched, letting in light
Fireplace/Hearth: Home, warmth
Rocking Chair: Warmth, safety
Rocking Horse: Childhood, the past, innocence

Not all these responses are crystal clear by themselves, but in the context of the play, with ideas in the text to bounce off of, they can communicate a great deal. Using objects in this way and contrasting them with objects of very different meaning can almost create a silent dialogue between the objects.

FIGURE 6.4 *Design for the play* Turn of the Screw

A Path to Finding a Designable Idea Can Be

- Study the characters and themes in the play

- Research the locations and things in the play

- Interpret the possible meanings of the things found in research in light of your ideas about the play's characters and themes.

To see how this process plays out, the following sections will use *A Streetcar Named Desire* as an example.

Study the Characters and Themes in the Play

Consider the character of Blanche Dubois and the effect on her of the environment in which she finds herself. She has come to stay with her sister, Stella, and Stella's husband Stanley in their small New Orleans apartment, because she has nowhere else to go. Blanche is disgraced by a situation in her previous job. Her major character flaw is that she lives with illusions of a genteel past that are now greatly at odds with her present. The apartment, to Blanche, is rough and confining, too small for much privacy. The people around her seem, to her, to be equally rough and unpleasant.

A notable poetic moment in the play is when Blanche buys a cheap colorful Chinese paper shade to put over the apartment's bare bulb. This is a metaphor for her needing to live in a world of soft light, not the hard light of day or the mirror's unkind reflection.

New Orleans is hot in the summer. This could be stressed to make the characters in the small apartment uncomfortable. Maybe Stanley lives in a state of undress because of the heat that to Blanche creates disturbing sexual tension.

The apartment is so small that Blanche, Stanley, and Stella have no privacy. Married couples often stop closing the bathroom door, which would disturb Blanche. They have set up a makeshift bed for her in the kitchen, and a curtain is all that separates it from their bedroom. She would clearly hear them in bed. The neighborhood around the apartment is crowded and busy, with garish lights at night and lots of people around.

Research the Locations and Things in the Play

The play was written in 1947, and there is no reason to believe it is not intended to take place in that year. It is set in New Orleans, in the Marigny neighborhood, next to, but not in, the French Quarter. It is a less desirable neighborhood than the Quarter. Do research that is as specific to the time period and that particular part of the city as you can.

When you have assembled these images, look through them and characterize what makes the architecture you are seeing specific.

List the common elements:

Crumbling brick or other masonry buildings
Porches and balconies
Shutters and French doors
Columns
Wrought iron, simple and more decorative

Now attribute meaning, within the context of *Streetcar*, to these elements. In other words, make them useful to yourself in designing this play.

Crumbling brick or other masonry buildings: Age, which is Blanche's enemy; decay; poverty.

Porches and balconies: Surrounding buildings, other people always around, watching.

Shutters and French doors: Shutters hide or reveal. They are like doors that still let some air move. They might be opened by Stanley and closed by Blanche to hide from the world outside.

Columns: Stately columns could suggest Blanche's genteel plantation past, now in decay.

Wrought iron, simple and more decorative: New Orleans ironwork can seem organic, based on plant forms but hard, rusted, decaying. Open ironwork can seem skeletal, confining, cage-like. As a construction material it allows openness, transparency.

If you were to write a designable idea written statement based on this process it might be:

The physical environment of the play will trap Blanche in a cage that both confines her and leaves her open to the scrutiny of others, a space physically uncomfortable to her due to its heat and lack of privacy that nevertheless has a fading, decayed beauty.

As explained here, the *designable idea* tends to come from more "inside" the play than the external feeling of concept.

Two terms of importance to consider are **reductive** and **inclusive**. In regard to scenic design, *reductive* means the designer reduces the different ideas about the play into a unified setting that contains them. It is an external approach; the play must be forced to fit in the box. *Inclusive*, in contrast, means that diverse ideas about the play are allowed to remain diverse, and the design reflects them all, even at the loss of unity.

We have looked at several ways to find a designable idea in the text: with adjectives, by making a clear written statement, and by finding meaning in the objects we will use. Following are three case studies of productions that came up with their designable ideas in different ways. Consider how they found ideas in their very different texts that, combined with research, led to strong, simple designs.

Production: *Carousel*

Carousel is another Rodgers and Hammerstein musical written two years after *Oklahoma!* It begins in Scene 1 at an amusement park on the New England coast in 1873.

A working carousel is the focus of the scene. Billy Bigelow, the carousel barker, meets Julie, a local girl in an elaborate scene that is largely an unscripted visual sequence. The carousel is a metaphor for life, implying we get on the carousel and life spins on and on beyond our control. The carousel itself is only seen in this scene, but requires a strong technical solution that will make it easier to shift out of, as well as enough detail and importance to carry through, the play as a metaphorical image.

In Scene 2, a romance sparks between them—Billy the rough, impulsive "bad boy" and Julie the "good girl,"—on a path along the shore. The key song here is "If I Loved You" and in the course of it they realize they do.

> I don't need you or anyone to help me. I got it all figgered out for myself. We ain't important. What are we? A couple of specks of nuthin'. Look up there. (He points up. They both look up)
> (He sings)
> There's a helluva lot o' stars in the sky,
> And the sky's so big the sea looks small,
> And two little people—
> You and I—
> We don't count at all.[3]

The next scene is set at a seaside café and boarding house a month later. Julie and Billy are married, but all is not well. He is unemployed and frustrated about it. Julie confesses to a friend that Billy has hit her, but defends him. Her love of Billy is constancy itself, no matter what he does. Julie tells Billy she is pregnant, and in the song "My Boy, Bill" we hear his thoughts for the future and stirring fatherly emotions. Later in the scene, though, Billy is talked into becoming involved in the payroll robbery of a ship owner being planned by one of his shady friends, Jigger. It seems to Billy that this is his only way to provide for his growing family. Act I ends with a sense of oncoming tragedy.

Act II begins at a clambake on an island across the bay. The plan is that the clambake will serve as Billy and Jigger's alibi; they will sneak away to commit the robbery and return after it. But things go very wrong, the robbery is botched, and when threatened with prison by the police, Billy stabs himself. Julie arrives and he dies in her arms. At the end of the scene, two heavenly figures come for Billy to escort him to heaven.

Heaven, in the next scene, is referred to in the script as "Up There." The God in this heaven, where a year on earth is just a minute, is called the Starkeeper, responsible for polishing and placing the stars in the heavens. Billy is told he hasn't done enough good in his life to get into heaven. Asked if he has unfinished business on earth, he asks about his child. He learns he has a daughter, and Billy is allowed to go back to earth to see her.

The action jumps 15 years, the earthly amount of time that Billy has been "Up There," to the cottage where Julie and their troubled daughter, Louise, live. Billy can let them see him if he chooses. He talks to Louise, telling her he knew her father, and learns that Julie has remained in love with him all along. Billy tries to get Louise out of her sense of despair but frightens her, and she runs inside. Billy doesn't allow Julie to see him, but she sings a reprise of "If I Loved You" with the lyrics now "How I Loved You."

The last scene is Louise's high school graduation, which Billy has asked to remain on earth to see. As the valedictory speech is given, he inspires Louise to go on with her life and not be held back by his mistakes. This earns him his entrance to heaven, and the play ends with the inspiring "You'll Never Walk Alone."

Some Ideas in the Play that Were Explored in the Search for a Designable Idea

- Julie's abiding love
- "Up There" keeping watch on earth "down below"
- The carousel as a metaphor for the way life spins on and on
- "Up There" as relating to the stars

Research was done on the New England coast and carousels. One research image of a carousel had a very strong circular base below its curved canopy that seemed to be almost cosmic (**Figure 6.5**). An image of earth seen from space had a similar shape (**Figure 6.6**). These two images were the key to the design. Early manipulation of their shapes developed a circular floor with a curved shape hung above it (**Figure 6.7**).

Continued research of New England brought up images of lighthouses. The lighthouse could be a symbol of Julie's abiding love, as a lighthouse is always there on the shore waiting, patiently, its eyes on the sea. It could also be metaphoric of heaven's

FIGURE 6.5 *Research—a carousel*
©Vitamin Co / Shutterstock.com

FIGURE 6.6 *Research—Earth seen from space*

© Triff / Shutterstock.com

FIGURE 6.7 *Diagram of set shapes*

FIGURE 6.8 *The Carousel*

constant watching of Earth down below. Detailed research of lighthouses found images of the big Fresnel lenses through which lighthouses shine their light. These lenses could be thought of as star-like.

In planning the carousel, it was decided that instead of using a turntable for the circular motion we would design separate rolling horses on which male dancers would move their girls. It would be exciting if the curved shape above could sometimes be sky and in Scene 1 be the carousel canopy. It was designed as light boxes covered with scrim. The scrim would be painted with clouds, and the inside of the boxes would contain the lights of the carousel canopy and fiber-optic stars. With a change in the lighting and the horses rolled off, the carousel would disappear easily.

Note in **Figure 6.8** that an additional piece was added for the carousel that flew in, opened like an umbrella, and then rotated at the speed at which the horses were moved.

"Up There" was designed as an abstracted lighthouse with a huge Fresnel lens and smaller Fresnel stars vacuformed out of clear plastic (**Figure 6.9**).

The lighthouse was also used in a realistic manner on the clambake island (**Figure 6.10**), and in a scaled-down unit used in other scenes to create distance (**Figure 6.11**).

In Act II, Scene 1 with all the lights in the light boxes off and their scrim fronts lit, the curved ring became a sky (**Figure 6.12**). A collage of architectural elements flew in to complete a seaside scene.

FIGURE 6.9   *"Up There"*

FIGURE 6.10   *The clambake*

FIGURE 6.11   *Scale lighthouse unit*

FIGURE 6.12   *Act II, Scene 1*

Connecting ideas in the text to research in ways that create simple, evocative scenic units can make a design rich, interesting, appropriate, and unusual.

Design Process Recap

*   Initial ideas about the interconnectedness of the locations led to research that could be abstracted into simple shapes that would always be onstage but which by varying the way they were lit either internally or externally could change their meanings.
*   Research of New England led to lighthouses, which had strong realistic and metaphoric uses.
*   By manipulating these ideas about the play and the objects from research in light of the meaning they could express in the context of the play, a small number of set pieces and the basic set of simple shapes could create all the elements of the set.
*   The resulting set both expressed the feel of its realistic locations and its metaphoric ones.

Production Credits

Carousel, Fulton Theatre, 2005
Director: Marc Robin
Set Design: Robert Klingelhoefer
Lighting Design: Paul Black
Costume Design: Beth Dunkleberger

Production: *And the Soul Shall Dance*

This production of *And the Soul Shall Dance* by Wakako Yamauchi used designable ideas about the realistic world of the play's location with elements from the characters' heritage. The play is about two Japanese families in 1930s California farm country. One family is getting along well in this harsh, new place and the other is not. The climax of the play has the wife of the unhappy family walk out into the desert, to her death in her kimono. Scenes take place in the houses of both families and the areas around them.

It was felt that the houses should seem somewhat fragile, as life is tough in this harsh land, as well as that there was the potential for beauty in it. Research images of desert mirages were found for this combination of harshness and beauty. A Photoshop mash-up of research images began to hint at an open space with small house units (**Figure 6.13**). The desert should seem harsh but beautiful.

The stage was not overly large, so the house units would have to be small and easy to shift. Thinking about this led to research of traditional Japanese Noh theatre, which uses small mobile abstracted set pieces to symbolize a mountain or a boat. The influence of this would lead to houses in *Soul* that were a visual combination of realism and Japanese tradition, a theme of conflict in the play (**Figure 6.14**).

The final design used a backdrop and floor cloth, each with painted shapes of two overlapping rectangles. These shapes gave focus to the placement of the house units and reinforced the contrasts between the two families. The desire for a big desert mirage look in the final moment led to putting gold Mylar on the floor US. When the distraught wife makes her final walk into the desert, lights would reflect off this plastic onto the actors and scenery. The paint job on the drop and houses incorporated metallic gold with gray and red in a way both real and symbolic. It also encouraged the Mylar reflections.

The overall look of the design merged realism with a longingly beautiful sense of tradition.

FIGURE 6.13   *Research mash-up*

FIGURE 6.14   *Noh theatre scenic unit*
Courtesy of The Noh.com—photograph ©Toshiro Morita

FIGURE 6.15   And the Soul Shall Dance *photo*

FIGURE 6.16   And the Soul Shall Dance *photo*

FIGURE 6.17   And the Soul Shall Dance *photo*

Design Process Recap

- Initial ideas were about the qualities of the landscape into which the characters had come to live and both its beauty and harshness.
- The physical size of the performance space and the fragile qualities of the house units were considered and made to work both physically and conceptually.
- A paint treatment was created that seemed both lushly beautiful and hauntingly lonely.

Production Credits

And the Soul Shall Dance, Pan Asian Repertory Theatre, 1989
Director: Kati Kuroda
Set Design: Robert Klingelhoefer
Lighting Design: Tina Charney
Costume Design: Toni Leslie-James

Production: *A Christmas Carol*

This was a new musical adaptation of the holiday classic. Key to the discussion of what could be done scenically was the desire to make the ghost effects in the play as spectacular as possible yet integrated in the Victorian period. The budget for this production was not as big as would be needed for a large realistic production with elaborate street scenes of London so ideas that might create a controlled approach were discussed. The designable idea breakthrough came when it was considered that this telling of Dicken's classic could be done within a Victorian Magic Theatre. The context of this could allow the use of projections that would seem to be in the style of magic lantern slides of the period but then morph into motion video. The ghost appearances would use what would seem like period illusions.

Because the video would give most of the visual interest of places traveled to by the characters, the set could be mostly these cabinet tricks and stage drapery

A first look was designed to be a framed rear-projection (RP) screen on a draped stage with the "show curtain" image being a period "Welcome Christmas" slide.

To change the mood of the stage, this drapery could shift from the festive red curtains to black ones.

Scrooge's bedroom became the most important set in the play because it was the launching pad for the effects of Jacob Marley and the three ghosts. In planning these effects the focus was put on three set pieces: the bed, an UC fireplace, and a wardrobe. The drapes that surrounded them were of gray Polysilk stenciled with a Victorian wallpaper pattern. The sheerness of the Polysilk and its color allowed these drapes to be backlit in a different color palette for each of the four sections of story that took place there.

The first effect was Jacob Marley's appearance. After a small moment of diversion in which a "mirror" of RP material over the fireplace had a video effect, the wardrobe which Scrooge had previously opened with hinged doors began to open like a drawbridge with smoke and light support and Marley and his girl backup singers entered. Lighting shifted the Polysilk to green.

> In approaching this play we began with the central idea that Dickens was writing about a change in a person's perspective. I remember that early in the process we decided that Scrooge's physical perspective might mirror what he was experiencing internally.
>
> The Ghost of Christmas Past flew Scrooge up over the action on his bed so that he was looking down on things he could not change or alter. The Ghost of Christmas Present placed Scrooge in the action but the Ghost itself was huge, dominating the physical space so that we never mistook this relationship with the more "realistic" opening or ending scenes. The Ghost of Christmas Future was enormous and Scrooge looked up at the action as if from the grave. These physical shifts were certainly supported by additional design but the concept created physically the distance and shifting perspective the actor was internalizing. Once these ideas were in place the play almost seemed to stage itself.[4]
>
> —Director Eric Johnson

For the first ghost, the Ghost of Christmas Past, the audience was expecting a big effect, and initially it was kept small, as a little girl with a glowing headpiece rose up from inside Scrooge's bed. Soon the bed with Scrooge and the ghost rose off the floor and white drapery that seemed like the bed dressing flew in to hide the other pieces of Scrooge's furniture and provide a surface for a video travel sequence that made the elevated bed seem to fly. Elements of the video throughout had a magic lantern style but departed from actual period effects as motion was allowed to change the way it was used.

Because the Scrooge's bedroom scenery was just the three trick pieces and drapery, most shifts were simply drapery pieces flying in and out to hide or reveal them.

For the Ghost of Christmas Present, the fireplace unit telescoped higher and wider until it was an opening through which the ghost could enter. Because Christmas Past had been small, Christmas Present was 12 feet tall, his long gown hiding a rolling rig pushed by a stagehand that also opened the robe to reveal puppets of Ignorance and Want. Lighting shifted the Polysilk to red.

For the final visitor, the Ghost of Christmas Yet to Come, another scale-based decision was made. A black silk drape flew in that framed huge skeleton hands and Scrooge played up to this spirit that was too tall to be completely seen. When it was time

FIGURE 6.18 A Christmas Carol *storyboard*

for the spirit to show Scrooge his future, the hands were rigged to tip and appear to open the black robe to reveal a flown-in RP screen for video effects.

The choice to context the play in a Magic Theatre enabled the focus to be on well-engineered tricks as opposed to a lot of realistic scenery. The designable idea and the technical movement of the production supported each other very successfully.

In the partial storyboard for A Christmas Carol shown in **Figure 6.18**, the top left sketch is the show curtain look with the "Welcome Christmas" image rear-projected on an RP screen set in a circular Victorian frame. The peripheral Victorian stage curtains were painted and in all the scenes. Red soft drapery flew in to frame the RP screen.

In the top right sketch, Scrooge's Bedroom is shown. Its pieces are the Bed Unit SR, the Fireplace Unit center, and the Wardrobe Unit SL. Note that the colors were kept dark and monochromatic and the way in which the gray Polysilk drapery gave a feeling of walls while being transformable in color by lighting.

The middle left sketch shows the Ghost of Christmas Past look with the bed flown and the bed dressing fabric flown in to hide the other bedroom units.

The middle right sketch shows the Ghost of Christmas Present look. The Fireplace unit has telescoped up and open to allow the 12-foot figure of the Ghost to roll in. The firebox component of the Fireplace was tracked to pull US as the telescoping occurred.

The bottom left sketch is the Ghost of Christmas Yet to Come in which his full-stage black robes fly in to conceal everything else onstage except his bony arms, which are shown in the bottom right sketch after they have been tripped by pneumatic cylinders to make it appear that they have pulled open his robe to reveal the round RP screen from the first sketch to be used for visuals of the cemetery.

Design Process Recap

- Thinking about what was needed to create the magic that the play required led to the creation of a context, a world onstage in which the play would be presented, and that would explain why things were being done in this way.
- This was both a technical decision and a conceptual one, made at the same time that guided all the remaining design decisions.
- The focus of the design was on the actions of the characters and the ghost stories instead of pictorial scenery that show a "real" world of locations.

FIGURE 6.19   *The Ghost of Christmas Past photo*

FIGURE 6.20 *The Ghost of Christmas Present photo*

Production Credits

A Christmas Carol, Fulton Theatre, 2001
Director: Eric Johnson
Set Design: Robert Klingelhoefer
Video Design: Adam Larsen
Lighting Design: Bill Simmons
Costume Design: Beth Dunkleberger

SUMMARY

- Work hard to develop a simple, clear statement of your designable idea.

- Make your technical solutions come from, and support, your conceptual ideas and vice versa. The more your solutions to both the practical and the conceptual are the same, the stronger they will be.

- Use objects for their meaning. Make the things you need to do the play also be things that speak to the ideas in the play.

- See *designable ideas* as coming from inside the play and its characters not as something from outside visual sources and then keep them as simple ways to explain and strengthen how you will do the play.

Project: The Designable Idea

Review all the work you have done so far on your project play. In this project you are to use the ways you broke down the play in Chapter 3, the text work you did in Chapter 4, and your research from Chapter 5 to come up with a designable idea.

- First, work on a short, concise written statement about the play. Remember to use visual terms.
- Interpret the possible meanings of things found in your research in light of ideas about the play's characters and themes.

Take your time with this; it is a crucial part of the design process. Consider alternate ideas. When you have decided on your approach, make a refined research collage that gets as close as you can to the feeling you have for *line, shape, form, color*, and *texture*. This collage should include more images than your first research collage from Chapter 5 did, but don't get carried away. Aim for economy. Cut away or color appropriately any white paper that shows around your research images. You may also go further in manipulating images than you did in your collage for Chapter 5.

When you have gotten the elements of your collage chosen, arrange them on a piece of black board. You may organize them into an arrangement that suggests what you envision for the final set, for instance, a floor texture along the bottom with doors or furniture on it and ceiling research above, but don't push it in that direction too far. As the last component of the collage, print your written statement and add it to the images. You may make the background to this text a color from the images or make the text a font that suggests the period of your design. You may put this text at the edge of the images or incorporate it throughout in some way.

Attach everything neatly. **Figure 6.21** shows a sample finished product.

If this is done in a class setting, I suggest having a presentation day where all students present their collage to the class.

FIGURE 6.21 *Project example*

NOTES

1. James Thomas, *Script Analysis for Actors, Directors, and Designers* (Burlington, MA: Focal Press/Elsevier, 2005), 196.

2. Thomas, *Script Analysis for Actors, Directors, and Designers*, 197.
3. Richard Rodgers and Oscar Hammerstein II, *Six Plays by Rodgers and Hammerstein* (New York: Random House, 1945), 109.
4. Statement from the director via email.

CHAPTER 7

SPACE

CONSIDERATIONS REGARDING SPACE

Space, for the designer, is both an abstract concept and a hard reality. It is the designer's job to define the space in which the performer does his work.

The stage, regardless of its configuration, functions as an optical focal point, and creates the impression we are looking through this lens into a boundless space beyond. In fact, for most spectators, it is the apprehension of space that may be the most profound and powerful experience of live theatre although, admittedly, it is one that is most often felt subconsciously.[1]

The volume of space the designer begins with is full of possibilities.

Even the simplest defining of an area inside that space creates a focus, an island where the performer is contained, supported, made important. As well as creating a "here" this also creates a "there," a positive and a negative space (**Figure 7.1**). This definition creates rules. The actor travels across the surrounding space to reach a destination. Straddling the line creates confusion. If the actor stands with one foot in a defined area and one foot out of it, where is he? The audience has to figure out what this means. Is it a mistake?

Emotional Space

Space has emotional qualities. Think about a lone figure crossing a vast open space, then consider a crowded tenement on a hot summer day. The designer will have reactions to the text in terms of the feeling of the space implied.

Some will be directly from the text, concerning the lives of the characters or the description of the location. Do these people live in a tiny cottage or a vast palace? Some will be an emotional reaction by the designer to the feelings the play evokes. Are the characters lost in their world or crushed under the weight of their past? The fundamental articulation of space can create a powerful reaction in the audience before all the other decisions of detail, color, or texture begin to be considered.

Movement in Space

How does the actor move in the space—in smooth sweeping arcs, or in fits and starts as he encounters obstacles that limit his movement? Everything the designer places in the space varies how and where the actor can move. What are the qualities of movement the text suggests? The answer can come from the period, specific action in the text, or the inner life of the characters.

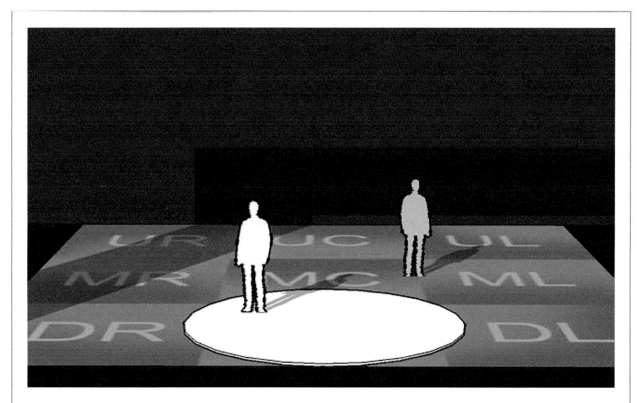

FIGURE 7.1   *Theatre Space: Here and there*

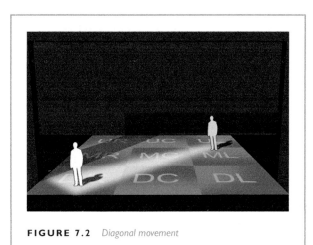

FIGURE 7.2   *Diagonal movement*

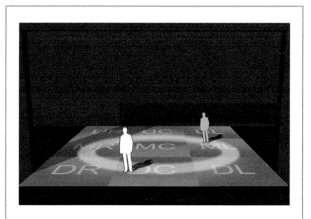

FIGURE 7.3   *Circular movement*

Diagonal lines create visual excitement when contrasted with horizontal and vertical ones. The same is true of lines created by objects in space whether they are static walls and platforms or the implied lines of an actor's movement. Diagonal movement is visually stronger than lateral cross-stage movement because it maximizes the sense of perspective over distance (**Figure 7.2**).

Circular movement involves the volume of the space (**Figure 7.3**). Any movement patterns of the actor begin to create a definition of space (**Figure 7.4**).

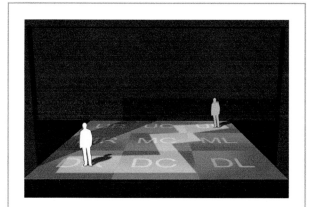

FIGURE 7.4   *Zigzag movement*

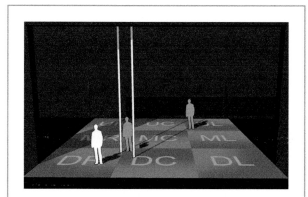

FIGURE 7.5   *Simply defined space*

FIGURE 7.6   Summer and Smoke

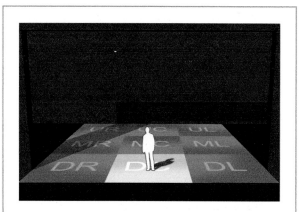

FIGURE 7.7   *Position in space*

Defining Space

It takes very little to give specificity to space. Two verticals become a door when used as such and create a sense of inner and outer space (**Figure 7.5**).

Objects of any kind can describe and divide space. Ramps and platforms create paths. Verticals and objects create obstacles that define how the actor may move.

Position of the Defined Area in Space

Placing a defined area within the stage space is largely determined by what else must be included onstage. Is more than one area necessary? If so, is there a hierarchy to the importance of the areas? If only one area is needed it will usually be placed DSC, in a proscenium or thrust space as this is the most important spot and has the

best sightlines for a high percentage of the audience (**Figure 7.7**).

Two spaces can share DS, one going right and one left. The third space will be pushed US and be a relatively less important place (**Figure 7.8**). If these areas have a realistic connection between them, for instance several

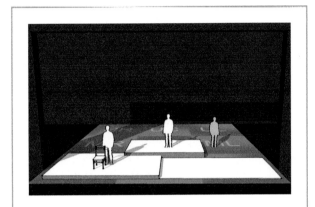

FIGURE 7.8   *Multiple areas*

what it needs to contain. Does the area need to contain multiple pieces of furniture?

You may need to plan the size of this area by drafting an arrangement of furniture, including space to move around and between them as needed and then wrestle with placing this new block on the groundplan. As the defined area is further developed, what it needs to contain will increase its size. This will alter the percentage of the overall space it takes up, affecting the amount of "other" space available. The designer must be clear about the furniture or scenic elements that are needed and accurate in how he represents their size. As they are positioned in the space, room must be left around and between them to allow the actor to move with a variety of possibilities.

In the planning stages it is helpful for the designer to treat small groupings of furniture as blocks. A sofa-armchair combination is a block. A Dining table and chairs is a block (**Figure 7.9**). A block is any grouping of furniture that will most probably remain together throughout the design process. When creating this

rooms in the same house, then the architectural logic of that house would be an organizing principle. If they are unrelated, they are placed in order of their importance to the story or by how much time of the performance takes place in each. The relative size of the area is variable by

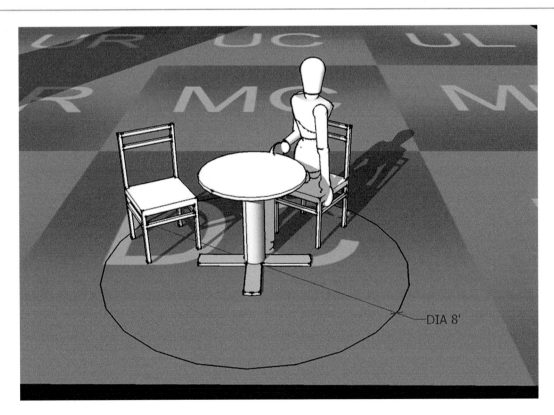

FIGURE 7.9   *Furniture blocks*

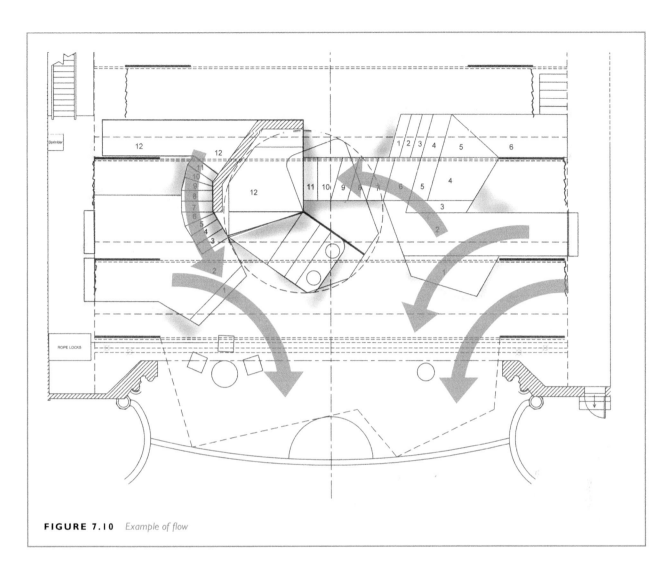

FIGURE 7.10 *Example of flow*

block allow room around the furniture to allow the actor to move or to push his chair back from the table. You are creating a "comfort zone." As you work on the groundplan, placing and re-placing this block's position, you will be working with the realities of the size of the objects and the amount of space necessary for their use.

Flow

It is a good test of any scenic design to consider the movement options, or flow, of the entire space. Take the time to consider the actors' options as they move through the space. Is the flow from space to space and level to level fluid with multiple options? Is there a bottleneck at any point? Any departures from a fluid flow should be because of a design decision not poor planning.

Angles or Parallel/Perpendicular?

It is common for the designer to make a very early decision as to whether the set should sit onstage parallel and perpendicular to the plasterline or be angled. In addition, the set may be composed of eccentric multiple angles or be composed of elements that are parallel and perpendicular to each other but set onstage at an angle.

This choice sets up some immediate responses from the audience. A set that is rigidly square to the stage architecture will seem formal, somewhat aggressive, and theatrical because it acknowledges the surrounding architecture (**Figure 7.11**).

A set which is angled will seem more informal and more realistic (**Figure 7.12**).

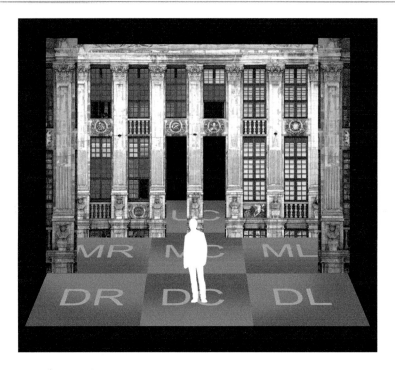

FIGURE 7.11   *A set square to the proscenium*

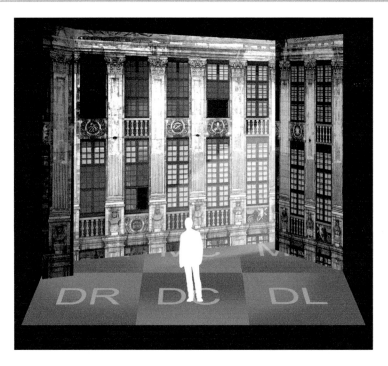

FIGURE 7.12   *A set with irregular angles*

This response may come from the way we experience architecture in the real world. While we realize that most buildings are built with 90-degree corners and true verticals, we generally experience them visually from an angle. Think about a structure as iconic as the Capitol Building in Washington. While we know it is a symmetrical building set directly at the end of the Mall, a surprising number of photos of it are from an angle. If we were asked to design U.S. currency, however, like the $50 bill, we would more than likely make the Capitol appear square-on to create the formality and power of that view.

Whether it is the angles you choose for a design, the angle at which you place elements onstage, or the direction of an actor's cross from UL to DR, diagonal lines are strong and powerful.

ARRANGING OBJECTS IN STAGE SPACE

Arranging elements onstage is not like arranging furniture in your living room. The architectural arrangement of the audience space and the stage space in any given theatre has already created a dynamic that the scenic designer must address when he does his work. The viewing angles created by the theatre will be the determining factor to his work. This being said, there are two basic approaches he can consider.

Planning Space by Architectural Logic

The first method that can be used to place scenic elements in space is to decide on the architectural logic of the spaces defined and then allow this to be the guiding principle of how to arrange elements such as furniture, doors, and stairs within this plan.

A first decision might be whether the set should sit squarely onstage or at angles. Then decisions could be made involving the shape, size, and position of areas, based on their meaning. In a single-set interior this would mean deciding where the two or three rooms involved would realistically be in relationship to each other. Then their relative sizes could be roughed in. Finally, the designer could begin to place elements of furniture in these empty rooms.

This approach can sometimes work, but in many cases the designer will find himself hard pressed to place furniture in positions that make sense for the angles of the room and for the angles at which the performer can be seen effectively by the audience.

Planning Space from the Performer's Perspective

The other method for placing scenic elements in stage space is to work from a performer-based perspective. In this method, the designer places key elements in space at angles that work for the openness of the performer first and then let successive decisions be based on that.

In this method, a Living Room would be designed by placing a sofa, an armchair, and a coffee table in positions relative to each other that made sense for their use as a conversational area. Then this block of three would be placed onstage and angled so that the performers using it would be at good angles.

If the overall setting was an adjoining Living Room/ Dining Room, the next decision might be to approach the dining table in the same way. Create a block of a table and the required number of chairs. Place it onstage and find an angle at which it works for the performer. In our Living Room/ Dining Room example, you would probably place one SR and the other SL. In working with the dining room table, consider where at the table various characters would sit. Tradition would say the most important person sits at the head of the table, but onstage, the designer might be able to make either end seem to be the head. Consider that it is impossible to place a table onstage in such a way that everyone at it is equally visible. Directors will often block the children in the family on the DS side of the table because they are small and won't block performers on the US side as much.

As you struggle with the table, look at the angles that are starting to be created between the Living Room block and the Dining Room block. Can you vary these angles, while maintaining their usefulness, in such a way that some architectural logic is created between the two rooms?

By starting with the most important furniture blocks and how they can best be placed in the space to work for the performer, you have let the most important decisions drive the remaining ones. Instead of trying to make furniture work in a box, you make the box work around the furniture.

Neither method described here is perfect, and truthfully, in practice, a bit of both is required to create an effective design. Thinking of these issues from a performer-driven perspective, however, is ultimately more helpful.

Loosening Up

When there are more areas than there is stage space, you may need to approach the problem by eliminating definition of the areas so one may blend into another.

FIGURE 7.13   *Generalized areas*

Let the furniture (and lighting) define the area and make the space around the furniture be common ground. A design that goes this direction may want to consider a background treatment that is generalized, or abstracted; in other words, as loosely defined as the areas themselves.

The design in **Figure 7.13** depicts three separate areas, but to make the most of the overall space the three are not sharply defined. Rather they are implied by the groupings of furniture that have some extra "separating space" between them, by three separate hanging elements that help the eye fix on each one and by the pools of light on the floor.

FINITE SPACE

Space on any stage, large or small, is finite. It is limited by the architectural envelope that surrounds it. One of the tenets of modern design is that accepting this is more effective than trying to imply it is not true.

This is in part a reaction and on-going rebellion against the painted illusory scenery of the past which in the postmodern period is open for reexamination. But since the widespread influence of Brechtian design took hold, in general, designers today approach the space in which they do their work as real and finite.

The Given Space

As the designer struggles with these initial reactions to conceiving the performance of the text in space in an abstract sense, he will also deal with the reality that this play will be performed in a specific theatre space. Regardless of the spatial reactions the designer has had to the text, in most cases the performance space has already been determined. Theatre companies have performance spaces of a specific size. Some are lucky enough to have multiple spaces of different sizes and types, but in many cases the decision of in which space to put a certain play will have more to do with the size of the audience desired or anticipated than the spatial demands of the play. The designer must attempt to be true to the space the text suggests and make it work in the space he is given.

Too Large

If the theatre space is very large and the play is an intimate piece with a small cast, the designer must work to bridge the gap. A common solution is to bring masking onstage and lower, but this can create sightline problems as well as an unwelcome sense of a weak set surrounded by dead air. Another solution is to scale the set to the performer and then design elements that expand the area around the set out far enough that the house masking can take over without becoming dominant.

The design in **Figure 7.14** represents a set that needs to be kept a realistic size, like a contemporary kitchen. The space in which it is to be presented has a 20-foot-high proscenium. Trying to make the kitchen fit the space will result in walls too high to be appropriate, so the decision is to maintain the walls at a realistic height and design elements that can float around and above the kitchen to fill the excess space. These could be anything from architectural pieces suggesting the house the kitchen is in, to more thematic pieces that tell something of the play as a whole.

Too Small

If the play has a large cast and multiple locations but the stage space is small, the solution may be to conceive of a set that somehow makes this limitation an advantage.

FIGURE 7.14   *Masking a large space*

Production: *Mother Courage*

A production of Brecht's *Mother Courage and Her Children* for the Jean Cocteau Repertory Theatre in New York had just such a problem. The stage is very small, about 20 feet square with no wing space at all. The stage ends at the side walls. There is little US space, only an exit to a staircase down. Brecht's play, of course, concerns the title character dragging her wagon across war-torn Europe. How does this play work in such a small space? Some consideration was given to using a miniature wagon or somehow using projections to suggest space and movement, but neither of these sounded right. There was just nowhere for the wagon to go but to turn around and around in one spot.

The acceptance that this was true, that the wagon had nowhere to go but round and round, eventually led to the solution.

If the wagon was a structure that just turned around and around it would seem to be more a machine than a form of transportation. If it seemed like a machine in the context of the play, it could seem to be a machine that Mother Courage had a desperate need to keep in motion, or a war machine that she was manipulated by as well as complicit in manipulating. Now the liability of the wagon not having room to move had been tied to some interesting conceptual ideas that came from the context of the play.

An art history reference pointed the way. Marcel Duchamp's *The Bride Stripped Bare by Her Bachelors, Even* (*The Large Glass*) (1915–1923) features a grinding machine of three large rollers that go round and round on a circular base (**Figure 7.17**). Duchamp was working in the Dada style in this work. Dada was an art movement that started at the end of World War I as a reaction to the horror and destruction of that war. *Mother Courage* is all about the horror of war and Brecht fought in World War I.

Using this image, and some additional research into wooden machinery, led to a deconstruction of the wagon into three different-sized wheels: two that went around on a round base center stage and the largest on the back wall. Several tongue-like beams provided places for the actors to turn the war machine (**Figures 7.15** and **7.16**).

FIGURE 7.15   *Mother Courage model*

FIGURE 7.16   Mother Courage *model*

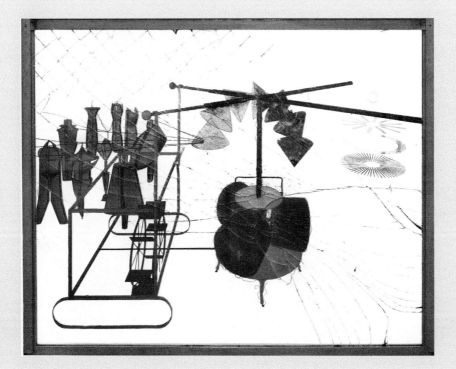

FIGURE 7.17   *Marcel Duchamp*—The Bride Stripped Bare by Her Bachelors, Even (The Large Glass)

TYPES OF THEATRICAL SPACES

The different types of theatre spaces are defined by the differing configurations of audience space to performance space.

The Proscenium Stage

The proscenium form is by a wide margin the most common theatre form today. It was developed in the late Renaissance, as a result of interest in linear perspective. The Teatro Farnese of 1618 is generally considered the first example. The placement of the audience in an arc viewing the performance space through the frame of the proscenium made the perspective scenery of the period "work." Proscenium theatres have changed very little in four centuries (**Figure 7.18**).

The audience seating is gently curved, facing the stage, and often arrayed in several levels. The Orchestra Level begins at the edge of the stage and slightly lower than it, and rises as it gets further away. Beginning part way back and overhanging the orchestra is a higher seating section, the balcony. If there is another balcony, the first is sometimes called the mezzanine.

Over the stage, typically, is a fly loft allowing the raising and lowering of battens that are parallel to the stage's plasterline and can be hung with lights or scenery.

The proscenium frame creates a strong cone of sightlines from the extreme reaches of the auditorium that forms a triangle of space DSC that can be universally seen by all audience members. This is the first thing the designer should explore when working in a new proscenium space.

Another sightline issue common to proscenium spaces with balconies is that the balconies may block the sightline from the rear of the orchestra, restricting the height an actor may be raised, as when the play calls for a second floor, or the first rows of a balcony may block the sightline from the rear of that balcony to DS.

The limited viewing angle means that scenery is seen mostly from one angle, as opposed to the thrust stage where it is seen from many angles. This and the linesets being parallel to the plasterline can make for a flatness, a strong similarity to the scenic style that this type of stage was designed for originally. The designer today must be aware of this tendency and use or avoid it as will best suit the design at hand.

Generally, it is desirable to get the action of the play as close to the audience as possible. The designer may choose to deck over the orchestra pit to accomplish this, but that will move the action DS of the main curtain making it impossible to use. Many proscenium theatres have a fire curtain that must legally be kept unobstructed. This can limit the possibilities of having scenic units play DS of the proscenium.

FIGURE 7.18   *Proscenium theatre*

FIGURE 7.19   *Proscenium productions—left:* The Secret Garden; *center:* Pig Farm; *right:* Amadeus

Things to Consider in a Proscenium Theatre

Sightlines: The sightlines are the first thing to look at. How will they effect where you can place elements in the space? It is not essential that everyone in the audience see every inch of the set, but all important characters and action in a scene must be seen by all. Mark the DS triangle created by the sightlines from far HL and HR seats.

Offstage and upstage space: This is space for storing scenery if it is a multiple set production, or space that needs to be masked depending on the production's demands.

Actor access to the stage: How do actors access the space? Are the wings deep enough to mask space offstage for entrances? Is there access to the stage from the house, either permanently, or if you designed it?

Traps: Are there traps in the stage floor that would allow actors or scenery to access the stage from below?

Access to the stage, loading doors: How is scenery loaded into the space? Are there doors, corridors steps, or elevators that limit the size of scenic pieces that can be brought to the stage?

Backstage traffic, crossover: Is there a way for actors to get from SR to SL other than by crossing the stage? If not, you will have to include a crossover US to allow this. If there is another way for the actors to cross, will it take a long time? If so, designing a crossover will still be important.

Linesets, dedicated linesets for electrics, acoustic shells, screens, and so on: What are your options for hanging and flying scenery? What linesets are dedicated to other uses and cannot be used for scenery?

Sidelight options: Lighting is important. Sidelight will sculpt the space, the actor, and your set. Booms or equivalent positions onstage will help the overall look of the production. In this theatre is sidelight commonly accomplished with booms that sit on the floor or ladders that are hung from above?

Other stage equipment: Is there any other stage equipment, like onstage elevators or a turntable, that can be used?

Main curtain: Where does the main curtain hang and how does it work. Does it guillotine, travel, or tab? What color is it?

Fire curtain: Where does the fire curtain hang and how does it work? What are the rules of the local fire marshal and the house crew in terms of how it must be used? Can scenery break the fire curtain line? Can scenery or furniture be DS of the fire curtain if it does not interfere with the fire curtain's operation?

Fighting the Frame

To counteract the proscenium's frame, the designer may wish to push the set as far toward the audience as possible. Many theatres that have orchestra pits have a pit elevator that can be played at stage level when an orchestra is not being used. Many others have a system of platforms that can be used as a pit filler.

Generally, it is always a good thing to have the performers as close to the audience as is practical. The designer must be aware, though, that pushing the space he uses downstage of the proscenium frame may cause difficulties. The theatre's main curtain obviously will have to stay US of the proscenium, and therefore will not be available if the scenery extends DS of it. Many theatres have a fire curtain just US of the proscenium that in case of fire creates a barrier between the stage and the house. The theatre company may have rules as to whether this fire curtain must be able to come in to the floor.

Additionally, in some theatres moving the acting area too far downstage may make the theatre's lighting positions not work as well. Sidelight positions especially may be affected.

In some productions the presence of the proscenium, the frame, may be oppressive to the design of the scenic space, or seem to create a letter box that the audience see the production through. There are some options to help alleviate this:

- Design black velour covered panels to hide the proscenium. This is helpful when the traditional Beaux Arts style of the proscenium conflicts with a spare, modern design.

- If scenic portals are being used, place the furthest DS, or visually dominant, one far enough US that a good amount of playing area is DS of it, thus creating the illusion that the actor is breaking the frame.

- Use decking out over the orchestra pit. If an orchestra is not being used, a pit elevator can be used at stage level. If an orchestra is needed in the pit, it is usually possible to build out over at least part of the pit.

The Thrust Stage

The thrust stage pushes the stage space out into the audience so that the audience wraps a significant degree around it (**Figure 7.20**). The proscenium frame is eliminated or significantly diminished. In a thrust space there is a much greater sense that the audience and actors are in the same architectural space.

This creates an exciting energy as the performer is close to, and wrapped by, the audience. It also means that the sightlines are much more difficult and that most vertical scenic elements need to be kept US of the primary performance space.

Frequently, thrust stages may have stage access from the house aisles or voms (vomitorium), tunnels which let the actor appear from the house and enter the stage.

Thrust stages may have no, or very limited, moveable linesets to fly scenery in and out, or these may be restricted to the most US part of the space. Typically, there will be a grid over the stage for hanging lights and scenic elements.

FIGURE 7.20   *Thrust theatre*

FIGURE 7.21   *Thrust productions—left:* The Visit; *center:* The Clean House; *right:* Blood Wedding

Designing for the thrust stage, the designer must be very aware of the range of sightlines and create a variety of positions that will allow the director to place the actor at different angles to the audience.

Things to Consider in a Thrust Theatre

Sightlines: The wider degree of sightlines in a thrust space creates challenges for the designer. Generally, this means he needs to design options for the director to be able to keep moving the actors around so they do not play to any one section of audience too much. This may mean placing furniture pieces in what in a proscenium space would be considered a DS position. Also, scenery will be seen from a greater degree of angles so may need finishing on more sides.

Offstage and upstage space: Generally, in a thrust space wing space will be in an US area where it will not be as useful for entrances or bringing on set pieces. The US space may be the only area in which scenery may be flown. Because of the side degree of sightlines to the acting area however, generally less scenery is used DS.

DS entrances, voms, and aisles: Because the acting area is so surrounded by audience, the options for actors to enter it are made more important.

Traps: Are there traps in the stage that would allow entrances from below?

Backstage traffic, crossovers: Because the acting area is so surrounded by audience, the distances to crossovers or dressing rooms may be greater than in a proscenium space.

Access to the stage, loading doors: These are important in any space.

Grid, Hanging Options: While flying scenery may not be possible, there may be options to hang scenic elements in the space that can create very three-dimensional effects. Making these work with lighting positions will be a collaborative solution.

Lighting positions, coves: Lighting positions in a thrust space may be in a wider range of angles due to the wide degree of audience views. Hung scenic elements must not interfere with important lighting positions.

Stage equipment: This is not generally as available in a thrust space as in a proscenium.

The Arena Stage

The arena stage surrounds the performance space with audience, creating the least sense of separation between them (**Figure 7.22**). Typically, aisles or voms are placed at the corners for actor entrances and exits. Some arena stages feature the ability to open up the floor and create entrances and exits through it. In some cases the entire stage floor is an elevator that can lower scenic elements out of sight where they can be changed.

Even more than in a thrust space, the designer and director, working together, must create positions so that the actor has options to move and angles that vary to which section of audience he plays.

Obviously, the 360-degree sightlines prohibit much vertical scenery such as solid walls. Floor treatments and level changes carry most of the burden of defining specific areas. Units like door frames or fireplaces are often placed in front of a vom where they provide the least obstruction. The designer looks for ways to define and animate the space without compromising visibility.

The space above the stage can be used in interesting dramatic ways if there is enough height available. Careful collaboration with the lighting designer is needed to make the scenic elements and lights work together.

Things to Consider in an Arena Theatre

Sightlines—verticals and obstructions: Because the sightlines completely wrap the space every vertical element can be an obstruction. But the designer still needs to define space so he sometimes carefully introduces skeletal vertical elements that give definition without blocking anything important.

Actor access, voms, and aisles: Because the audience wraps the performance space, how the actor can enter and exit the space is made even more important.

Traps: Having access through the stage floor from below is a very desirable feature in an arena space.

Hanging options: Because his options are so limited in the arena space, hanging elements can be one of the few options the designer has.

FIGURE 7.22   *Arena theatre*

FIGURE 7.23   *Arena productions—left:* World Builders; *left center:* Fifty Words; *right center:* Stick Fly; *right:* Summer and Smoke

Other Stage Types

Many other stage forms exist with too many variations to discuss here, but the issues to consider in approaching them are basically the same.

SIGHTLINES AND MASKING

The designer does more than create a set; he also shapes and conceals areas of the stage, which allows the audience's focus to remain on the acting areas. Much of

this is done by carefully considering the sightlines of the audience's view of the stage and the use of masking to conceal what will distract them.

In this section of the Walnut Street Theatre in Philadelphia (**Figure 7.24**), notice the sightlines drawn from the first row position that check the masking, confirming that each border masks the top of the next upstage one. These sightline lines also will tell the lighting designer at what trim his electrics will need to be to be hidden. These are the most common vertical sightlines

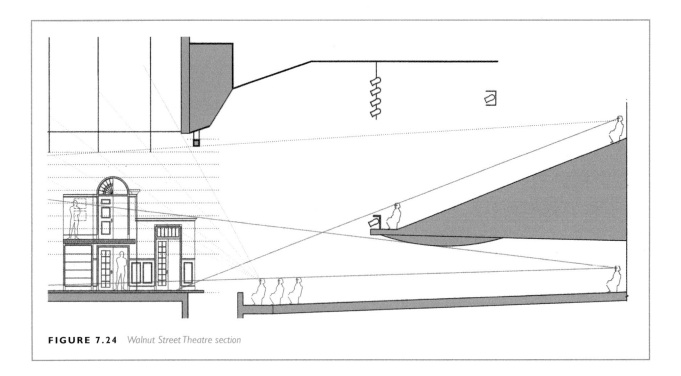

FIGURE 7.24 *Walnut Street Theatre section*

a set designer draws. In this section note the additional sightlines drawn from the back of the orchestra level, checking the height limitation caused by the overhanging balcony, and the degree to which the DS area is cut off by the heads of audience members in the balcony first row.

All types of theatre spaces have equipment and systems that the designer must understand to be able to use effectively.

In examining the linesets, be aware of any designated as *electrics*. Most theatres have a semipermanent system of which linesets are used for lighting equipment. These may be prewired with circuits and/or be a truss as opposed to a pipe to accommodate the heavier weight load of lights. Any of these situations may make linesets unavailable to the set designer.

Additionally, many stages have permanently hung features like orchestra shells or projection screens, which cannot be moved. These can make more linesets unavailable.

Most theatres have a stock inventory of soft goods. These drapery items may include black borders and legs as well as assorted cycs, scrims, and full black drops. The designer should be aware of what these stock items are and their sizes, as this will affect how he can use them. On most production budgets you do not want to buy a lot of new or custom soft goods if at all possible. Some theatres have a semi-permanent hang for masking, too, that the designer may have to work with.

Many proscenium theatres have very restricted wing space. The designer will be responsible for planning where his scenic elements store when they are offstage as well as where they play onstage, so he must be very aware of wing space offstage as well as space that may be available upstage of where his set ends. Additionally, access to the stage for loading and unloading may connect to an offstage space that may be used to store scenic elements. Knowing where this space is and how big it is may significantly affect the set design. In many theatres, any large unit must come from a particular side as that is where the largest offstage space is.

Things to Identify in the Plan Detail of **Figure 7.25**

    Plasterline
    Legs
    Tabs
    Borders
    Electrics
    Sightlines from first row seat

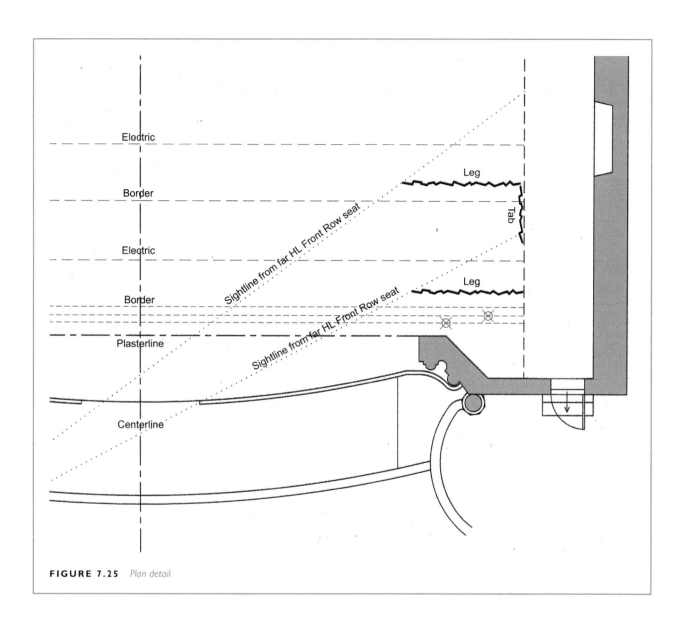

FIGURE 7.25 *Plan detail*

Things to Identify in the Section Detail of **Figure 7.26**

 Plasterline
 Legs
 Borders
 Electrics
 Sightlines from first row seat
 Sightlines from back of balcony
 Note: The first electric in this example does not mask
  for the first row.

Setting Trims

Trim is a term used to describe the height at which a flown element, a piece of masking or an electric, hangs above the stage floor. When referring to masking, the trim is to the bottom of a border. The trim of an electric is customarily set to the pipe. Trims are planned in the section with the scenic designer setting the trims of the masking and initially the major electrics. These heights should soon be reconsidered with the lighting designer and modified if necessary.

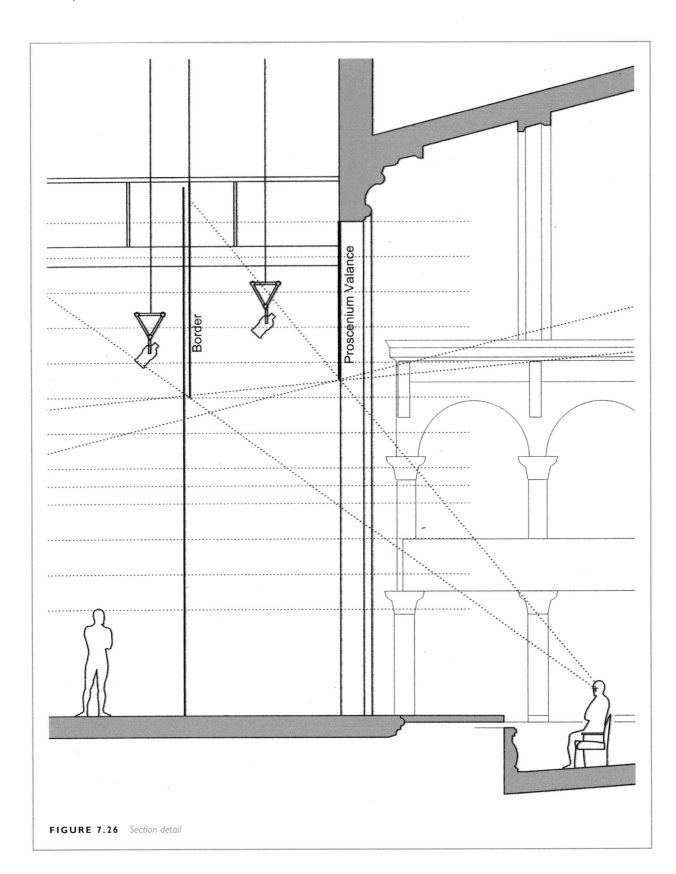

FIGURE 7.26   *Section detail*

Whether the lights on an electric can be seen by the audience or not is an aesthetic decision agreed on by the director and designers. In some shows seeing the lights can add a strong sense of theatricality. In others it can ruin a sense of reality of the imagined world.

If the design has scenic units that fly in and out, those units have an in-trim and an out-trim. The in-trim is the height at which it plays and the out-trim is the height at which it stores, usually in a masked position. Both are figured to the bottom of the unit.

During the load-in of a show, the scenic designer is usually called on to set trims. Some masking units may be set to the dimension planned in the section with a tape measure attached to the pipe or the bottom of the border as it is raised. Once these borders are at trim, the designer eyeballs the in- and out-trims of the scenic units. Sometimes these are done by measurement, but this is the designer's first chance to see this scenery onstage, and he may want the ability to tweak the heights he planned in the drafting.

In a perfect world everything is trimmed from the front row so that all elements meant to be masked are masked to all audience members. The designers can, however, choose to set trims from the second or third row. The theatre's architecture can make "perfect" masking difficult to accomplish while maintaining lighting angles that work well for a certain effect, DS back light, for instance. Some theatres tell designers that they customarily set trims from the second row or even the third because of idiosyncrasies of the theatre's architecture. It is desirable to make your hang mask as well as possible for the desired effect. If you need to depart from that, it should be discussed with the design team and theatre's staff.

WORKING IN SPACE

After spatial options have been considered and explored, the groundplan is the first solid step the designer will take. The two sections that follow explore ways to take first steps toward arriving at a groundplan. One is for a single set play and the other for a multi-set musical.

First Steps on a Single Set Production

Some initial work on a design can be done before decisions are made as to designable idea or theme. You know from just a quick read, for instance, that the play

involves a living room, or a kitchen, or a bar. Most likely this will not change drastically no matter what direction you go stylistically or what your research will bring later in the process. This relationship of furniture in space will be a building block in wherever the design will go. If this block is important in the play, key action takes place there and you know it should be in an important spot onstage both in proximity to the audience and in a strong position in regard to sightlines. This block is something you can work on as other elements of the design come into focus.

Take as an example *Yankee Tavern,* a play by Steven Dietz. It is a 9/11 conspiracy-theory thriller set in a run-down New York bar that has more ghosts than patrons. Regardless of what you think about architectural details or colors and textures that might be used, it is quickly apparent that the most basic need of the play is a bar that can seat two patrons and a position for a bartender. These three characters are in conversation most of the play.

This is enough information to work with. A bar is most often a straight counter-height structure with patrons seated in a row on one side and the bartender on the other.

This creates a problem. In this spatial relationship at least one side of the bar will force an actor to face away from the audience. Probably the best choice is to put the bartender US facing DS and have the two patrons angle toward each other on either side of him (**Figure 7.27**).

This works but gets better if you think of how diagonals are always a strong choice and more interesting than parallel and perpendicular lines and place the two patrons on adjacent sides of a corner bar. This turns them to each other more naturally, lets them use the bar more normally, and creates a nice triangle between the three actors (**Figure 7.28**).

The next step is to place this block onstage. On a proscenium stage this is no problem. Place the block on centerline fairly far DS (**Figure 7.29**).

On a thrust stage it is trickier. The block must be US enough to keep the bartender open to the side sections of the audience (**Figure 7.30, 7.31**).

In an arena space you would orient the direction that is DS in the proscenium to the most important side of the seating if there is one or just pick one if they are equal (**Figure 7.32**). It would be a valid choice, all things being equal to the audience, to aim this direction at the lighting booth or because of some other consideration like the

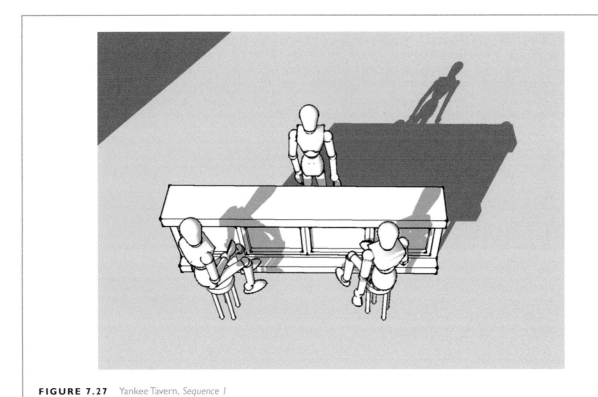

FIGURE 7.27   Yankee Tavern, *Sequence 1*

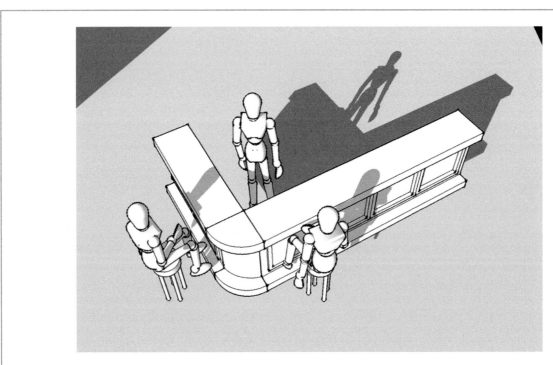

FIGURE 7.28   Yankee Tavern, *Sequence 2*

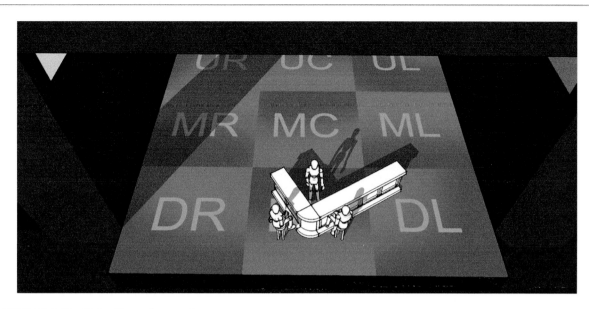

FIGURE 7.29   Yankee Tavern, *Sequence 3*

FIGURE 7.30   Yankee Tavern, *Sequence 4*

FIGURE 7.31 Yankee Tavern, *Sequence 5*

FIGURE 7.32 Yankee Tavern, *Sequence 6*

direction a majority of the audience enters the space from. In an arena, the next elements you would place needs to give movement options to the actor to keep him turned open to different sections of the audience (**Figure 7.33**).

In your proscenium design, the next things to place are two table/chair groups. Since you placed the bar on center, as is appropriate for the most important block, place one of these SR and one SL (**Figure 7.34**).

FIGURE 7.33   Yankee Tavern, *Sequence 7*

FIGURE 7.34   Yankee Tavern, *Sequence 8, complete rough*

All that remains is to place three entrance/exits, one from the street, one to a back room, and one to a set of stairs to the floor above.

Because the bar choice set up strong diagonals, you would consider following that decision in placement of walls. Your walls would create an architectural logic if they were at 90 degrees to each other, and all set onstage at the bar's angle.

By no means is design work on *Yankee Tavern* finished. But you have made initial decisions based on a performer-driven decision and how the block of the bar unit will play best for sightlines to the actors involved, and used that crucial initial decision to build a basic space. The next decisions would be more visually based, adding treatments, textures, color, props, and dressing.

In this design for a large proscenium theatre, it was important to keep the walls relatively low to suggest a below-street-level bar. This meant that a lot of empty space was above the set. A scaled-down expression of the exterior of the whole building the bar was in was added above the set walls to fill this space (**Figure 7.35**).

First Steps on a Multiple Set Production

As in the example given for *Yankee Tavern*, a single set production, work on a multiple set production can be begun with a series of spatial and technical decisions even before visual design ideas have been formed. To give an example of this type of decision-making process for a multiple set production, we will use *Crazy for You*—book by Ken Ludwig, music and lyrics by George and Ira Gershwin—as an example. *Crazy for You* is a very complex production set in the 1930s with locations in a Broadway theatre, on a New York street, and in multiple locations in Deadrock, Nevada, a Wild West ghost town, that includes interiors of a saloon, onstage, and in the lobby of a theatre, and an exterior town street. The biggest challenge perhaps is the saloon set, which requires a second level, quite a bit of furniture, and several special effects. The toughest shift begins in this saloon with a dance number that has the lead characters move out of the saloon door into the street as the saloon shifts a vista out of the way.

In the following section we will list the steps of the decision-making process in the order that a scenic designer might use in designing this production.

FIGURE 7.35   Yankee Tavern *photo*

You are designing *Crazy for You* in a large proscenium theatre. Begin by looking at the groundplan of the stage. Identify the wing space and other potential storage areas. Look at the sightlines. Identify the dedicated electrics (**Figure 7.36**).

Because it is a multiset show, it is probably a given that you will use portals to mask the electrics and define entrances and exits. Identify the linesets you will use for the portals (**Figure 7.37**). These will be the closest lineset DS of each electric. Sometimes the designer may choose

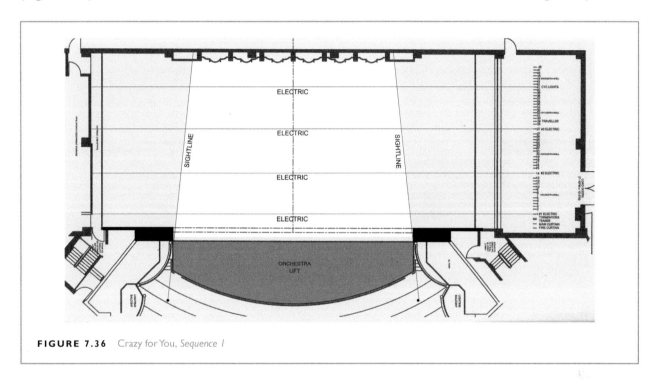

FIGURE 7.36   Crazy for You, *Sequence 1*

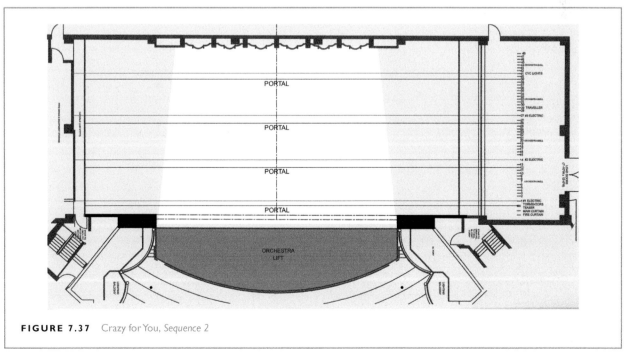

FIGURE 7.37   Crazy for You, *Sequence 2*

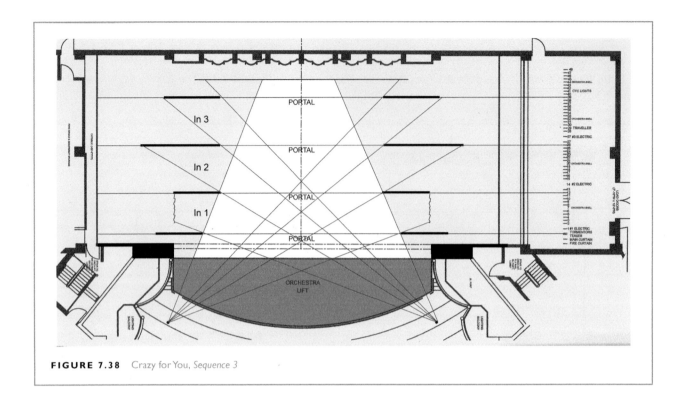

FIGURE 7.38 Crazy for You, *Sequence 3*

to skip the nearest DS lineset and use the second one DS of the electric to allow a little extra clearance around the electrics which, in a big production will be heavily packed with lights. For the same reason, the lineset immediately US of each electric is also frequently not used to eliminate a potential trouble spot.

You have decided where your portals will go but not how large a portal opening to use. Depending on the size of the stage and the available wing space, you may want to make the portal opening significantly smaller than the proscenium width. Look at your groundplan and make a decision. You decide a 36-foot portal opening is plenty big, and helps create a useful amount of wing space. Draw these portal openings on the groundplan and then check the sightlines to these portals. Extend each portal offstage until it masks the sightline from the nearest DS portal or the proscenium (**Figure 7.38**). Don't worry about these decisions too much; you can change them later.

Now look at the section of the theatre (**Figure 7.39**). Mark where your portal headers will be in the section. You will need to make a decision about the height of your portal. This will be determined by three factors: the sightlines from the highest seats in the

theatre, usually the second balcony, the height at which the electrics will have to trim to be accessible for focus, and an aesthetic decision on the proportion of the portal's width to height. Generally, in a large proscenium theatre borders and portal headers want to trim at more or less 20 feet. Standard Genie lifts used to focus lights give access to heights up to approximately 25 feet. Draw your portal headers at 20 feet, and check the sightlines from the first row and the highest balcony seat. If these sightlines force an electric to trim much over 25 feet, redraw your portals at 18 feet and check again.

When you have a portal height that works with the sightlines, draft a rectangle the width and height of your portal and draw within it a 6-foot-tall figure (**Figure 7.40**). This will be a front elevation that you will use later. For now, look at the scale and proportion of your portal in reference to the figure. Does it dwarf him or make it seem he is in a volume of space that is appropriate to the play? Does the size of this portal opening seem appropriate for the scale of the sets you will design within it? If your answer to either question is yes, consider modifying your decisions. If you make changes, check their sightlines in both groundplan and section.

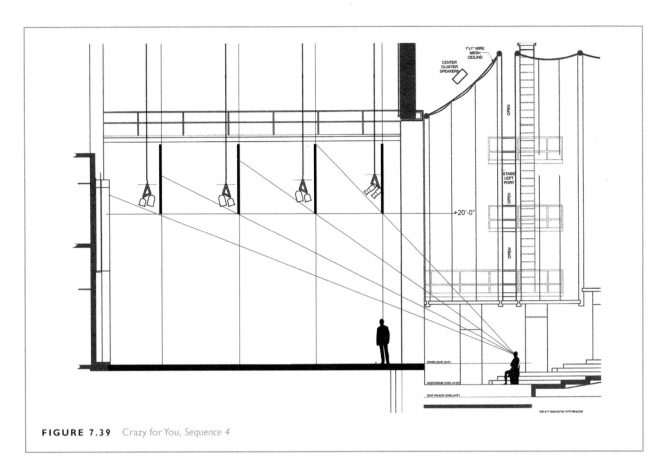

FIGURE 7.39   Crazy for You, *Sequence 4*

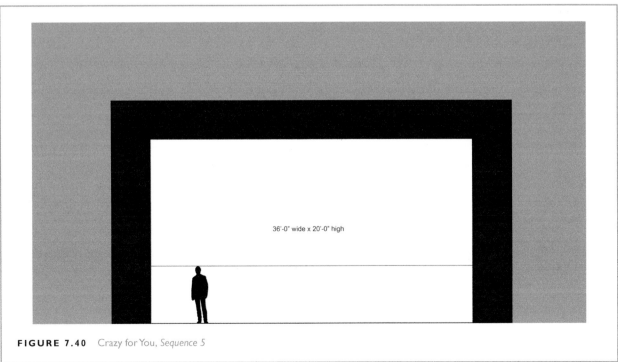

36'-0" wide x 20'-0" high

FIGURE 7.40   Crazy for You, *Sequence 5*

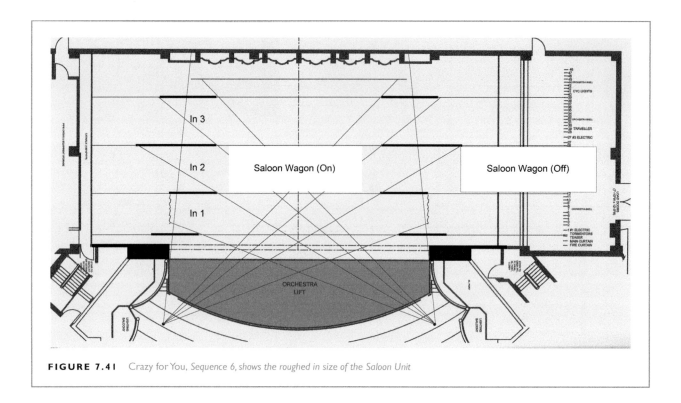

FIGURE 7.41   *Crazy for You, Sequence 6, shows the roughed in size of the Saloon Unit*

It is always good to attack your biggest problems first, so begin with the saloon. As described earlier, it is reasonably large and detailed set. Look at your groundplan, and assess your options for storing this large unit offstage. Remember that it is seen as a full interior at center stage and in an exterior view in the street scene (**Figure 7.41**).

> You might consider that there could be an Interior Saloon and an Exterior Saloon set, and not one which changed positions, but your goal in designing a multi-set production is to make it move in exciting ways. As the shifts in and out of the saloon are á vista changes, leave the Saloon unit as one element that will change positions.

Look at your storage options. Generally, your choices to store this unit are probably SR, SL, or US. Let's say your best storage space is SR. The saloon will have to shift from offstage through one or more portal openings into a position in which it will show its exterior face just onstage, and then to a second position fully on, in its interior

position. Look at what those positions mean to the size of your unit. Think what those positions tell you about the angles the main entrance into the saloon will have to play at. The different angles this main entrance wall must play at probably means it needs to change angles, to be pivoted as the complete unit moves from position to position. The rest of the saloon unit would be simplest if it moved straight on and off through one or more portal openings.

You have now blocked in sizes and shapes for the saloon wagon. Now using these wagon sizes spend some time designing the details of the unit. Work on its full interior position. Its other requirements are a long bar, a player piano, at least two tables with two to three chairs each, and stairs to an upper level with three doors on it—two to guest rooms and one to a hall. Design this unit as if it was a single set (**Figure 7.42**). When you have made progress, move the wagons into their mid-onstage street position. Design the main entrance wall to pivot from an interior viewpoint to an exterior one. Also consider that the upper level doors will need an escape platform. This could be a separate unit that could roll into position unseen after the bigger unit moved into its onstage position (**Figure 7.43**).

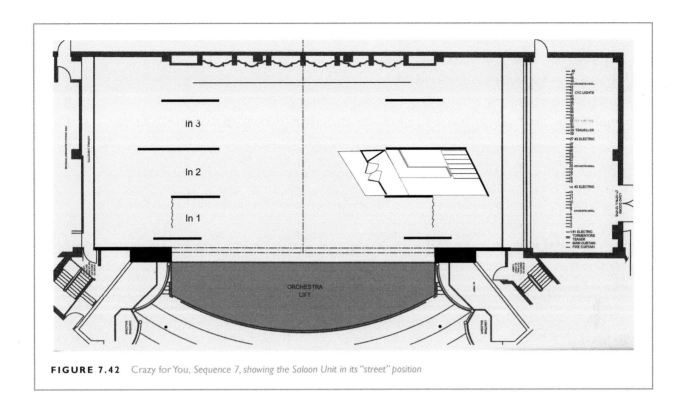

FIGURE 7.42   Crazy for You, *Sequence 7, showing the Saloon Unit in its "street" position*

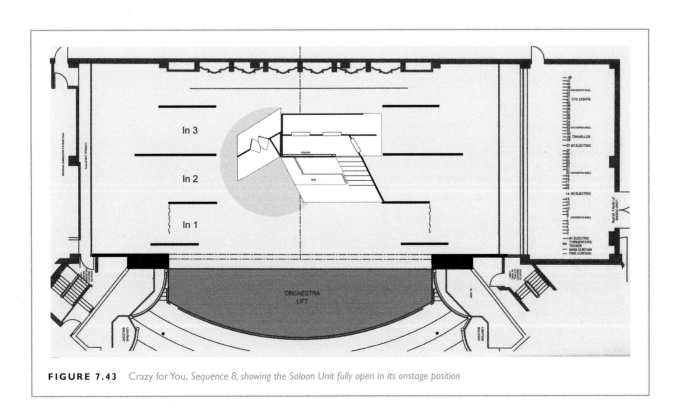

FIGURE 7.43   Crazy for You, *Sequence 8, showing the Saloon Unit fully open in its onstage position*

In the preceding steps, you have certainly not completely designed *Crazy for You,* but you have set some spatial boundaries and guidelines that can be a solid beginning on which to work. By doing this spatial and technical investigation first, you can be comfortable with knowing that the more purely visual decisions to come will work within them. You should on no account resist making changes to what you have done so far as problems and solutions present themselves.

SUMMARY

•   Design space from a performer-based perspective.

•   Use conceptual ideas to make the performance work in the space.

•   Use the space; don't fight it.

Project: Model Play

This project illustrates that space can be approached very quickly and directly. It challenges the student to spontaneously create without hesitation or long thought.

Create a collection of furniture, figures, and shapes that could be used to mock up ideas in the model box. These can be quickly built foam board pieces, as in the example below, or leftovers from previous models, or purchased elements. Cut rectangles from foam board in basic incremental sizes used in scenery: 4′ x 4′, 4′ x 8′, 8′ x 8′, 8′ x 12′, and so on. Supply T-pins and masking tape.

> Use the model box for the theatre your school produces the most in. It is also interesting to do this project in both a proscenium and a thrust space.

Develop a list of possible scenic locations. You can do this in class or prepare it ahead of time. Give each student a location and then one at a time give them five minutes to set their location up in the model box. The rest of the class can watch and comment or question. When time is up, have the student explain why they did what they did. If you have a different solution, demonstrate it.

The Concepts to Stress

•   Overall placement of objects in the space

•   Effectiveness of angles for actor openness

•   Finding the space's sweet spot

•   Sightlines

•   Show how considering blocking opportunities first can lead to effective design

•   Effectiveness of the set in conveying the location

•   Minimalism: How few pieces can you use and still communicate location

Some Ideas for the Locations

A Coronation
Court Room (this can be one of the most technical)
An adjoining Living Room/Dining Room
A Living Room in one house and a Dining Room in another
A Hotel Room
Two adjoining Hotel Rooms
Living Room and Porch
Facade of Whole House, Front Porch, and Small Yard

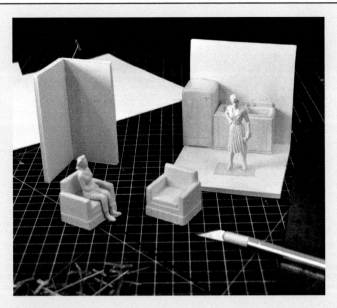

FIGURE 7.44 *Model play*

Project: Space for the Project Play

The first decision in this project is one a designer seldom gets to make in the real world: What type of theatre space do you want to do your project play in? You may do it in a proscenium, a thrust, or an arena theatre. Before you decide, think about what happens in the play and how these actions will work in different spaces. Where do actors enter from? Is there a need for elements that will be difficult to make work in an arena, for instance, with sightlines from all sides? Be prepared to explain the reasons for your choice.

You will be given a groundplan of your choice of space that you can print at 1/4″ = 1′-0″ scale to use as a base for a model box.

Using your **Stage Pictures project** from Chapter 3 and your **Breakdown** and **French Scene projects** from Chapter 4, determine the elements needed for your play. Thinking about the Stage Pictures project, decide what the two or three most important moments in the play are and what pieces are needed for them.

Place these two or three most important elements in your model box in strong positions relative to each other and the theatre's architecture. How will these positions force the actors to move? What will the moment look like in terms of their positions and the objects? What is the next most important object? Place it in a position relative to the previous ones that both works for the performer and makes some architectural logic. Continue this process, making the best choices possible. Each decision is influenced by the previous one. Try in this phase of the process to make decisions based solely on creating spatial relationships between objects on a performer-driven basis, not an architectural-logic one. Continue until you have placed all the important elements.

Take a photo of your model now.

Look at what you have done. Look at your research images from the project in Chapter 5. How can you apply them to the construction you have made? Consider the architectural logic of the setting. Depending on how realistic you intend to make the design, the architectural logic can be very important or not important at all. Make any adjustments you need to improve the architectural logic of the set without destroying the strong relationships between objects you have made.

Take a photo of your model now.

Now consider your design statement from Chapter 6. What is the key idea to your approach to the play? How can you make this idea immediately clear and bold in the space you have created? Add whatever you need to make this happen, rebuilding anything you have to in order to get the result you want.

Take a final photo of your model now.

NOTE

1. Arnold Aronson, *Looking Into the Abyss: Essays on Scenography* (Ann Arbor: University of Michigan Press, 2003), 1.

CHAPTER 8

DESIGN AND REDESIGN

In the previous seven chapters, we have looked at the various aspects of scenic design: the nature of the work, the history of the field, collaboration, text, research, idea, and space. In this chapter we will look at how all of these areas are brought together to create an effective design.

THE DESIGN PROCESS

No two design processes are the same. With experience, you will find a process that serves your skills and temperament. Still, the demands of a specific project's schedule, your collaborators, and problems inherent in the project will make it unique in its own way.

First Phase of the Design Process

- Research Images
- Thumbnail sketches
- Rough groundplan
- Rough 1/4-inch model

This first phase of the work may take a while. In some projects it will be a steady, if perhaps slow, progression of development in a single direction. In others, it may be a scattershot trying of a variety of options. At some point, the designer will need to, or be pushed to, share where he

is with the director or the whole design team, depending on the production circumstances.

> Developments at all stages of the process must be reflected in all media. A change in the groundplan should be shown in the model or the sketch, and vice versa. Keeping everything up to date is time-consuming, but having versions that are not all current can be confusing for you and your collaborators.

A major goal in this phase of the process is to get, rather quickly, to a point at which you can have a representation of the design (in whatever media) that shows a sense of the complete design, with a sense of detail and color.

This is a skill that is very important to develop. Whether your media choice is a sketch in traditional media with, perhaps, a quick wash of color, or a rendering done in digital media, it is important that you develop a way to do a nice-looking representation of your design to show (**Figure 8.1**).

Because all the elements of a design are so interdependent, it is very difficult to assess the whole without all the parts shown.

FIGURE 8.1   *Early "complete" sketches*
These are a quick SketchUp model with Photoshop effects added, done to explore a design for Romeo and Juliet and A Funny Thing . . . Forum in rep. While rough they show a sense of space, color, and detail. While a long way from finished, they give a "complete" first look at the idea.

DESIGN STRATEGIES

Elegance and Economy

Because of the huge range of projects, styles, and interpretations the designer will come across in his work, there are not many concepts that hold true for all. One that seems to remain viable is that the designer should look for an **elegant solution**. Elegant, of course, here does not imply formality, but a simple, appealing "rightness."

> **Elegant** *(adjective)* pleasingly graceful and stylish in appearance or manner (as in a scientific theory or solution to a problem); pleasingly ingenious and simple

Tied to the goal of creating an elegant solution is **economy**. Generally, there is beauty in simplicity. An elegant solution usually implies few unnecessary elements are used. Also, economy is often necessary when the production demands do not match the budget.

Selection, Abstraction, and Transformation

Three basic design strategies are frequently called upon. They can be used in different ways, in different combinations, and at different points in the process. They are fundamental ways in which the designer can turn research and ideas into effective designs.

Selection is simply choosing which elements to use and which not to use, so in a general sense it is the most basic thing a designer does—select what to put onstage.

But it can also be a way to take what is first seen as a complete and realistic image and make it more focused and artistic by selecting elements that best convey its essence and eliminating others. The results can be subtle or profound.

Two different degrees of selection are **selective realism** and **minimalism.**

Selective realism strengthens a design by eliminating unnecessary details but retaining a complete, essentially realistic look.

Ming Cho Lee's design for Tennessee Williams's *The Gnadiges Fraulein* carefully crafts a sculptural design with a poetic realism using selected elements (**Figure 8.2**).

This design for the opera *Street Scene* presents a realistic tenement facade, but as it reaches the edges of the proscenium, it eliminates elements surrounding the building in favor of some laundry and cropped panels suggesting adjacent buildings (**Figure 8.3**). A design like this essentially takes a complete image and then picks away at it, eliminating the unnecessary.

Minimalism is a different approach, in which the goal is to limit the elements used as much as possible to create a very spare look that is often more aesthetic than realistic. The challenge is that what remains must be very

FIGURE 8.2   *Ming Cho Lee's 1/2-inch model for* The Gnadiges Fraulein, Broadway, 1966
From *Ming Cho Lee: A Life in Design* ©2014 by Arnold Aronson. Reprinted by permission of Theatre Communications Group

FIGURE 8.3   *Design for the opera* Street Scene

focused as it is all there is to communicate ideas to the audience. Minimalism is often more about idea and mood than location.

This arena production of a multiple location play (**Figure 8.4**) needed to be simple just to let the play move quickly from one scene to another, but conceptually it was not about the real locations anyway. The lives of the characters are dominated by their past in the Guantanamo Detention Camp. The action in the play takes place in their current homes in Minneapolis. The design idea was that the present locations should be kept minimal, and a massive chain-link structure representing Gitmo would hang over the space as it does over the character's lives.

This design for the play *Dragonwings* (**Figure 8.5**) attempted to create a sense of multiple locations with the same scenic elements. The play involves a Chinese American boy who helps his father invent the airplane. Two simple panels were used to suggest the two wings of their biplane hung within a frame of delicate struts and wires that would further suggest the plane's construction. In the top left image, actually the last scene in the play, the panels are their most wing-like. The top right look was used for interior and street locations with the addition of a few furniture and prop pieces. The bottom left image was to suggest sky, and in the bottom right one of the panels fell to the stage floor for a scene during the 1906 San Francisco earthquake. This design is an example of both minimalism and abstraction in that the idea of a biplane was abstracted into a construction of materials and shapes that communicated the original idea but had lost any realistic sense of that image.

FIGURE 8.4 Lidless

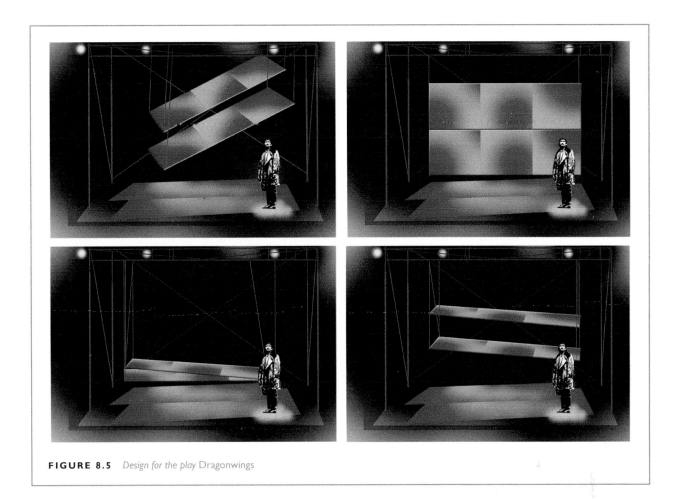

FIGURE 8.5   *Design for the play* Dragonwings

Abstraction is at its simplest a refining of shape, eliminating detail and unnecessary complications. Abstraction can help find simple visual elements that can suggest a lot yet retain a simplicity. Extreme abstraction can reduce visual information too far, leaving no meaning.

In Chapter 6 the design for *Carousel* took research of carousels and planets and lighthouses and created a simple abstraction of two shapes, a circular floor disk and a suspended horizontal band that could suggest some of the ideas in the play (**Figure 8.6**), but in their extreme form did not convey much mood. It needed to be transformed by tricks of paint and light to work fully as a background for the entire production.

Abstraction can be used in many ways and to different degrees. It is important to remember that one element onstage cannot be abstracted—the actor! Not only is the actor the given scale reference for stage design, he is the only given, immutable element. Though there have been many attempts to abstract costume, notably

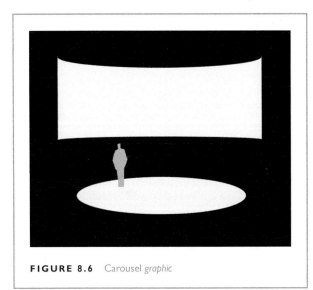

FIGURE 8.6   *Carousel graphic*

in Russian Constructivism, it is somehow never very satisfactory in most plays.

This is an idea that is used a great deal in stage design: **The actor and the objects he uses are realistic but the space can get more and more abstract as it moves away from him.**

Transformation is changing one thing into another. Transformation is always a part of scenic design, as the designer transforms his ideas and research into visual and physical elements that will work in the finite and focused space of the stage.

Working with Transformation

The conflict in the play *Riders to the Sea* is between the family in their small cottage and the power of the sea around them. The sea is really the antagonist in the play. The following is in the form of an inner dialogue that is a common part of a designer's process:

If I want to make this relationship visual, how would I represent the sea?

A painted drop is the first idea that comes to mind, but while it will add a visual image of the sea, it will lack any sense of the physical presence and power of the sea, largely because it will be perceived as a common, safe choice. It is not the sea; it is a picture of the sea.

How could I make the sea a dimensional, dangerous element? What materials would I use?

Fabric is frequently used to represent water onstage. Lightweight fabrics like China silk can be manipulated to flow like water, but fabric seems soft and gentle. The sea in *Riders* is strong, powerful, and elemental.

What other materials could I use?

Wood is the most common theatrical construction material; what about wood? Elements made of **wood** usually appear as man-made, constructed, and this doesn't seem right.

How could I give a wooden sea an accidental, non-constructed feel?

The characters are a fishing family who go to sea in ships—wooden ships. When their ships are wrecked they become part of a great flotsam and jetsam of debris that the sea continues to throw around. Could I suggest the sea by arranging wooden pieces resembling wrecked ships, suspending them to appear like a great wave of debris about to crush the cottage?

Another choice might be metal. Metal seems cold and heavy. Could I create a sculptural sea that seemed to be made of metal plates that arced up into a frozen wave above the cottage?

This exercise has been about talking through possible practical options, while assessing the meaning each will bring to the design until you have turned one material that had some difficulties as a solution into another that works to solve the problem.

Transformation is not always about materials. In Chapter 7, the case study of *Mother Courage and Her Children* was about the transformation of the wagon, which could not do what was intended of it in such a small space, into a war machine that could suggest a wagon while making a bigger statement about the play.

In the case study of *Into the Woods* in this chapter, the design process is about transforming the idea of a forest from something literal into something more interesting using color, texture, and shape.

COLOR

Color is an extremely important element to consider because of the very strong reactions to color in the human eye and mind.

Choices of color can be arrived at in many ways:

- Many objects if used in a realistic manner come with color choices already. The sky is blue. Grass is green.

- If an element is transformed to seem like it is made of a different material than its common look, then the new material would give it its color. Example: a steel forest.

- Color can be chosen for the emotional response it will create in the audience.

- Unexpected color choice or intensity can create estrangement.

- Because the reaction to color is so strong, it can act as a strong unifier to balance or connect very dissimilar elements.

Sharing Color

Color is the aspect of design that is most shared by scenery, costumes, and lighting, and as such should be amply discussed during the design process.

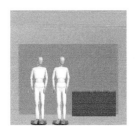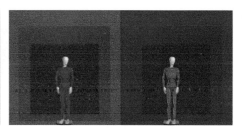

FIGURE 8.7 *Color*
These three images show some aspects of the use of color. The first one, at left, shows the emphasis that color can create. A red shape in a gray set commands the eye. The second image, center, shows the emphasis created on the actor by only slightly making his costume more intense a color than the background. The third image, right, shows the principle that warm colors advance and cool colors recede.

Some considerations in talking about color:

- Color is so intense that it can easily create emphasis in your design. Imagine a red sofa on an all-gray set. It would be hard to look anywhere but at the sofa.

- Generally the thing that wants to create the most emphasis onstage is the actor. Color is a major tool used to make this happen. The most intense and emphasis-creating colors are commonly reserved for the costumes, with the colors of the set kept at least a little reduced in saturation or hue.

- The color used in light will affect the paint colors of the set and the dye colors of the fabrics used in the costumes, so a major consideration for the lighting designer is how his colors will blend or transform all the other colors on stage.

- Color can connect a design that has very diversely shaped or sized elements.

THE REDESIGN PROCESS

All the things we have discussed so far will inevitably, finally, magically coalesce into a design that seems to have possibilities. This point may come quickly and smoothly, or only after much discussion and many attempts to pin it down. It has been said about the writing process that **"writing is easy; rewriting is hard,"** and the same is true of design. However promising your first design seems, you will almost always have more to do to make it better. The strategies of doing this involve **assessment**, **development**, and **refinement**.

Assessing Your Work

It is important that you develop ways in which you can assess what works in your project and what does not. In most cases you will know what's wrong but be somewhat unable to express it. This can be because of visual fatigue caused by the hard work of getting to this point or the fear that you won't be able to make it any better than it is right now. There are always things to do to make a design better, but to do so you have to look clearly and think clearly about where you are and where you need to go.

One strategy is to look at the design quickly and say out loud the first thing that strikes you as wrong. Don't think, just react. This will often work surprisingly well.

When you know what needs work but don't know what to do, develop a mental list of possible things you could do. Don't think about what these choices would mean to the play or whether they are right or wrong, just quickly run through a list of what you could do:

- Make it bigger.
- Make it smaller.
- Make it a different color.
- Make its color more saturated.
- Change its position.
- Change its scale.
- Change its proportion.
- Eliminate it.

Again, don't think, just consider quickly all the options you can think of, and then decide if any of them will help.

Sometimes you get stuck, not knowing how to get past where you are. In this situation it can be helpful to have some ways to force yourself to reexamine what you have done. Two tricks to do this involve forcing yourself to look at the design with fresh eyes and editing.

Reversal

A good way to help you see the design with fresh eyes is to reverse the set; that is, flip SR and SL (**Figure 8.8**). Of course, if the set is symmetrical, this won't help much, but if it is asymmetrical, the reversal will make you reevaluate it completely. Look at where your eye goes. Note the things that look odd or seem to be out of proportion. This process is easiest to do in a digital media, of course. You should make a copy of the original design before you start, so you have an unedited backup that you can go back to. After you've looked at the reversed copy for a while and identified some areas that you feel need work, begin to make the changes. When you have finished this, save the file and then reverse it again to its original orientation. See what differences your changes have made. Do you now like the design in its original form or the flipped one?

Eliminate an Element

There is an expression in writing that the writer should always be willing to "kill his babies"; in other words, to sacrifice something he loves if it is getting in the way of the overall story. For the designer the equivalent of "kill your babies" is to see what happens to the design if you eliminate one element. Again, digital media can make this quick, easy, and painless. By turning on and off layers in Photoshop, you can see what it is like to eliminate any element of the design. A minimalist design aesthetic can, in many ways, be perfect for the theatre. In most cases having the fewest pieces onstage forces you to evaluate what you really need to say to the audience. A test of minimalism is that removing one element diminishes the design. If you can eliminate something and the design still works then why wouldn't you? Budget and labor hours will improve, and you will have strengthened the design.

Development

There are many ways in which a design can need development. There may be elements that want to become stronger or that want to be toned down to not be as bold. There may be an aspect of the design or a particular unit that doesn't quite work yet. These aspects of development are really just continuations of the initial process.

Show Me the Magic

It is common for the first design arrived at to be a good solution to the problems of the production that is solid and practical but lacks something intangible that elevates it to the magical. We must never forget that as scenic designers, we are called upon in every project to create magic spaces, not just practical ones.

FIGURE 8.8 *Reversal*

Some Options to Make the Design More Exciting

- Eliminate an element or two.

- Make surface treatments or textures bolder.

- Add a bold image (go back to your research) as a surface treatment rather than a realistic material or texture.

In this design for *West Side Story* (**Figure 8.9**) the usual brick textures of New York tenements were replaced with harsher, colder concrete that, while less correct for the period, created an effect of modern timelessness and an extremely inhumane world.

Refinement

The preceding tricks can help give you fresh eyes, but the refinement phase is more about finesse—making everything a little more perfect. There are many ways that this can be done.

Refine Line

In drawing and especially in drafting the initial design, it has grown in fits and starts. You have drafted it quickly and made revisions in some places and not in others. In the refinement phase you will need to go back and correct, or improve, many things but chief among them is often line. This is true especially in the groundplan.

Look Closely at Your Groundplan

- Are there lines that should be parallel but are not?

- Where three lines converge, does one miss by a little, and could it be made to land at the juncture of the other two?

- Check dimensions between parallel lines. Are they 3 feet, 5/16 inches apart? Can you make everyone in the shop's life easier by redrawing it to be 3 feet exactly? A good rule of thumb is to draft basic elements at standard dimensions, like a platform at 4 feet wide, not 4 feet, 3 1/2 inches, or a door's width

FIGURE 8.9   *A design for West Side Story*

at 3 feet even, not 3 feet, 1 inch if you can. Then as you move on to other elements things can be the odd dimension they need to be to make things look the way you want. This will use materials better, which will save money and make your shop happy.

Refine Proportion

Chief among aspects of the design that may need to be finessed is proportion. Almost any first-pass design can be made better by examining the proportion of elements and the space between elements.

You should have done a front elevation by this point from the groundplan to determine heights to build the model or do a rendering, but you probably have not looked at individual units with an eye to proportion. It can advance the process if at this stage you draw individual units of scenery as front elevations. This will also serve as work that can be turned into the finished designer elevations when you are ready to draft them.

Draw a unit and draw a figure beside it. Think about what could be improved. If it is a wall with a door, window, or molding, are all these the heights and widths you want them to be? Are the doors and window a good proportion for the period and economic status of the characters? Look at any horizontal lines of molding. Do they cross the actor's body at unfortunate places like through his head or directly through his knees? This can be incredibly annoying on stage to see a badly placed line cut though the eye-level height of the actor or cut his head off by lining up with the top of his neck.

Check the scale and proportion of doors and windows. Are they correct for period and for the door's purpose?

The Front Elevation

As the design develops, a very valuable tool can be the front elevation. This is a straight-on look at the whole stage with no perspective. Its primary value is that it allows the designer to work on the size and proportion of scenic elements. A proscenium-sized rectangle is drafted in either 1/2-inch or 1/4-inch scale. A scaled figure is added.

This rectangle's size and proportion could be arrived at as discussed in the *Crazy for You* example in Chapter 7.

The placement of scenic elements is transferred using construction lines from the groundplan. Heights and elevations of things you know, such as upper level heights or standard door heights, are added and then the heights of units you have not previously decided on are worked out. Many problems present themselves at this point and are solved by adjusting scale and proportion.

A Photoshop rendering can be done over this drawing. While in some designs the sense of perspective will be missed, it will be clear in the model, and usually any design that looks good in front elevation will look better in perspective. Perspective distorts the actual measure of things so it cannot be used to check relative proportion. It is worth noting, also, that in many proscenium theatres the audience viewing angle from the orchestra level is low enough as to be very close to a front elevation as opposed to the view from the balcony, which will show a much greater depth.

The following case study illustrates a design that went through several stages of design, development, and refinement:

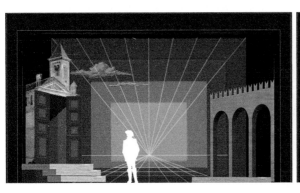 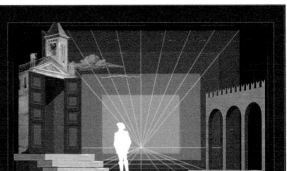

FIGURE 8.10 *A front elevation for Kiss Me Kate showing variations in proportion*

Production: *Into the Woods*

Movement is always important. The actors' movement as it is guided by the set design is critical to how the audience will perceive the rules of the stage world and how the scenery actually shifts, from scene to scene, is key to how smoothly and quickly the production will move.

The design for a 2005 production of *Into the Woods* had its initial decisions made about both these types of movement.

Most of the story involves the show's many characters on their adventures in the woods.

One way to design this scenario is to design a forest look that remains predominantly the same. This sets up a Shakespeare-like situation where characters enter and exit from various offstage locations into a somewhat common onstage one.

Another choice is to vary the forest look to a greater extent, adding and removing scenic elements to create multiple locations. This is perhaps more useful. The choice to move scenery brings with it a number of other considerations. Because moving scenery will ultimately be a budget consideration, an early strategy would be to look at the stage machinery that is available in the particular theatre.

Most proscenium theatres have some system of linesets for flying scenery in and out. The use of an existing form of stage machinery will always be considerably easier and cheaper than adding equipment of another type. But using the house linesets for *Into the Woods* would create a type of movement that is theatrical as opposed to realistic. Regardless of the eventual theatricality or realism of the scenery yet to be designed, using the house linesets will create tree elements that fly in from above. Realistically as a person walks through the forest their movement is lateral, on the ground. Realistically, of course, trees do not move, but as the walker moves the vista of the trees seems to change in a horizontal, lateral way.

Decision one was made: it would be desirable if the forest could move in a lateral, more actor-movement-oriented way.

The next factor considered in this production's design concerned the only location in the play that was not "in" the woods. Each act begins with overlapping scenes in three separate locations: Jack's House, the Baker's House, and Cinderella's House. A necessary element in each of these locations was that they should have a practical door. Practical doors are difficult to do in flown scenery as all manner of tipping and shaking can result. So the decision to use practical doors led to seeing these as units that should also move laterally.

Now two major considerations have steered the design toward lateral movement. Thinking about common stage machinery, other than linesets, might lead to choosing a traveler track system for trees. The difficulty with this would be that the trees could only shift SR to SL, never in a more fluid way, and this would accentuate the flatness inherent in the proscenium form. Adding to this negative was that the theatre in question had very little wing space. The offstage storage for traveler track trees and the house units could be a major problem.

Thinking of other movement options led to considering winched movement in various directions.

I remembered the groundplan for a production of *Oedipus/Antigone* by Josef Svoboda that I thought might be helpful. It featured a number of elements that formed a wall DS and moved US independently, at angles away from each other, into more irregular US positions. Adapting this idea to *Into the Woods* would mean the trees could shift at will to a variety of forest positions.

The sketches in **Figure 8.11** show this idea. The panels were somewhat irregularly shaped to create interest. Something about the DS wall position seemed like a show curtain, and the next sketches played with an image of a woodcut map of the woods (**Figure 8.12**).

In their US positions the sections of this map would appear split into tree-like units that if individually winched, would be capable of moving separately, or in groups, into a myriad of other forest configurations.

To work as winched towers, these units would need a stable base, which would mean they had to have some size. This might work well with some other requirements of the show; for example, the tree from within which Cinderella's mother appears and Rapunzel's tower could be in these tree-like units.

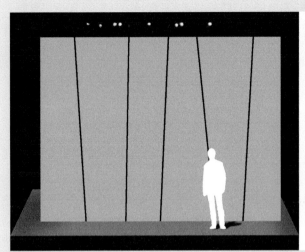

FIGURE 8.11 *First sketches: Basic spatial idea*

FIGURE 8.12 *First sketches: Show curtain map look*

And if the towers were to have interior levels and window openings for these two effects, could they have practical doors and be used in some way for the three houses required in the opening of each act? The sketch in **Figure 8.13** was the first exploration of this idea, showing openings in three of the towers with scenic treatments within. Three different color palates would reinforce that each was a different locale.

FIGURE 8.13   *First sketches: Cottage idea*

Groundplan

In a show with this much movement, getting the groundplan to work is the most important thing and should be done early.

As stated elsewhere, the designer's process is working equally, and at the same time, on practical things and visual things.

Note on the plan in **Figure 8.14**, the dashed lines of the tower paths, from DS wall to US spread. The cuckoo clock and a ramp/step unit sit in the UC area created between towers.

Note also the steps to the loading areas that allowed actors to access the inside platforms of Towers 3 and 5 which were used for the "Mother Tree" and Rapunzel's Tower.

Sketches

Successive sketches explored some variations. To counteract the massiveness of the towers, I tried adding slender tree elements, but with the map image on the towers, these became the trees, and the towers were just panels (**Figure 8.15**).

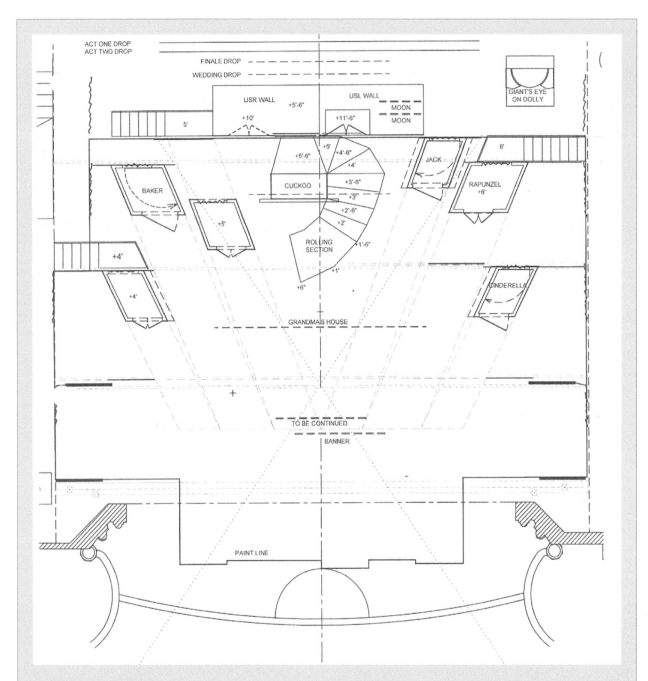

FIGURE 8.14 *Groundplan*

The cuckoo clock was always in the mix, because it supported the character's race against time to find the four ingredients that will lift the witch's curse, and because of its Black Forest style and quirkiness. It could be whole in Act I and broken in Act II to help the visualization of the Giant's destruction.

FIGURE 8.15   *Second sketches*

FIGURE 8.16   *Second sketches*

Back to attempting to solve the towers versus trees problem: I tried eliminating the map image in favor of a more abstract forest image, and still wasn't happy with the results (**Figure 8.16**). First, the slender trees were still there and second, the abstract image was a bit vague.

Working in Photoshop on abstracting a forest image led to thinking of an enlarged woodgrain treatment (**Figure 8.17**).
To add an element of forest leaf canopy and some color, a new version was done in which the woodgrain towers now faded from bark-brown at the bottom to leaf-green at the top (**Figure 8.18**).

FIGURE 8.17   *Forest image*

FIGURE 8.18   *Woodgrain and green*

The next round of sketches kept the woodgrain effect and added the image elements of the map idea on top of it. The results were encouraging but seemed heavy, and the map image was confusing (**Figure 8.19**).

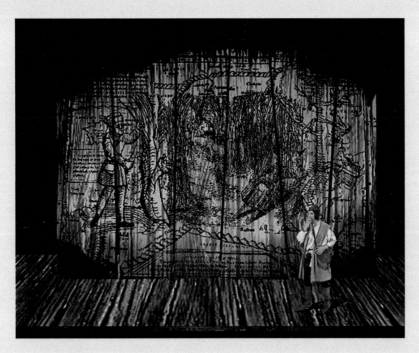

FIGURE 8.19   *Third sketches*

FIGURE 8.20   *Third sketches*
This sketch also plays with two new elements: the title scrolling banner, and the three cottage doorways with different color palettes.

Final Design

In the production photo of the opening three cottages, you can see that the inside of the doors in the DS face of the towers opened fully and were given a colorful collage of images specific to each character's story (**Figure 8.21**). Another door in each of the US tower faces had a colored door that was the entrance to the cottage. Note that Cinderella's "birds" was a moving projected effect.

The collage of images on the doors was mostly enlarged period ads. This started to set up a scale-change effect. Since the play already had a giant, what if we suggested that the characters were a little smaller than average humans? This brought to mind *The Borrowers*, a children's fantasy novel by Mary Norton in which a family of little people live among regular-sized humans and borrow things from them. This idea led to some other uses of scale change. The carriage was a flat cutout that looked like a scrap from an advertisement for a stable (**Figure 8.22**).

The map graphic was greatly simplified at this point to where it became some woodcut images suggesting fairy-tale characters. This kept the fun of the image without all the details that were needed if it was a map.

FIGURE 8.21   *Final design: Cottage look*

FIGURE 8.22   *Carriage*

In the Act I forest model shot in **Figure 8.23**, the cottage doors have closed, the scrolling banner has flown out, and the towers have winched to US positions, around and through which actors can move. The cuckoo clock, moon, and backdrop are revealed as the tower-trees move.

Granny's House (**Figure 8.24**) became another play on the cuckoo clock. It was a flown unit with a translucent center panel for shadow play of the Wolf eating Granny.

FIGURE 8.23   *Final design: Act I model and drop paint elevation*

FIGURE 8.24   *Final design: Granny's House*

The Act II model shot (**Figure 8.25**) shows the increased "giant damage." The Act I cuckoo clock was replaced by a broken version. The Act I drop was replaced with one showing broken trees, and the moon was rigged to change to a tipped position.

In Act II the Giant's Wife peered onstage (**Figure 8.26**). The face was carved Styrofoam, and the large Styrofoam ball eye could be rotated by an US stagehand.

FIGURE 8.25 *Final design: Act II model and drop paint elevation*

FIGURE 8.26 *The Giant's Wife*

FIGURE 8.27   *The final look*

The end of the play featured a flown-in 1920s ad for "A Fairy Tale Wedding" (**Figure 8.27**).

The fence unit DSL rolled onstage so that a cable that flew in with a bird attached could be hooked to the Beanstalk that the fence unit contained. It was made of semi-stiff hose so it had some 3D dimension as it grew. Note the cuckoo clock mailbox on the fence.

Design Process Recap

- Ideas that solved how the production could move in a way that seemed appropriate for the setting but also practical for the stage space came first.
- Solving the problem of the three houses within this idea was an indication that the design was going in a good direction.
- This was followed by many attempts at visual looks that enhanced the movement idea.
- The tree look went through a lot of possible options.
- The idea to put enlarged ads and other images on the doors of the houses opened up scale change ideas elsewhere and resulted, finally, in the Giant's eye unit.

Production Credits

Into the Woods, Fulton Theatre, 2005
Director: Michael Mitchell
Set Designer: Robert Klingelhoefer
Costume Designer: Beth Dunkleberger
Lighting Design: Paul Black

SUMMARY

- Your first pass at your design is just the start. Develop your ideas!

- Use *selection*, *abstraction*, and *transformation* to grow your design.

- Manage color.

- Refine line and proportion.

- Make magic!

Project: Project Play Complete

Your project play design should be complete at this point. Use any of the techniques in this chapter to assess, develop, and refine your design.

See Chapter 9 to consider what final form you want to present your design in, rendering or model.

THE ART(WORK) OF COMMUNICATION

The true product that the scenic designer creates is the finished set in performance in combination with all the other elements of production. In the creation of that design, he will use many art techniques to plan and communicate his ideas. He will create many beautiful objects, from drawings and color renderings to models and drafting, as he plans his design. The fact that his objective is the final set in performance is important to remember. Beautiful drawings or models do not necessarily produce effective designs. It is important for the designer to look at the artwork he creates while designing and communicating the design as steps toward a final goal, not finished products in themselves.

Many successful designers have not had ideal skills in drawing or painting. They found ways to communicate their ideas to those they worked with and produced successful designs onstage. Many employed assistants to do their renderings and/or models.

In common practice today, the scenic designer will create visualization tools in several different media: sketches, renderings, models, and drafting. The beginning designer must attempt to master proficiency in all these forms.

SKETCHES

Drawing is a skill that is fundamental to all design work as a step in the process itself and a foundation for the other steps that follow. The first thing most designers do is pick up a pencil and make a few quick sketches. These thumbnails get the ideas out of your head and onto the page where you can see and assess them (**Figure 9.1**). These first drawings are most commonly intended for your eyes only. Developed a little further, early sketches

FIGURE 9.1 *Sketchbook page*

FIGURE 9.2   *Rough sketch:* Three Sisters

FIGURE 9.3   *Sketch:* Love's Labour's Lost

are the first thing shared with the director and other designers (**Figures 9.2** and **9.3**).

Some designers, notably Ming Cho Lee, develop their designs through a series of very precise small sketches on tracing paper with overlaid layer after layer as changes are

made. If the tracing paper used is the buff onionskin type, white colored pencil highlights can be added.

Pencil drawings may continue to develop the design or the designer may move quickly to a rough model to explore his ideas in 3D. If a traditional (nondigital) rendering is done, a same-size pencil drawing is often done first and transferred to the watercolor paper or illustration board using graphite transfer paper.

Cross-Hatching

Hatching is the pencil technique of shading by creating lines with variations in value and separation. This hatching can be in any direction and be straight or curved lines. If lines go in two or more directions the technique is considered cross-hatching. It is a desirable technique because it produces a wide variety of values while retaining a very clean appearance.

> Because any part of a sketch, rendering, or model that appears sloppy will call attention to itself, techniques that are clean and clear are always preferred.

Pencil Technique

Proper pencil techniques and choices are important. Drawing pencils come in a variety of lead weights. Harder leads produce lighter marks. Softer leads produce darker marks. A good range of drawing pencil weights would be 6B-3B-1B-B-HB-H-1H-3H-6H, from darkest to lightest.

In planning the drawing, work from background to foreground initially with a light lead. Progress to darker leads as the drawing develops. When you are done, finish with very dark lines, used very selectively to pop out the most important elements, usually the figure and the elements around him.

Combining Media

Even if you want to stay with pencil drawing as your main presentation media, there may be ways that digital media can help you. For instance, if you were to draw elements of your design individually and then scan them, you could digitally edit them in Photoshop. This could allow the turning on or off of various elements or changing their

FIGURE 9.4 *Cross-hatching and pencil technique*

position. This can be especially helpful with changing the position of the figure.

Perspective can be an issue, in this method, because an element drawn at one perspective angle cannot be digitally altered to a different perspective. Also, changing the scale of an element will change the scale of your pencil lines as well so that may look odd, but if you keep within these limitations, you will be able to revise drawings rather than totally redoing them. You could also take your finished digital drawing into Photoshop to paint in color over or under it making it possible to try multiple color choices from the one drawing.

Storyboards

A storyboard is a series of sketches of all the looks of a unit or multiple set production shown together to give an overview of the entire production. The storyboard of

scenes for a production of *Ragtime* in **Figure 9.5** shows the advantages of digital media in a large production.

Digital media makes it much easier to create the multiple sketches required to create a storyboard for a multiple set production. In a master Photoshop file with all the elements of the set in it, individual layers can be turned on or off until a certain scene's look is created. This look can then be saved as a .jpg. The production of *Ragtime* from **Figure 9.5** had 39 sketches that were plotted on a 4' x 9' panel that was hung in rehearsal.

Storyboards can also be done as pencil sketches as they are frequently in film, as renderings in digital or traditional media, or as models of each look.

Resources: Materials for Drawing and Sketching

Drawing pencils 6B-3B-1B-B-HB-H-1H-3H-6H
Pink Pearl Eraser

FIGURE 9.5   *Storyboard for* Ragtime

Erasing shield
Sketch pads
Drafting Vellum like Clearprint 1000
Onionskin tracing paper
White colored pencils for highlights

RENDERINGS

A fully developed image a designer creates of a proposed set is called a rendering. It is an image that shows the design as accurately as possible and that should ideally have no style of its own but be an objective view of the finished design, whatever its style. The designer should therefore develop techniques with which he can best capture this verisimilitude.

The rendering, unlike the model and the paint elevations, has the ability to show the magic in a production moment. It is the only tool the scenic designer has to communicate his view of the complete effect of scenery, lighting, and costume. This may be very important in helping the production team visualize the ideas being

discussed. Lighting designers do not typically do any form of visualization, so if the production depends on specific lighting looks or effects, the set designer's rendering may be the only place those looks will be able to be looked at prior to Tech.

Traditional Rendering Techniques

Renderings may be done in a wide range of media. The traditional benchmark is to use watercolors as the transparency of the dyes in washes on watercolor paper or illustration board can create luminous effects that convey light well.

In this form a drawing prepared using a mechanical perspective method to lay out the elements of the set is commonly done first and used to guide the watercolor painting. The drawing, on vellum, can be transferred, using the graphite-transfer method, onto illustration board for painting (see the example in **Figure 9.6**).

Whatever the media chosen, the beginning designer should work hard to develop rendering techniques with

FIGURE 9.6   *Rendering for The Lady in Red*
The drawing in this rendering was done initially in pencil on vellum and then transferred to illustration board using graphite transfer. After the vellum was removed the transferred lines were strengthened in pencil. Cross-hatching was added around the perimeter that faded out to give a feeling of a dark surround without a sense of weight. Color was added in transparent layers by airbrush, with colored pencil and watercolor details added with small brushes.

which he can clearly, easily, and quickly present his design ideas.

A rendering should show the set as it looks finished, onstage, and lit. (**Figure 9.7**). If only one rendering is going to be done for the production, it should be of a moment when the set is brightly lit enough to have all its parts visible. A moody, dark moment may make a beautiful rendering, but may not be very helpful as a tool to show what the set is like. Rendering the set as lit by stage lights may require the designer to make some assumptions as to what the lighting will be like months later when technical rehearsals begin. If the lighting designer is onboard early enough, consulting him or her may be helpful. If not the designer takes his best educated guess as to what the lighting may be like. The paint elevations discussed later will show the true color of how the designer wants the set painted.

Rendering Darkness

One of the problems faced in a rendering is how to convey darkness. Sets are experienced in the theatre as a lit volume of space surrounded by darkness. For the audience, with their focus on the lit area, this darkness seems to fade away. When the designer attempts to render this darkness, however, the results can seem heavy, dead, and wrong.

Some Ways to Convey Darkness in a Traditional Rendering:

- In a watercolor and pencil rendering, cross-hatch the dark areas with the darkest zones closest to the set and fading out as they move farther away (**Figure 9.8**).

FIGURE 9.7   *Rendering for Wilderness*

FIGURE 9.8   *Rendering for Lucky Come Hawaii*
This rendering is in pencil on illustration board with watercolor wash and bleed-proof white highlights. The dark perimeter was heavily cross-hatched, while at the bottom the hatching was allowed to fade out.

- Using an airbrush, spray the dark colors, again, with darkest areas closest to the set and fading away. Linear streaks can also suggest light beams in space to help the illusion (**Figure 9.9**).

- Consider using black illustration board as the base for your rendering. This means you will need to build up all the light tones, and this can be difficult (**Figure 9.10**).

The renderings for a production of *The Wizard of Oz* in **Figures 9.12–9.14** were created very quickly using a collage of pre-printed elements (the house, the landscape, and the spirals) with quick spray work in both flat black spray paint and floral sprays done with stencil mattes to create the cloud-shaped portals. This production fell in a period where digital techniques were very new, and I was mixing the digital images as printed collage pieces and painting over them.

Digital Rendering Techniques

There are many software options for digitally creating renderings.

Digital media offers several advantages over traditional methods:

- **Speed:** Rendering digitally can be faster than traditional techniques, especially when you consider the time spent to redo a traditional rendering.

- **Ease:** Many aspects of rendering are easier digitally than in traditional media. Very detailed or photographic-looking elements can be found and reworked for sharper looks than by panting from scratch.

- **Duplication:** If you are doing a multiple set production, a master image rendered digitally can allow you to turn on and off layers and save many looks as separate images.

FIGURE 9.9   *Rendering for an Armstrong Industrial*
This rendering for a small set in an Industrial is drawn in colored pencil with liquid watercolor airbrushed over it that fades out to the white board. Final painting and highlights are added in the center-focused area.

FIGURE 9.10 *Rendering for* The Elephant Man
This rendering was done on black board. The first step was to mask the perimeter and lightly dust the center with white enamel spray paint. While this is an unusual technique, the spray paint creates a resist that can be worked over with opaque watercolors and colored pencil for a nice effect that preserves a feeling of light beams visible in the air in a dark space.

FIGURE 9.11 *Detail of a rendering for* The Glass Menagerie
Always consider that in a rendering you are not painting "things." You are painting light and shade that allow you to see things. Combining watercolors and colored pencils can give some rich lighting effects.

FIGURE 9.12   *Rendering for* The Wizard of Oz: *Kansas*

FIGURE 9.13   *Rendering for* The Wizard of Oz: *Munchkin Land*

FIGURE 9.14   *Rendering for* The Wizard of Oz: *The Wicked Witch's Castle*

- **Revision:** Any time you need to revise something the time saving in digital work will be to your advantage.

- **Clarity:** By working with digital images and textures, you are from the very beginning of the process working with "real" looking materials, not trying to render the feeling of a material or texture using a media that doesn't convey its power or complexity.

But digital techniques can also tempt the user to make "one-click" choices, to use preset options, to go the easy route to achieve his intentions. Digital rendering techniques must be held to the same standards as traditional media.

- Does the rendering capture the magic of the setting, its presence onstage?

- Does the rendering clearly show all the parts of the set and serve as a tool for its understanding?

I generally prefer the more basic digital tools mentioned in this chapter, and I resist becoming a slave to the latest version of everything. I don't want programs that do a lot of the work for me; I want good solid tools that I can use in much the same way as if I was working with traditional tools.

In pre-digital days, the designer commonly did water-color renderings of the set. These were beautiful but very time-consuming. A common, terrible moment in the process would be when you presented the beautiful rendering you had spent days creating, and the director would say, "That's great, but can we move this over here and make it blue?" Your spirits would sink as your beautiful rendering became obsolete. There would be the urge to defend the way it was, to resist the changes just to protect the rendering. Digital media has made this less of an issue today as changes are much easier to make.

SketchUp

There are several 3D rendering programs that can be used as a final rendering technique or as a step in creating a rendering in another digital technique. Trimble SketchUp is an easy to learn and use program that allows the user to draw simple shapes to scale, and then expand them in different directions to make 3D forms (**Figures 9.15**). The drafting of the shapes is like a very simplified CAD

FIGURE 9.15   *Basic SketchUp*

FIGURE 9.16   *SketchUp with imported textures*

program. The space you work in is 1:1, and you assign lengths to the lines you create. You can very quickly create complex 3D shapes. Viewing options include Zoom, Orbit, and Pan, which let you move around the model in any direction and see your digital model from many viewpoints.

Quick visualizations can be made and then exported to use as the basis of a Photoshop sketch, supplying an accurate perspective view of the set, or can be finished in SketchUp with textures added to the shapes. By creating paint elevation-like images in Photoshop and importing these as textures onto the faces of your SketchUp model you can create a clean, clear 3D digital model (**Figure 9.16**).

By making a SketchUp model of the theatre space you can see the set in the theatre's architecture from multiple viewpoints to check sightline issues (**Figure 9.17**).

SketchUp 3D Warehouse is a website on which other SketchUp users have uploaded things they have made to share. There are a wide variety of furniture items, figures, and assorted oddities. While there may seldom be exactly what you are looking for, these can be effective mock-ups as you design, and then replaced or exploded and worked on to make them more appropriate.

SketchUp can be a very effective design and visualization tool but its look doesn't really allow much in the way of atmosphere or mood. Lighting effects are limited to simple directional effects and basic shadows. Exporting your most complete SketchUp into Photoshop to create atmospheric effects can help give a more polished look.

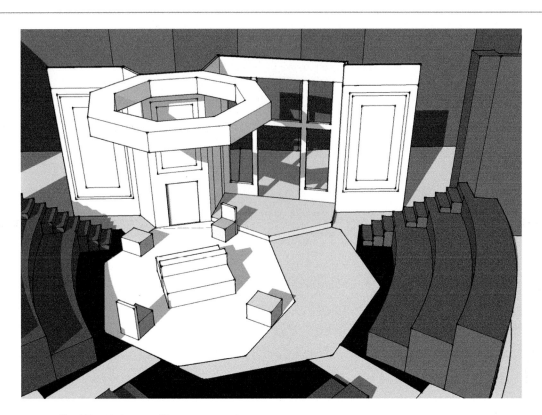

FIGURE 9.17   *SketchUp with theatre architecture*

Photoshop

Adobe Photoshop can be used to create a rendering from scratch, to make elements to add as a texture to SketchUp or to add post effects to a SketchUp rendering.

The rendering in **Figures 9.18** and **9.19** for a production of *Bus Stop* was done entirely in Photoshop using a number of flat textures and objects found online or created from scratch.

The rendering in **Figure 9.20** and a production photo of the scene onstage, **Figure 9.21**, of a production of *Dracula* show how accurate a pre-visualization can be. This design featured video of a stormy sea projected on a DS black scrim.

Resources: Materials for Renderings

Software for Rendering

Trimble SketchUp
Adobe Photoshop

Some Websites for Textures

www.textures.com
www.mayang.com/textures

Materials for Traditional Renderings

Surfaces

Illustration Board	Brands include Crescent and Strathmore Sizes are 15″ × 20″, 20″ × 30″, and 30″ × 40″. Cold Press surface has a degree of texture; Hot Press is smooth.
Watercolor Paper	Brands include Arches, Canson, and Strathmore Sizes are 16″ × 20″, 20″ × 30″, and 32″ × 40″
Black Board	Brands include Crescent and Strathmore Sizes are 15″ × 20″ and 20″ × 30″.

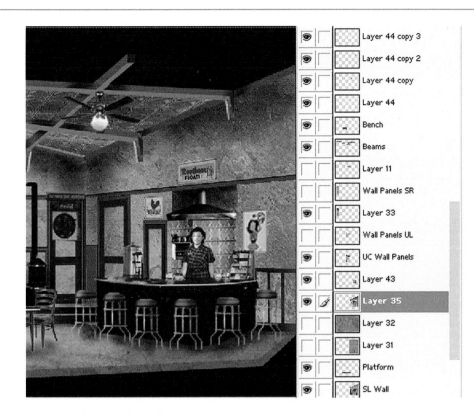

FIGURE 9.18   *Screenshot of rendering for Bus Stop*

FIGURE 9.19   *Photoshop Rendering for Bus Stop*

FIGURE 9.20 *Rendering for* Dracula

FIGURE 9.21 *Production photo of scene from* Dracula

Media

Colored Pencil   Brands include Prismacolor
Gouache   Brands include Winsor & Newton
Liquid Watercolors   Brands include Luma and Dr. Martin's
Inks

Tools

Watercolor Brushes   red sable preferred
Airbrush   Brands include Badger or Paasche
Technical Pens   Brands include Koh-I-Noor
                       Rapidograph

MODELS

In the last century stage design has become more and more a three-dimensional form, and in the process the scenic model has become more and more important. Many designers create a very quick rough model at an early stage of the design process. Models are made to scale with the most common scales for theatre work being 1/4″ = 1′-0″ and 1/2″ = 1′-0″.

The Importance of Models

The scale model is the only form in which the set can be fully understood in 3D and the best tool with which the designer can sculpt space. It is also the most important tool for collaboration as all involved can get a true sense of the 3D space and even get their hands in it and play.

The two most common types of models are the 1/4-inch White Model and the 1/2-inch Color or Final Model.

White Models

The White Model, so called because it does not show color, is fairly quick to construct and easy to transport (see examples in **Figures 9.22** and **9.23**). Cardstock or Bristol board are used because they can be easily cut, scored, and folded to create many scenic elements, with white foam board used for larger, thicker

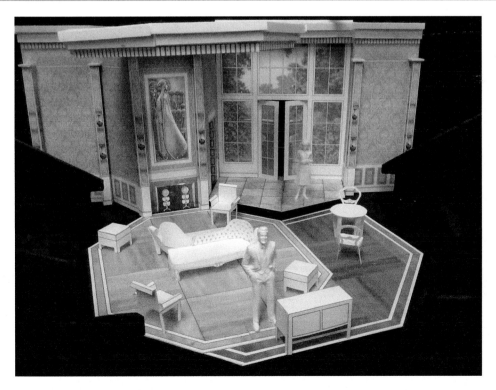

FIGURE 9.22   *1/2-inch White Model for Blithe Spirit*

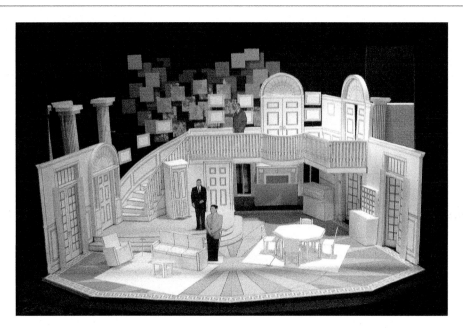

FIGURE 9.23 *1/2-inch White Model for* The Eclectic Society

elements and black foam board used for the theatre model box. Gray tones can be used in a White Model if value differences are important to conveying the design accurately. Cardstock can have drafted detail printed on it. If images are involved, for instance, a detailed backdrop, the image should be drawn, painted, or digitally prepared in black, white, and gray only, as any color will create an unduly strong point of emphasis.

> All scenic models should include a scale figure so the proportions of the design can be gauged. The use of two or more figures can help to show spatial relationships, the relationships between different areas, and even a sense of story depending on how the figures are placed.

Full-Color Models

Finished color models show all details exactly as the designer plans them to look onstage. This usually means the actual texture desired on set pieces is rendered in scale. In a realistic interior set there may be a great deal of furniture, props, and dressing that needs to be made. This detailed work can be extremely time-consuming for the designer or his assistants. This can cause the designer to do a less detailed model and/or a very complete rendering.

Sometimes the designer may create a color finished model in 1/4-inch scale, especially if the model is to be transported often or the theatre is very large, but it is more common to build a 1/2-inch model of the set with all its details. This form is the clearest way for the director and the production team to understand the proposed design. A 1/2-inch scale model is big enough get your hands into as you make changes or manipulate the position of scenic pieces. One-half-inch scale models can take a great deal of time to make especially if the set is very complex or prop-heavy.

In the model for *Good People* in **Figure 9.24**, the wall of venetian blinds and the stone of the fireplace are printed flat textures spray-adhesived onto illustration board or foam board. The high-gloss black deck is a piece of black Plexiglas that had the turntable line scratched into it. The sofa and armchair are built-up foam board coated with gesso. The bookcase is built of illustration board pieces individually covered with printed woodgrain texture before being glued together. Figures are from Plastruct and glued with zap-a-gap onto 1/16-inch clear acrylic bases.

In the model for *Wilderness* in **Figure 9.25**, the walls are foam board and illustration board. The branch structure is different thicknesses of wire glued to a 1/8-inch dowel pipe structure and textured with gesso

FIGURE 9.24   *Model for* Good People

FIGURE 9.25   *Model for* Wilderness

before painting. The furniture is illustration board and various-sized pieces of basswood and balsa.

In the model of *Miss Ever's Boys* (**Figure 9.26**) the walls were made of 1/8-inch-wide strips of 1/16-inch-thick balsa wood glued onto illustration board shapes. Balsa and basswood were used for the beams and other structural

pieces. The hung lamps were disks of Bristol board gusseted into a shallow cone and mounted on pieces of floral wire. The corn was cut from a straw broom and set into hot glue rows. The figures were cut from illustration board and painted.

The model for *A Flash of Lightning*, in **Figure 9.27**, like the actual set had very little built detail and was mostly 2D

FIGURE 9.26 *Model for* Miss Ever's Boys

FIGURE 9.27 *Model for* A Flash of Lightning

painting. The model pieces were drawn with black ink in a technical pen and then painted with watercolors. Figures were made of specific characters to help show the usage of the sets in this nineteenth-century melodrama.

For the model of *Ready for the River* (**Figure 9.28**), the car parts, seats, front grille, and hood in the collage

of elements at the rear were from a 1:25 scale plastic car model. The doors were cut out of single-thick illustration board with their open panels backed in Bristol board to create the panel depth.

In the 1/4-inch scale model of a production of *Hamlet* (**Figure 9.29**), double-thick illustration board

FIGURE 9.28   *Model for* Ready for the River

FIGURE 9.29   *1/4-inch model for* Hamlet

was stacked to create the stairs. The columns were pieces of single-thick illustration board glued over a built-up form to create the gaps between panels. The torches were inverted pyramids made of Bristol board glued onto piano wire supports. Jeweler's chain was used UR.

Model Boxes

Usually, before a model of the set can be built, a model box of the theatre must be made (**Figure 9.30**). It is important that this model box be accurate in the size of the stage space. It need not include all the architectural detail of the theatre. If it is a 1/2-inch model of a fairly large theatre, the model box itself can be quite large. It is not unusual for a model box to be 3′ wide × 2′ deep × 2′ high.

This leads to several considerations:

• **The weight of the model box.** A large model box can be quite heavy. Building it from black foam board can help keep the weight down.

FIGURE 9.30 *A model box*
In these images of a typical proscenium model box, note how the sides have sections missing to let light into the model, and in the detail how the construction of the box creates some structural points that help make a relatively light box seem pretty sturdy.

- **Strength is important.** The model box will be moved around a great deal and needs to be strong to stand up to so much handling. Use foam board to build up structural shapes that have thickness that gives them stability, and join them in ways that create strength. Consider a 1/2-inch-thick foam board base.

- **Let light in.** Leave out side walls as much as possible to let light in. The real set will be lit. Your model can seem awfully dark if you don't let as much light into its box as possible.

- **Build it to breakdown.** There are several methods to build a model box to break down to a flattened form that is easier to ship, but to do this the model of the set must break down as well, and this can be trouble. Also the idea of sending a model to afar-off theatre unassembled can make you worry if it will be put back together correctly.

To Print or to Model?

An important consideration in model making is where to stop. Low-profile detail like the indentation of mortar between bricks can be difficult to replicate at some scales. In 1/2-inch scale there are techniques like spreading modeling paste on the surface and stamping or drawing the mortar lines on it, and materials like pre-made brick panels, to consider. In 1/4-inch scale, this thickness is difficult to reproduce, and printing a brick texture to scale can often be cleaner. In general, it is a good idea to consider anything less than 1 inch thick in 1/2-inch scale or 2 inches thick in 1/4-inch scale as better drawn or printed than built.

Printing also has the advantage of allowing greater control in representing detailed scenic art treatments. If your scenery is a brick wall with a trompe l'oiel sky painted on it, the model will seem more accurate if you make the image in Photoshop of the sky with an added brick texture and print it than if you build the brick texture and try to paint the sky on it. The digital method will also let you use the image as the paint elevation as well.

Scale Tolerances

It is important in any model, at any scale, that the model look clean and elegantly made, that no part of it calls attention to itself as seeming clumsy. This is a challenge

FIGURE 9.31   *Model options*
This fireplace from a model of Good People *was made of a foam board core and covered with a printed stone texture that matched the vacuform brick panels used in the actual scenery.*

not only to your model-making skills, but to your decision-making skills as well. If an element will look cleaner if you print it or build it in a simplified manner, that probably means you should. The thinnest common model-making sheet material is probably Bristol board or cardstock, which is roughly 1 1/2 inches thick at 1/4-inch scale and 3/4 inches at 1/2-inch scale. Anything thinner than this you should consider drawing, painting, or printing.

Furniture and Detail

A model of a set that contains a great number of furniture pieces, props, and set dressing can take a great deal more time to make than one that does not. Many designers will opt for a simpler white model of such a set and do a rendering to show the completely detailed set.

Furniture and detail in a model can be a great deal of fun to make, if there is time, and really show what the set will look like completed. There are a few options of furniture that can be purchased that will work in a model:

- **Pop-Out Furniture** is a series of kits created originally by a set designer that feature cardstock sheets of furniture in various styles that are already die-cut. You cut the tabs that hold them to the sheet and then score and fold them into their 3D form. They are white with printed detail. They work very well in white models. They can be painted, but in a fully detailed model still look flat and unrealistic.

- **Doll house furniture** is available, especially in 1/2-inchscale, and sometimes smaller. Care should be taken to choose pieces that are well made and don't look clunky. Sometimes antique stores have plastic doll furniture that is an appropriate scale.

- **Model railroad elements** can sometimes be of use. Model railroad items come in scales designated by letters like HO and O. O scale is basically 1/2″ = 1′-0″.

Material Thickness

Probably the most important consideration in model making is the choice of the proper material in regards to its thickness and suitability for how it will be used. Nothing ruins the illusion of proper scale quicker than a material whose edges appear too thick in a flat shape or a join between two pieces. Solutions to this problem can be proper material choice, or covering joined elements with filler, like gesso or modeling paste, or a final layer of a thinner material, like cardstock or Bristol board.

Scale Thicknesses of Materials for Scenic Models

Materials vary in thickness brand by brand and are not perfectly dimension-able, but for the sake of consideration, here are some common thicknesses of model materials and their scale thicknesses.

Real Thickness	In 1/8″ scale	In 1/4″ scale	In 1/2″ scale
1/64″ (paper)	1 1/2″	3/4″	3/8″
1/32″ (cardstock)	3″	1 1/2″	3/4″
1/16″ (single-thick illustration board)	6″	3″	1 1/2″
1/8″ (double-thick illustration board)	12″	6″	3″
3/16″ (foam board)	18″	9″	4 1/2″

Adhesives

Using the right adhesive for each material used in the model is a very important matter in determining the strength of the bond and a clean appearance.

Some basic adhesives commonly used include the following:

- **Hot glue** can be used where a quick bond is helpful, such as between big pieces of foam board in a model box where the join will not be seen. For detail work it is in most cases too clumsy.

- **White glue** can be used for many model materials including wood, cardboard, paper, and foam board. Its slower drying time requires the pieces to be temporarily joined using T-pins or a jig.

- **Zap-a-Gap** is a cyanoacrylate super glue that bonds most materials. It is easy to apply to small pieces and has a dry-time accelerator, Zip Kicker, which dries it virtually instantly where that is an advantage.

- **Spray adhesive** is perfect for applying large printed paper elements onto illustration board or foam board. 3M Super 77 is the strongest, most dependable brand. Types labeled as *artist's adhesives* often have a repositionable delay in their bond, which can make them prone to slipping in assembly and to not bond as strongly when dry.

Finishing and Painting

Since accurate scale and a clean appearance are so important in model making, the finishing and painting of the model must be done with care.

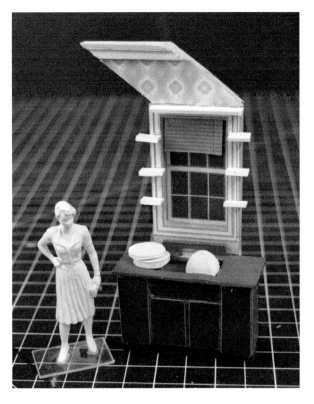

FIGURE 9.32 *Model furniture options*
In this kitchen sink unit from the 1/2-inch model of Good People the wallpaper, molding lines, and blinds in the window are printed. The basic structure of the cabinet is illustration board with the break lines of the cabinets cut partially into the front.

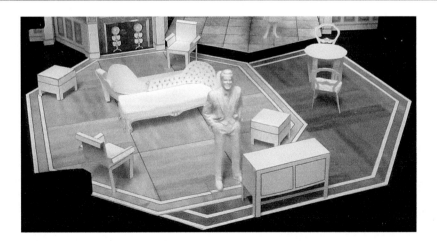

FIGURE 9.33 *Model furniture options*
In this 1/2-inch white model for Blithe Spirit the chaise and balloon-back chairs SL are Pop-Up Furniture. The other pieces were made for this model by designing the flat pattern for the piece, drafting it, printing the drafting on cardstock, cutting it out, and scoring, folding, and gluing it into its 3D form.

To finish elements that were made from dissimilar materials, such as basswood and illustration board, a coat of white gesso can give a common surface before painting.

If the desired painted image is detailed, digital printing is probably a better choice than painting by hand. Modeling paste is product made for acrylic painting that can be applied to many materials and worked to create a variety of textures including stone and old, rough brick.

Figures

Models, like all scenic representations, must include the figure of the actor to show appropriate scale. Three-dimensional figures are available from Plastruct (www.plastruct.com) and PeopleScale (www.peoplescale.com) in all common architectural scales or figures can be printed to scale from historical photos or previous productions of the play or other plays of the period and spray-adhesived to Bristol board and cut out. Simple white Bristol board silhouettes are an acceptable, simple alternative (**Figure 9.34**).

3D Printing

3D printing is now a viable option for creating all manner of elements for the scenic model, from moldings to furniture. It is especially nice when multiple pieces are needed, as 3D printing will make all copies identical.

Resources: Materials and Tools for Model Building

Boards

White and black foam board are basic materials for model making because their thickness can give some strength while remaining lightweight and easy to work.

Illustration board is available in Hot Press (Smooth) and Cold Press (lightly textured) in single thick (1/16") and double thick (1/8") and with one good side, two good sides, and black, which is black throughout.

Bristol board is a thin cardboard that bends easily for curved forms and cuts easily for detailed work.

FIGURE 9.34 *Figure options for models*

Cardstock is similar to Bristol board but generally a little thinner. It is sold in 8 1/2″ x 11″ size and can be digitally printed.

Wood

Balsa is a lightweight, easy to cut wood available in sheets of various widths and thicknesses of 1/16 inch to 1/4 inch. Because it is soft it is easily damaged and prone to breaking along the grain.

Basswood is stronger and more durable than balsa but still relatively easy to cut.

Hardwoods, including walnut, mahogany, and cherry, are available in the same range of sizes, but in most cases it is a better choice to build from basic materials and paint the desired finish than to use hardwoods due to the scale of the grain and difficulty to work.

Manufacturer: Midwest Products (midwestproducts.com) Available at most craft stores.

Metal

Wire in a variety of materials and sizes can be used in scenic models. Wire wound on spools can generally never be straightened enough to use.

Floral wire can be purchased in straight 18-inch lengths that can be bent as desired. It is especially useful for hanging flown scenery.

Piano wire is stiffer and more difficult to bend but stays very straight and is strong.

Brass rods, tubes, and shapes can be very useful. Brass is available in L-shape and U-shape and in small gauge hollow tube. Brass rod can be soldered to make very strong hanging structures for flown scenery.

Manufacturer: K&S Metals (ksmetals.com)

Aluminum rods, tubes, and shapes are available in the same shapes and sizes.

Manufacturer: K&S Metals (ksmetals.com)

Plastics

Thin clear acrylic sheet, 1/16-inch thick, is useful as glass and as a base for plastic scale figures and other small, free-standing elements as it lets the floor show through but provides support.

Other Materials

Found objects: Anything is fair game. Jewelry and jewelry parts can be useful. Remember that what you use in the model will need to be re-created in full scale.

Doll house molding and details: A wide range of doll house products can be used, but some is in "iffy" scales that can seem odd next to other items.

Model railroad items: Many items intended for model railroading adapt well to scenic models. O scale (RR) is 1/4″ = 1′-0″.

Sand and Aquarium Gravel can be mixed with modeling paste to create strong, stable textures.

Tools

X-acto Knives and blades: X-acto #11 blades are a good basic choice, but many specialty blades are available.

Miniature saw: Small, very finely toothed saws are useful for clean, square cuts in thicker balsa and basswood pieces. Miter boxes for these are available.

Metal straightedge: Make all straight knife cuts using a metal straightedge to guide the knife.

T-Pins are perfect for temporary assembly of parts while glue dries. Several sizes are available.

DRAFTING

Scale drawings are a part of the designer's process from the very beginning. There will be a large chunk of time required late in the process for the creation of the final drawing the designer will supply to the shop that will build the set, but scale drawing must be a part of his process from the very beginning. It is common for a designer to do a rough groundplan of the set while he is doing thumbnail sketches. As he develops the design he must do drafting that works out how the scenery he envisions in his sketches works in the theatre's space.

Switching frequently from drawing or model making to drafting to set the actual size of elements as you design them is good practice.

Hand drafting is a good way to learn basic concepts and techniques, but is increasingly losing ground to CAD due to CAD's clarity and ease of revision.

Designer drawings is the term given to the set of drawings the scenic designer creates for the shop that is building the scenery and from which the shop will do its own construction drawings. The designer drawings give the size and appearance of all scenic pieces and how they fit onstage and off if they have a stored position. The drawings include different views as needed to explain the scenery. The three most common views used in drafting are Plan, Section, and Front Elevation.

The Groundplan

The groundplan is generally the first drawing the designer drafts. It is a view of the whole stage, at floor level, of the set looking straight down from above. It shows the size, in the horizontal plane, and position of all elements. The designer receives a plan of the stage to be used for the production from the theatre organization, usually from the production manager. This groundplan will include the theatre's architecture as it pertains to the limits of the stage space; the theatre's equipment, especially linesets; and the array of audience seating. It allows the designer to begin to sculpt the theatre's space for the particular production. It lets him check the sightlines from different positions in the audience space. Important reference lines in the plan are the centerline and the plasterline (if the theatre is the proscenium type). The centerline is an imagined line that runs US–DS in the center of the stage. Its value is as a point from which element's positions on stage can be measured. The plasterline (so called because it springs from where the fancy plasterwork ends on a traditional proscenium) is an imagined line perpendicular to the centerline from the back of the proscenium on one side to the comparable position on the other side.

The Groundplan: Things to Consider

The groundplan is the single most important drawing the designer will create. It is the essence of how the design will work in space.

There are some basic things to consider while creating the groundplan:

The Architectural Relationship of the Audience Space to the Performance Space

This is the fundamental relationship that will determine the audience sightlines and what and how much space the designer can use.

The Correct Actual Size of the Scenic Elements Used

Walls and platforms can be any size, but furniture items have somewhat standard dimensions, as do common doors and windows. The designer may choose to use larger or smaller than "normal" elements, but when he intends to use standard sized items, he must know their correct dimensions and show them in the groundplan.

Resources: Standard Sizes of Common Furniture Items

Many furniture items have no standard and may vary a great deal, but following are standard sizes or approximate sizes, rounded up generally, of many common items.

Modern Sofa: 7′ long × 2′–6″ deep
Loveseat: 5′–6′ long × 2′–6″ deep
Armchair: 2′–6″ × 2′–6″ (3′ × 3′ if heavily padded)
Straight Chair: 18″ × 18″ × 18″ high (seat)
Mattress (Full): 54″ × 74″
Mattress (Queen): 60″ × 80″
Dining Tables: Extremely variable. Allow 2 feet of length per person

four people: 36″ × 48″ × 30″ high
six people: 36″ × 72″ × 30″ high
eight people: 36″ to 42″ × 90″ × 30″ high

Sideboards: 6′–7′ long × 36″–39″ high
Stoves: 3′ × 3′ for an apartment stove up to 6′ × 4′ for a period woodstove or contemporary professional stove
Refrigerators: 3′ × 3′

If the designer draws an item on the groundplan at an incorrect size, he misleads himself on the amount of space he is using.

The Section

The groundplan gives the size of elements in the horizontal plain but little information about their heights.

Platform heights are dimensioned but not shown. Elements hung above the stage are shown as dashed lines indicating their position but not their size or how high they are. This is the information that the section will provide. The section is drawn as if the theatre was cut in half and the halves separated. The view is from centerline looking directly into one half. The decision to draw the view looking SL or SR is made based on which view is more helpful in showing important elements in the particular design. Because the section shows the vertical plane, it should show a figure as a scale reference. The section is the drawing that the designer uses to also check vertical sightlines and masking.

Elevations

These are front views of scenic elements. A front elevation of the entire set is a helpful tool to plan and assess position and proportion. This is a view directly from the front, on centerline, with no perspective. All horizontal surfaces are simply horizontal lines. Draw a figure here, too, as a reference.

Drawings that show elements of the set individually are called elevations, because a front elevation of the unit is the key view, but these drawings show a plan view of the unit as well and, frequently, a side view or section through the unit to explain all its dimensions. These drawings also include details of molding and other components.

When drafting, make sure that you are using line weights appropriately to make your drawing easy to understand, and double-check each unit you draft to make sure you have included all the views and details that are needed to understand that unit. Look at it as if you were seeing it for the first time and see if you understand it completely.

SUMMARY

- Use all your media to advantage, moving back and forth from drawing to drafting to model making and back.

- Remember the set in performance is your final goal. All your renderings, models, and drafting are only tools to get you there.

CHAPTER 10

CONSIDERATIONS FOR SINGLE SET PRODUCTIONS

A single set production can be any type of location from a forest to a ship. By definition it is simply a play that takes place in only one location. But the most common type of single set production is a room or rooms in the interior of a building or house (**Figure 10.1**).

BOX SETS

A *box set* is a term used for a realistic single set interior with complete walls, that is, one that is like a box with furniture in it and windows and doors. Since realism became the dominant style of plays in the nineteenth century, box sets have been a typical approach. While a set can have the form of a box and not be realistic, the term has come to mean a fully realistic interior set in a proscenium theatre (**Figure 10.2**).

THINKING OUTSIDE THE BOX

Since the 1950s or '60s there has been an increasingly common trend to not design an interior set as a complete box set. This is due in part to the influence of Brecht and Neher, and partially to a desire to have the set be a little more flexible and interesting than a full, enclosed space. Sometimes the ideas in a play feel too big to be contained in a box, and the designer feels he should open the set up to give them room. Whatever the reason, the result can be a set with an attractive sculptural shape (**Figure 10.3**).

SHAPING EDGES

Where does the set stop? A realistic set on a proscenium stage can be designed to fill the stage space so that everything within the proscenium frame is complete. Sometimes aesthetically, or because of budget, the designer will choose for the set to stop at some point before this. As was noted in a previous chapter, one approach is to have things around the actor, that he sits on or holds, be complete and realistic, and things farther away from him get progressively more incomplete and/or abstract.

There are many ways to do this, from surrounding a completely realistic set with other realistic elements that have more and more space between them, to ways in which the set can seem to break away, exposing its construction. More abstract choices tend to make their point more clearly. Choices that break away showing bricks, for instance, run the risk of communicating to the audience that this structure is damaged or decayed if that is not what is intended.

Choosing how to end the set gives the designer the opportunity to sculpt the outside edges into an attractive or meaningful shape (**Figure 10.4**).

ELEMENTS OF A SINGLE SET INTERIOR

The common interior set has many elements that other types of sets do not, like a ceiling, detailed floors, doors and molding.

FIGURE 10.1 The Eclectic Society *photo*

FIGURE 10.2 *A box set:* Arsenic and Old Lace

FIGURE 10.3   *Not a box set: Ming Cho Lee's sketch for Lolita, My Love (Broadway try-out) 1971*
In his design for a planned Broadway musical Lolita, My Love, Ming Cho Lee created an interior set that was far from a complete box set. Pieces selected were placed in realistic relationships with each other. A platform defined the space of the room. But the degree of selection used was quite severe and used a collage approach with scraps of architecture of the house, and other buildings were merged with a surround of tree and sky patterns.

From *Ming Cho Lee: A Life in Design* ©2014 by Arnold Aronson. Reprinted by permission of Theatre Communications Group

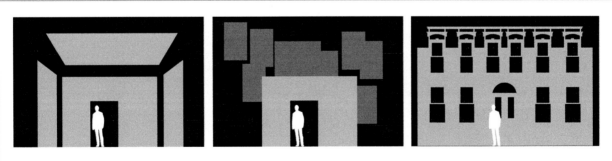

FIGURE 10.4   *Edge options*

Ceilings

A real room would have a ceiling. Yet in a theatre, where much of the lighting that will illuminate the actor comes from above, ceilings can severely limit what the lighting designer can do and therefore must be approached with care and collaboration.

Some solutions are found in **Figures 10.5–10.8**.

Floors

Other types of scenery have designed floors, but a single set allows more detail to be given to the floor's design as it does not change, and in an interior set there are many choices of floor materials that could be imitated, such as parquetry, marble, and many others, depending on the characteristics and period of the location.

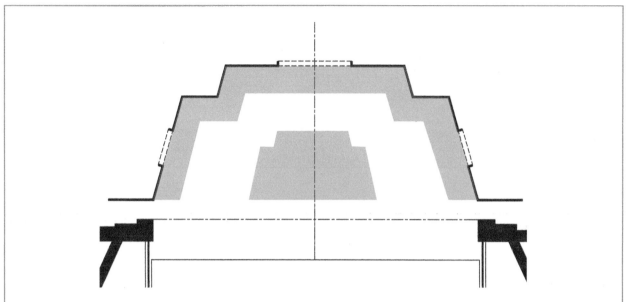

FIGURE 10.5 *Island/ring ceiling*
In this option, a ceiling is suggested by a band that follows the walls and a floating section in the center, leaving the remaining area open for lights. This would require borders to be hung in a traditional way above the ceiling to mask the lights. Molding that followed the edges of the ceiling pieces would give them a finished look.

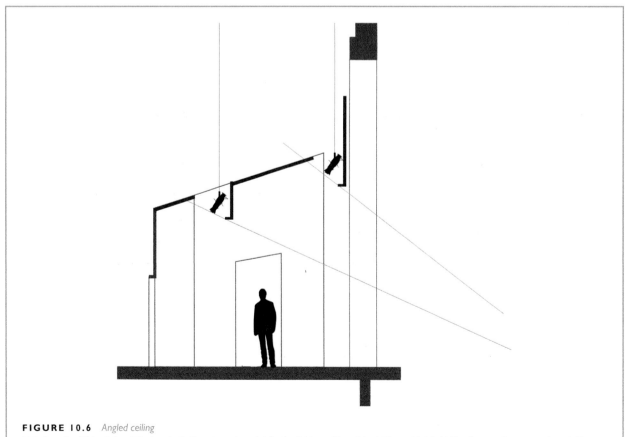

FIGURE 10.6 *Angled ceiling*
Note how the DS portal and the header in the set create a slot for the lights and how this slot is completely hidden from audience members in the front row.

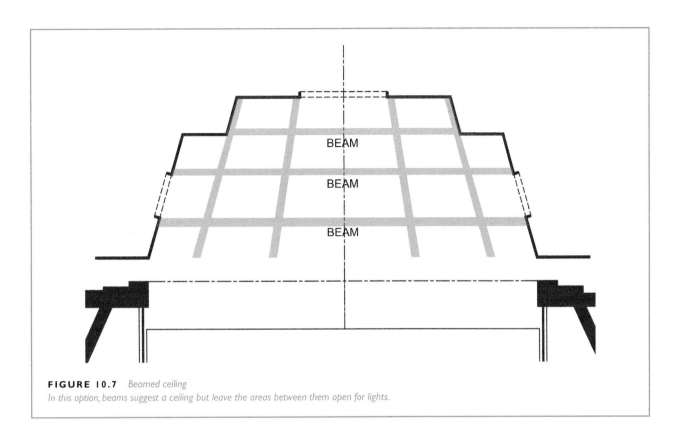

FIGURE 10.7 *Beamed ceiling*
In this option, beams suggest a ceiling but leave the areas between them open for lights.

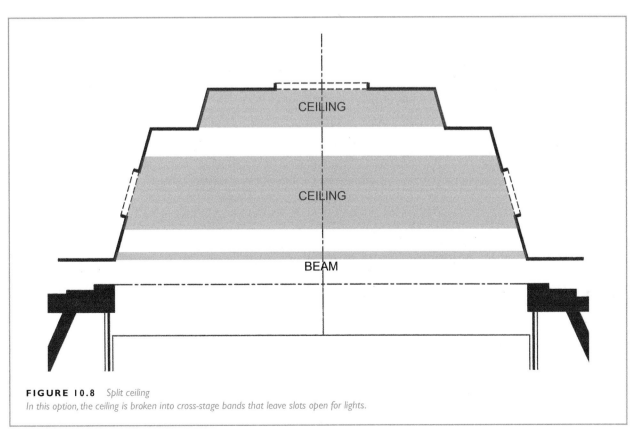

FIGURE 10.8 *Split ceiling*
In this option, the ceiling is broken into cross-stage bands that leave slots open for lights.

Some Considerations in Designing Floors

Floors are often painted on MDF or Masonite sheets. These sheets are typically 4′ × 8′. If possible, the designer should incorporate the 4′ × 8′ sheet break lines into the design so they do not appear arbitrary or at odds to the design of the floor. It may help to cut the sheets into 4′ × 4′ sections as this produces a more regular grid of break lines, as would even smaller squares of 2′ × 2′ or 1′ × 1′. Odd dimension shapes are possible as well if they fit the floor's design, but would waste material when cut from the 4′ × 8′ sheet size.

If material waste is not a concern, irregular shapes can be cut that follow lines in the design of the floor for a seamless effect. All shapes must be kept within the 4′ × 8′ sheet size by creating designed breaks (**Figures 10.9** and **10.10**).

Other floor options are rolls of vinyl flooring, painted with the desired effect and installed like a dance floor on the stage. Seams between rolls should be back-taped to make a clean seam.

An older technique, not as common today, is the canvas floor cloth, which is essentially a heavy canvas drop that is painted and then stretched on the stage floor. It can be difficult to stretch a floor cloth completely and wrinkles can be an issue.

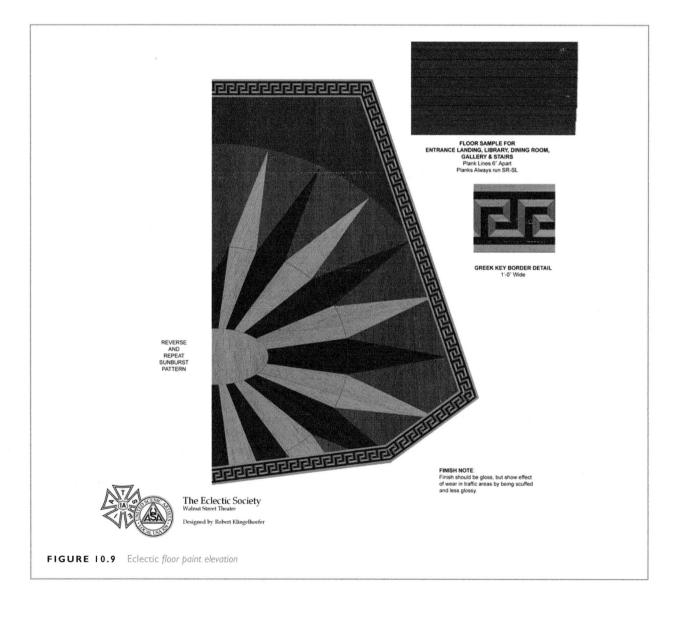

FLOOR SAMPLE FOR ENTRANCE LANDING, LIBRARY, DINING ROOM, GALLERY & STAIRS
Plank Lines 6″ Apart
Planks Always run SR-SL

GREEK KEY BORDER DETAIL
1′-0″ Wide

REVERSE AND REPEAT SUNBURST PATTERN

FINISH NOTE:
Finish should be gloss, but show effect of wear in traffic areas by being scuffed and less glossy.

The Eclectic Society
Walnut Street Theatre

Designed by Robert Klingelhoefer

FIGURE 10.9   Eclectic *floor paint elevation*

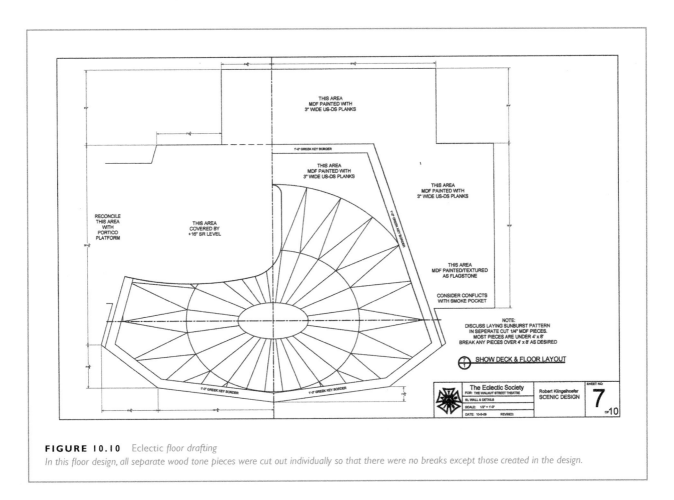

FIGURE 10.10   Eclectic *floor drafting*
In this floor design, all separate wood tone pieces were cut out individually so that there were no breaks except those created in the design.

If a plank floor is desired (like the one in **Figure 10.11**), a nice treatment is to have planks ripped from Lauan, other wood paneling, or MDF of a desired width, and paint or stain them separately. They can then be laid at random to give a natural variation in grain and tone.

Raked Decks

Raking a stage floor, making the US higher and sloping the floor lower as it comes DS, began to be done in the Baroque period because it enhanced the illusion of the perspective scenery. It is done today because it makes action US a little easier to see, and simply because it looks dramatic and sculptural. It is most often used in single set productions, as moving scenery would be difficult to move on the rake.

While the most common rake is higher US than DS, with the direction of the rake coming straight DS, a rake can be in any direction.

The degree of rake is important to consider so it is not too steep for the actor to comfortably and safely move on it. Actor's Equity insists a rake be no steeper than 3/4":1'. In other words, the rake rises no more than three-quarters of an inch for every foot it goes US (**Figure 10.12**). This ruling is generally the industry standard, though it was originally created to prevent actors in a long-running show from having injuries due to the time spent on the raked stage. Ramps are exempt from this ruling, but should not be too steep for safety in any event.

Doors

In an interior set that needs to contain multiple doors, there are considerations as to variations in door size and hinging direction depending on the kind of door it is. The hierarchy of doors dictates that front doors or main doors are larger than doors between interior rooms which are, in turn, larger than doors to closets or

FIGURE 10.11   *Plank floor*

less important rooms or spaces. Door hinging is variable. Exterior doors in domestic architecture open into the building. Exterior doors in modern public buildings open out so in case of emergency they allow quick escape. Doors from main rooms open into smaller rooms. Closet doors open out into the room because there would not be enough room in the closet for the door to swing in. The side a door hinges on is determined by the desired position once opened (**Figure 10.13**). Generally, a door hinges toward a dead side, like toward an adjacent wall rather than into the room where it might block traffic patterns.

Period and economic status greatly affect doors, with earlier periods having much more variety of size than today's standard door sizes (**Figure 10.14**). Wealthier people have always lived in bigger houses with bigger doors.

Door sizes range from the 30″ × 80″ and 36″ × 80″ modern standard to all manner of period sizes from small sizes in a fisherman's cottage, which might be 24″ × 66″ to the immense doors of an ancient palace, which might be 4′ wide × 11′ tall or more (**Figure 10.15**). Width of doors is affected by period costume as well. Eighteenth-century

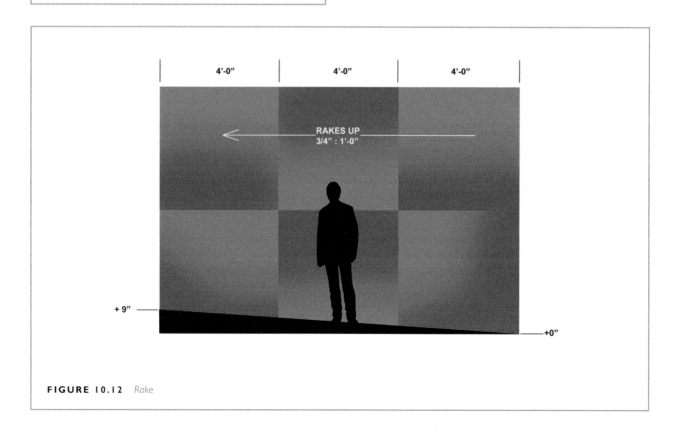

FIGURE 10.12   *Rake*

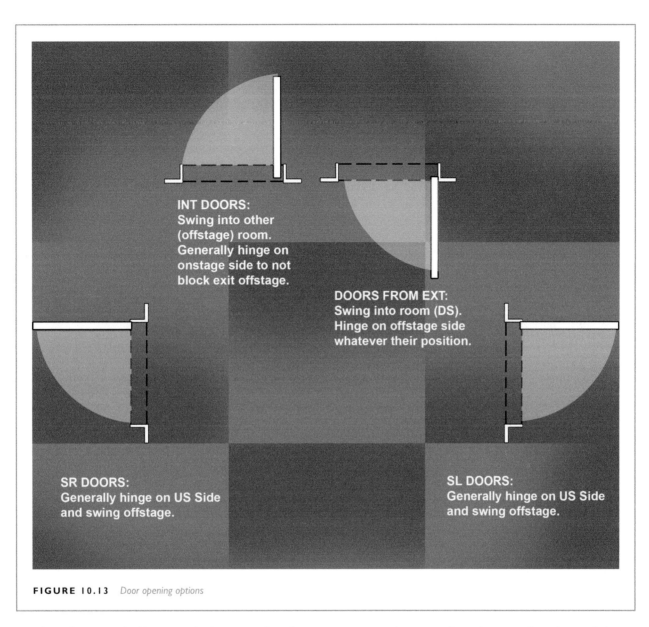

INT DOORS:
Swing into other (offstage) room. Generally hinge on onstage side to not block exit offstage.

DOORS FROM EXT:
Swing into room (DS). Hinge on offstage side whatever their position.

SR DOORS:
Generally hinge on US Side and swing offstage.

SL DOORS:
Generally hinge on US Side and swing offstage.

FIGURE 10.13   *Door opening options*

panniers of a woman's skirt can make her up to 5 or 6 feet wide. Doors onstage in this period must clearly be big enough to allow her to enter and exit.

Windows

The most important consideration in size of windows is to be found in the history of glass manufacture. Until the seventeenth century, panes of glass could only be made quite small. Many small panes made up windows, which overall were quite small themselves due to cost, except in the homes and palaces of the wealthy. In France in the late seventeenth century, float glass manufacturing made larger panes possible creating examples like the Hall of Mirrors at Versailles. Large plate glass windows are a product of the twentieth century.

Molding

The history of molding begins with the classical architecture of Ancient Greece, and the general rules for its use have remained much the same, a mixture of aesthetics and practicality. In interior sets there are six general types used:

FIGURE 10.14   *Door proportions*

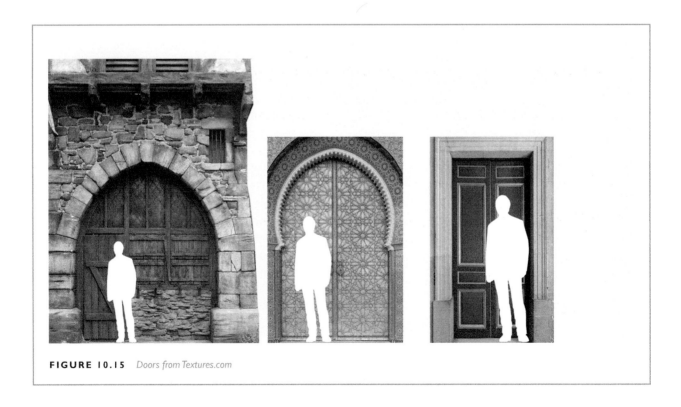

FIGURE 10.15   *Doors from Textures.com*

FIGURE 10.16 *Windows*

Crown #1 in **Figure 10.18** is at the top of a wall where it meets the ceiling. Aesthetically it makes an attractive transition between the two planes, and practically it is an element added to cover any construction flaws where they meet. The crown shown is a composite, or built molding using a commercially available crown with added pieces of 1x on both top and back. It would be common in his type of crown to add a routed cove in the bottom edge of the back piece and a piece of half round on the edge of the top piece.

Picture Rail, #2 in **Figure 10.18**, is a horizontal molding in the upper part of the wall below the crown. Aesthetically, it helps to break up a tall wall, and practically it is where nails might be attached to hang pictures below, thus its name.

Casing, #3 in **Figure 10.18**, is any molding that frames a door or window. Aesthetically a transition and practically it protects the wall from wear and tear and covers any flaws in the window insertion.

Chair Rail, #4 in **Figure 10.18**, is a horizontal molding at about 3 feet above the floor, whose practical purpose is to protect the wall from damage by chair backs being pushed against it.

Panel Molding, #5 in **Figure 10.18**, is used to subdivide a large unbroken surface into panels.

Baseboard, #6 in **Figure 10.18**, is the molding used where a wall meets the floor to protect the wall from being damaged from floor mopping, and to visually transition between the two planes. Baseboard is often made by using base cap molding on top of a 1x strip of the desired dimension.

Nosing, #7 in **Figure 10.18**, is traditionally used where a horizontal surface and a vertical surface meet with the nosing placed flush at the top of the vertical surface. Nosing is also used on stair treads unless the same profile is routed in the stair tread.

Cove, #8 in **Figure 10.18**, is a square-profiled molding with a quarter-round shape removed from

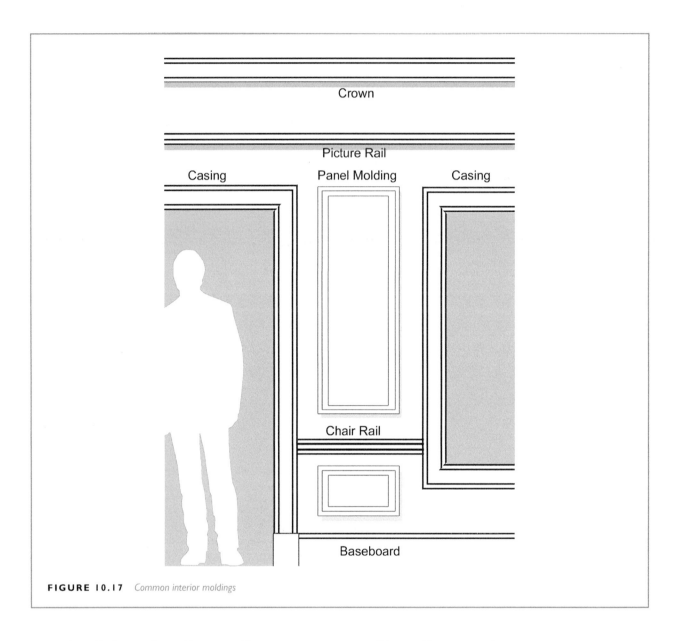

FIGURE 10.17   *Common interior moldings*

it and is frequently used in composition moldings.

Bead, #9 in **Figure 10.18**, is another small decorative molding used in composite molding or routed around window muntins.

Half Round, #10 in **Figure 10.18**, is a small molding often used in a composition molding with other elements. In profile it is one half of a circle with a flat side where it meets its wall or base.

Quarter Round is simply half of a half round, with two flat faces at 90 degrees to each other.

Other molding terms to know:

Cornice is a large molding at the top of a wall, especially used at the top of an exterior wall. It may be used for an interior wall if especially large; otherwise crown is more correct.

Ogee is any molding with a prominent s-curve shape to its profile. It may be large or small and is frequently used in composition moldings.

A Pilaster is a vertical element reminiscent of an engaged column, a partial column that adjoins a wall or other surface, rather than being freestanding.

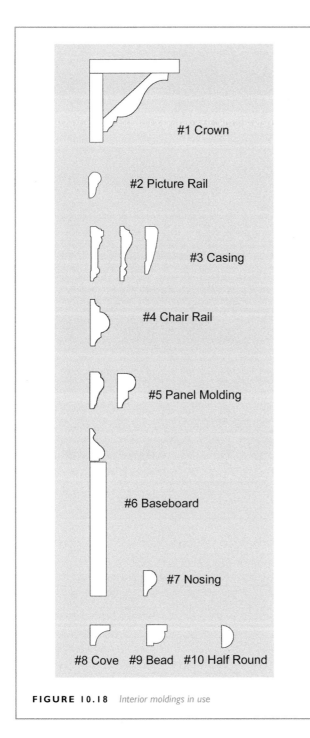

FIGURE 10.18 *Interior moldings in use*

FIGURE 10.19 *Break lines*

of the designer to plan at least some of the break lines needed and approve any others the shop considers necessary. Corners are obviously a common place to break. Molding can be used to hide a break line as well. A last choice would be to place a break at the edge of a door or other opening—as then at least the break is only visible in the area above the door (**Figure 10.19**). If the set is a one-time install, plan to fill and touch up the breaks.

Walls

Finish for Painting

Set walls are commonly made of MDF or Lauan and there will be seam lines where two sheets meet that need to be hidden. Muslin covering the scenery can hide these seams and provide a good paint surface. If the walls are textured, this can hide the seams.

Break Lines

All sets will be built in smaller pieces than they will appear onstage simply because of the need of easy handling in the shop, truck sizes, and the size of loading access areas in the theatre. It is the responsibility

FIGURE 10.20   *Ming Cho Lee's 1/2-inch model for* Angels in America Part One/Millennium Approaches, *Broadway, 1966*
From *Ming Cho Lee: A Life in Design* ©2014 by Arnold Aronson. Reprinted by permission of Theatre Communications Group

Texture

Various textures can be applied to walls, from a shop-made mixture of joint compound and white glue applied in different ways to create different effects, to vacuformed sheets of plastic available in several stone, brick, and other patterns. Jaxsan is a commercially made product that is a thick white paste used to create textures. Crumpled brown paper can make a good quick texture but should be covered with a flameproof coating like Jaxsan.

Wallpaper, Commercial or Plotted

Commercially available wallpaper can be used on scenery, though sometimes the scale of the pattern is too small to read well onstage. Wallpaper patterns can be created in Photoshop and plotted to use on scenery. This allows control of the scale of the pattern and control of color.

It is a good option for period wallpapers that can be researched but are not commercially available. Plotting is also an option for other low-relief treatments like tile work because it gives a lot of detail with little labor.

Walls with Unrealistic Treatments

Sometimes walls are treated in unrealistic ways, such as applying an image of a sky onto the wall as Ming Cho Lee did in the design for *Angels in America: Millennium Approaches* (**Figure 10.20**).

Stairs and Platforms

Stairs are very common whether between levels in a multilevel design or as conventional staircases in an interior. Typically the depth of a stair tread is called the run,

FIGURE 10.21 *Examples of stairs*

and the increment of height is called the rise. The run and rise of stairs can vary onstage, but building code standards usually require a rise of no more than 7 inches and a run no more than 10 inches. For the stage a height of 7 1/2 or 8 inches works well simply because these dimensions multiply nicely into easy to draw and build overall heights (7 1/2", 15", 22 1/2", 30", and so on, and 8", 16", 24", 32", and so on, respectively. For runs at these heights 10 or 12 inches works well and again is easy to draw and build.

Widths of stairs vary as well, but generally onstage staircases in an interior are between 3 and 4 feet wide. Stairs of course can be monumental and extremely theatrical depending on the scene design. It is important to always consider safety, however, no matter the design.

In designing curved or spiral stairs, where the tread may taper, always remember that the depth of tread should be measured in the middle of the tread.

Offstage escape stairs may stretch the boundaries of run and rise but still should be designed with safety in mind.

Railings

Stair railings can be made using commercially available components or custom made to a wide variety of period styles. Generally, platforms over 4 feet in height need a railing on at least one side. Escape steps and offstage platforms require railings on both sides for safety.

Using Levels

We have previously seen how any defined space onstage creates support of and focus on the actor. When that area is raised it becomes even more powerful in that an actor on it is now raised above another who is not.

Levels combined with other architectural elements create even more focus. A landing inside a front door creates a place where an actor entering can draw focus more easily. It gives him a spot to stop and address the others in the room. A landing in conjunction with a staircase, whether at the top, the bottom, or a midway turning point, creates variety, and possibilities to stage the actor in many interesting ways. Landings at front doors and bottoms of stairs are very common in interior sets as the raise the actor at points where he might seem weak because he is behind DS furniture for sightlines from the first rows of the orchestra.

Run-Offs

Most raised levels in a scenic design should have a run-off platform at their height that will let the actor enter or exit the level; see the example in **Figure 10.23**. Dead-end levels and levels that are only accessible by onstage stairs are usually avoided.

FIGURE 10.22   *Examples of levels*

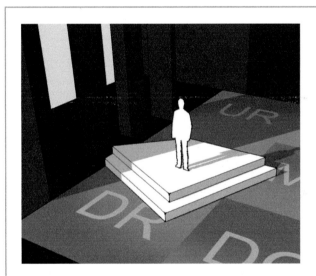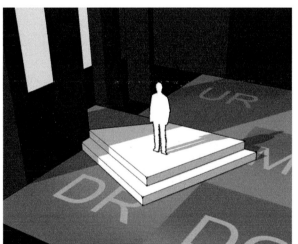

FIGURE 10.23   *Examples of a run-off*

A Transitional Space

It is sometimes helpful if the structure of the play involves a narrator or instances of a monologue or short transitional scene with two actors, to place this space outside the main area of the set so it can be tightly lit while actors in the main area exit or scenery is changed. This can be done DS on either side but gains some power if raised. The Inner Above of the Elizabethan stage works in this way.

Production: *The Eclectic Society*

FIGURE 10.24   Eclectic Society *photo*
This is a photo from the balcony that shows the three-dimensionality of the set.

The Eclectic Society was a new play by Eric Conger produced by the Walnut Street Theatre in Philadelphia and directed by Ed Herendeen. It is set in a fraternity house on the campus of an old East Coast college in 1962 (**Figure 10.24**). The set is the common room of the house with a front door and exits to other rooms on the ground floor and upstairs. The feeling of the set is of a classic WASP world of tradition and money that is about to change as the brothers consider inducting an African-American member.

The design eliminated the US walls above the wainscot level to show a cluster of hanging panels that could be lit as leafy trees, or other exterior effects, and had a subtle tie-dye paint treatment. Metaphorically this was to represent the changes taking place in the outside world. The size of the panels was chosen to match picture frames of previous classes of the fraternity that lined the curving staircase.

A large two-step landing was created inside the front door to tie together that door, the stairs, a telephone booth, and door to a powder room, and elevate an actor playing there above the DSR sofa. This platform created a strong position for an actor to have command of the room.

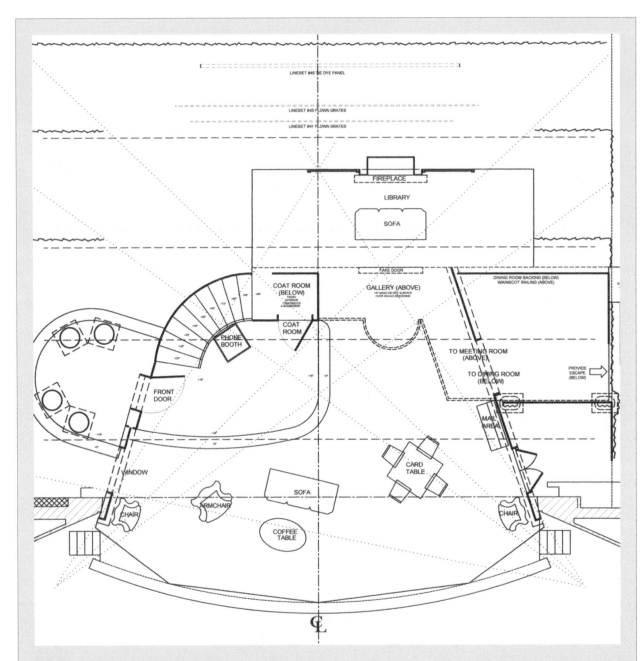

FIGURE 10.25 Eclectic Society *groundplan*
In this groundplan, note the multiple levels and how notes have been used to try to clarify them.

A problem with the theatre's sightlines, seats at the back of the orchestra's view of the upper level being blocked by the overhanging balcony, was carefully worked out in the section. A compromise that gained 6 inches was to make the powder room door under the stairs less than standard height, a situation that occurs in real-life architecture in older houses.

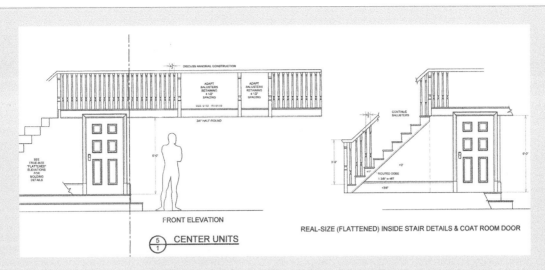

FIGURE 10.26   *Eclectic Society drafting: Stairs*
The stairs are shown in a combination of views to reflect real and flattened dimensions. Note the powder room door which was shortened by 6 inches to help the sightline to the upper level.

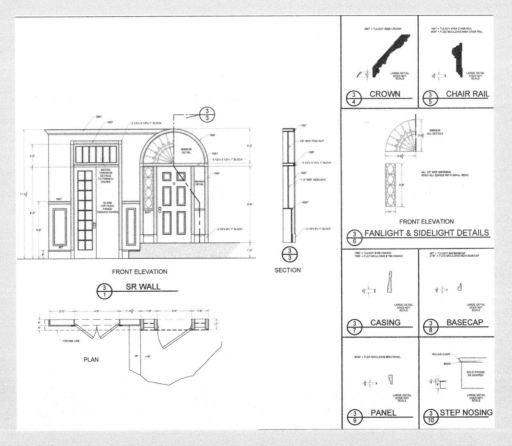

FIGURE 10.27   *Eclectic Society drafting: Elevations and molding details*
A detailed interior set requires careful drafting to communicate all the molding and other construction details the designer intends.

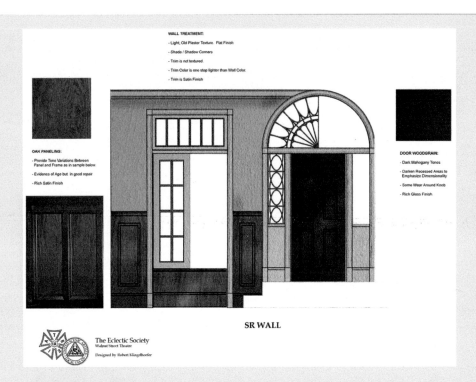

FIGURE 10.28   Eclectic Society paint elevation
This digital paint elevation of the SR walls was built over a scan of the drafting and used flat textures from an online source for the woodgrain and plaster treatments.

FIGURE 10.29   Eclectic Society panels
This is a straight-on view of the US panels, which were made of recessed ceiling fixture diffusers cut in half and hung with 1/16-inch aircraft cable.

FIGURE 10.30   Eclectic Society *photo from orchestra level*
This photo from the orchestra level shows almost no floor, but a good angle for the US panels

Production Credits

Eclectic Society, Walnut Street Theatre, 2010
Director: Ed Herendeen
Set Designer: Robert Klingelhoefer
Lighting Designer: Paul Black
Costume Designer: Colleen Grady

Production: *1001*

This design for Jason Grote's kaleidoscopic reimagining of the Scheherazade stories, produced by the Contemporary American Theater Festival, was a single set. It had one flying panel that changed the look of the UC area and a large special effects moment, but was otherwise a single set transformed by lighting and a few actor-driven props.

The play is a whirlwind of scenes in many different times and locations. It would be impossible to design it as a multiple set production, so it wanted a single set that could contain some required practical elements and give a look to the mix of the modern western world and the past of the Islamic world.

Key requirements were:

- An enormous explosion effect, which, though unnamed, paralleled the 9/11 event.
- The feeling of a great library.

FIGURE 10.31   1001 *photo—basic set*

- A tower where the Genie could appear.
- A transitional space, a sort of home for Scheherazade, the storyteller, which would put her above the main acting space. This would allow her narration and introduction of new scenes to be lit tightly as actors and elements were shifted below her.

Because this UC structure was essentially symmetrical, the main acting area—a raised, raked deck—was set at a slight angle to break up the symmetry a little (**Figure 10.31**).

Scheherazade's area needed an architectural element to focus it, and a research image of an Islamic muquarna arch was adapted to provide a sweep of architecture that would frame it (**Figure 10.32**).

The space below this area was a series of doors hidden in tile work that could provide entrances and exits (**Figure 10.33**). These doors worked independently but could also be connected to pneumatic cylinders that would let them blow open DS for the explosion, which also featured air cannons that blew debris and aircraft landing lights that blinded the audience. Smoke effects were also used, and the two towers of books on the set were rigged to collapse.

For the Genie Tower look, a spiral unit reminiscent of the constructivist tower of Vladimir Tatlin's 1920 *Monument to the Third International* was created US (**Figure 10.34**). A flown panel would reveal or conceal the spiral. The design of the flown panel was a combination of Islamic designs with a street map of lower Manhattan. The rim of the muquarna sweep was decorated with toy cars and a toy airplane heading toward the book towers.

FIGURE 10.32   1001 *research: Muquarna*

FIGURE 10.33   1001 *photo*

FIGURE 10.34   1001 *photo—the Genie after the explosion*

FIGURE 10.35   1001 *photo—Sinbad*
During the telling of the Sinbad story actors manipulated a China silk sea.

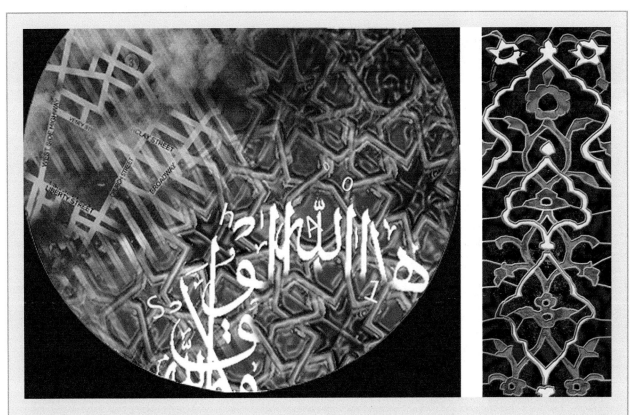

FIGURE 10.36   *1001 plotted disk design and tile*
The design on the flown disk and all the tile work were prepared in Photoshop and plotted on gloss photo paper. They were applied to the scenery with wallpaper adhesive.

Production Credits

1001, Contemporary American Theatre Festival 2007
Directed by: Ed Herendeen
Set Designer: Robert Klingelhoefer
Lighting Designer: D.M. Wood
Costume Designer: Margaret McKowen

UNIT SETS

A unit set is simply a set that represents two or more locations but because of aesthetic choice, the need for smooth quick changes, limited stage space, or economy does not change completely from location to location. Certain elements may change from scene to scene, but most elements do not. Lighting often plays a huge role in making the locations specific.

Neutrality

Because a large proportion of the scenery does not shift and is always in view, the designer must treat the set carefully. If the locations in the play are related—for example, are all different parts of a boy's school—then the unit set elements can represent that greater location. If the locations needed are not related, the designer must treat them in a way that relates to the mood, or greater

FIGURE 10.37 *Jo Mielziner's design for* After the Fall, *1964*
Courtesy of the Mielziner Estate—Bud H. Gibbs

world of the play, or neutralize them by stripping down the visual information they give to a bare minimum and let the pieces that do change shoulder the burden of identifying the locations.

There was a type of unit set in fashion in the 1940s and '50s that was a neutral arrangement of levels varied by lighting, projection, and minimal set props. This style became used less as designers found the neutrality of it fairly inexpressive.

Figure 10.38 is a unit set that has some of the same basic levels as the design in **Figure 10.37** but which uses materials from the world of the play to create more specific choices.

A problem with this type of unit set is if certain levels are used for specific locations the director is trapped blocking scenes in tight spaces and specific areas that may seem cramped or far away from audience on the opposite side of the theatre.

These issues have led designers today to create unit sets with a wide range of other solutions. Like scenic design in general today, images are often very bold and sometimes not immediately understood.

Unit sets are now more often a large expanse of open floor on one level with groupings of objects specific to the locations set in amorphous areas with blurred definitions. Common elements are often abstracted into

FIGURE 10.38   *A design for* The Spitfire Grill

an evocative architectural space or a blatantly theatrical one with strong image treatments.

Commonality

The unit set represents ideas or elements common to the play as a whole, whether or not these elements are in any particular set.

This production of *The French Lieutenant's Woman* adapted by Mark Healey from the novel by John Fowles required a unit set for its many locations. The story concerns a Victorian naturalist and the mysterious woman he is attracted to. Its primary locations are all around the village of Lyme Regis in Dorset, England, in the late nineteenth century. Like the novel, though, the main action involves a character who is the author of their story, who looks at his characters as specimens in much the same way as the naturalist regards his finds until they begin to surprise him in what they do.

The design idea, therefore, was to create a space made of specimen drawers with objects used in the play in and around them (**Figure 10.39**). They would be "real" to both the world of the characters and the author.

FIGURE 10.39   *A design for* The French Lieutenant's Woman

SUMMARY

•   A single set interior, one of the most common types
    of set, in many cases requires intense attention
    to detail and tests the designer's knowledge of
    architecture and building techniques.

CONSIDERATIONS FOR PRODUCTIONS WITH MOVING SCENERY

DESIGNING MOVING SCENERY

The first rule of designing a multiset production is that the shifts from one location to another must be quick and smooth and that this is a more important consideration than the design of the individual sets themselves. This concept requires the designer to think about the production with different priorities. How should the show move? Can the scenery be designed to move in a way that complements the design idea? In the case study of *Into the Woods* at the end of Chapter 8, the desire to have the trees move in a grounded, lateral way, as opposed to flying in and out, led to the key decisions that shaped the design.

> How a production moves is both an aesthetic and a practical decision. As has been discussed throughout this book, the best design comes when the aesthetic and the practical decisions are totally integrated and complement each other.

Ultimately, any production is faced with the overwhelming question of practicality. How are transitions made from one scene to the next? The answer will be informed in part by the way in which
the director and designer interpret the structure of the play.[1]

Finding the Structure of the Show/Determining the Type of Movement

There are many ways a show can move and types of equipment that can be used. Determining which is appropriate is, like most good design decisions, made by choices from within the play. These can be based on movement patterns in the design or that the director will use in the blocking. Boris Aronson said he designed *Fiddler on the Roof* using a turntable because it metaphorically represented the circle of the family inside the circle of the village. Ideas for how the production should move can also come from the structure of the show. In Chapter 4 we discussed using the breakdown of the play to identify patterns in the order of scenes. This can be very helpful in determining a structure for how the show should move. Scenes that repeat should be considered as anchors— scenes that do not move, if possible, and which are concealed and revealed by other scenes. Short scenes can play with minimal scenery within a larger set with lighting keeping the focus on the current moment.

Since the 1930s, many critics have seen the inevitable influence of the movies upon the theater and have

*designated almost any play that moves through
multiple scenes as cinematic.*[2]

Cinematic Movement

How the production moves should primarily be addressed
as a theatre-based decision that combines ideas about the
play with practical decisions that support them. But when
a more cinematic look is desired, the two factors that may
be most helpful are the number of moving pieces and the
manipulation of the audience's focus.

In film, camera movement can put the whole scene
into motion. In the theatre, the motion of, for example,
a wagon moving SR to SL will seem very simple by
comparison. If, however, at the same time as the wagon
moves, panels US of it move and other units fly in, then
the effect becomes more cinematic. In most cases it is not
a good idea to add moving elements just to have multiple
things to move, but in a design that has created a system
of tracked panels, or some other combination of moving
elements, creating more complex and visually interesting
motion may be possible. Shifts need to be conceived
with the shift of the lighting and movement of the actors
considered as vital components.

By controlling what elements the audience focuses
on during the shift interesting moments can be created
that continue the life of the scene.

Consider this sequence:

- The scene ends: Lights start to pull down as elements
begin to move.

- The actor onstage takes a beat to regard this then
turns and walks off SR still in fading light, as panels
from the previous scene move SR also.

- A wagon comes on from SL with actors on it already
in conversation.

- As the wagon reaches its spike, lights up full, and the
scene begins.

This sequence has kept the focus on the actor from the
previous scene for a few extra moments as motion began,
and then let it shift to the forming scene SL. Instead of
trying to rush through the shift in a blackout, the audience
is allowed to see the shift. All elements—scenery, lighting,
and actors—have been a part of a theatrical moment.

A scene change in which the audience is allowed to see
is referred to as an **á vista** change. **Á vista** changes
are designed using movement in scenery, blocking of the
actors and changes in the lighting to create an attractive transition that in some cases can even be used to
advance the story.

*But the practical considerations still haunt the designer.
There is, after all, no button to click that will take
the viewer from screen to screen, leaping through
cyberspace in milliseconds. The stage is still bound by
the laws of physics, Euclidean geometry, linear time
and the limitations of human actors.*[3]

*The more elements that need to move on and
off the stage, the more one is dependent on actors
or stagehands to do the moving. In a play with so
many changes, this parade of furniture-toting figures
ultimately adds not simply an encumbrance or
distraction, but another level of text—a secondary play
about furniture moving that exists in the interstices of
the primary text.*[4]

It is common for the designer and director to discuss the
possibilities of this "secondary play." Who are these people
and why are they moving these things? If the answers
are well thought out, any audience confusion can be
minimized.

Some common solutions to consider:

- If actors move things it should only be lesser
characters. Hamlet does not carry furniture. If the
social structure of the period includes a servant class,
these characters moving things will seem appropriate.

- Having actors move things in character helps the
reality of the play to not be broken.

- If stagehands will be seen moving things, they can be
in period costumes and appear to be servants, or
characters inherent in the scenes, such as a waiter
clearing a restaurant scene or a bellboy setting a
hotel scene.

- Use the context of the design to find solutions. In
the *Christmas Carol* at the end of Chapter 6 set in a
Victorian Magic Theatre, the stagehands would be of
that world.

SOME COMMON APPROACHES AND SCENIC ELEMENTS USED IN MULTIPLE SET PRODUCTIONS

Systems

Systems are a way of designing a multiple set production by creating a series of panels or other elements that track or fly to modify the space and frame or reveal and conceal the scenery specific to each location (**Figure 11.1**). This can be done in bold or relatively

discrete ways. It can provide a visual anchor that remains from scene to scene even though there are major changes and give a sense of continuity. It can often also save space and money on a big show.

Portals

Portals are really just designed scenic elements that serve the same purpose as masking legs and borders. They are

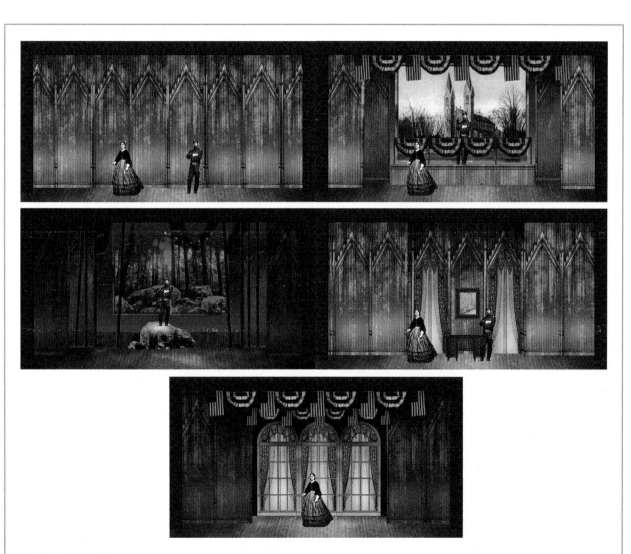

FIGURE 11.1   *Systems*
This production of Chamberlain at Maine State Music Theatre used tracking panels as a system. The panels were of the wooden Carpenter Gothic style prevalent in Maine in the early nineteenth century and evident in historical locations in the play. They could open and close in various combinations to reveal, conceal, or frame scene-specific scenery, which was flown, tracked, or preset behind the panels.

often framed scenery. A simple portal has legs on the SR and SL sides connected by a header (**Figure 11.2**). Portals can have a designed shape from the simple to the elaborate. They can be painted or fabric covered. They may have moldings or metallic trim. Their treatment may be designed to match other scenery or be independently decorative. Because they ordinarily are in view the whole show, they are commonly designed to go with all the sets in the production.

In-Ones

A portal system whether it is a designed scenic element or a simple use of black masking legs and border, defines entrances that can be made from offstage right and offstage left. These entrance points have traditionally been called In-One, In-Two, In-Three, and so on, starting DS and working US. Stage directions for the actor may be recorded as "from In-One Right" or "from In-Two Left."

In the period that saw the creation of the great musicals, it became a common technical device to alternate scenes with large sets and scenes with smaller sets so that the smaller set could play DS and cover the set change from one big set to the next. These small scenes often were backed by a drop playing far DS in In-Two. Because playing space was therefore limited to the In-One these scenes and the concept in general became known as **In-Ones** (**Figure 11.3**).

This idea of an In-One scene covering the shift of a bigger set upstage of it is written into many of the great musicals and can still be very useful to the designer even if he chooses to design it in a more modern way.

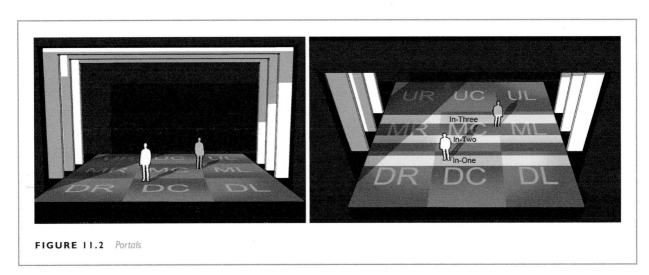

FIGURE 11.2 *Portals*

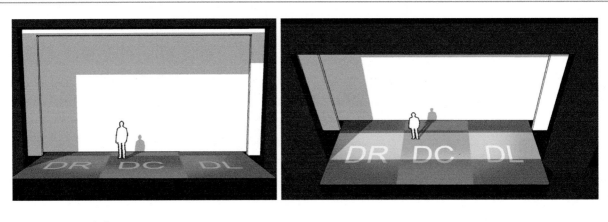

FIGURE 11.3 *In-Ones*

Drops

A backdrop is a basic element of scenery that can be used in many ways. It can be made of a wide variety of fabrics, but the most common drops are made of muslin and are usually painted.

In regard to design decisions, the choice to paint a drop with a literal image should not be the default. A drop can represent anything; from a realistic subject to an abstract design of color and texture. It is truly a blank slate that the designer can use to fill a large area of space with one simple element that is reasonably cost effective.

A drop can be painted opaquely or translucently, allowing it to be backlit for a wide range of effects.

The choice to go translucent involves a few other considerations:

- There are different weights, or thicknesses, of muslin; lightweight, medium weight, and heavyweight. The standard used by a company that makes drops is usually medium weight or heavyweight if a drop is large. For a translucent drop medium or lightweight is preferred.

- Muslin comes in a range of widths from 44 inches to 39 feet. The wider it is, the more expensive it is. The standard width used in a commercial shop is usually 120-inch muslin. Drops are made with horizontal seams so they hang flat. A drop that is taller than the width of muslin used will have seams that don't matter in an opaque drop but will in a translucency. The designer must spec whether a drop is to be seamless or seamed. If seamed and he wants something other than standard 120-inch muslin used, he must spec where he would like the seams. If the translucent drop designed can have an opaque bottom section, for example, and a translucent upper section that are both under 120 inches (minus seam allowance), then the drop can more cheaply be made with 120-inch muslin than if it were seamless.

- The designer also specs how the edges of the drop are finished. Standard is webbing with grommets and ties on 1'-0" centers at the top and a pocket for lightweight pipe or chain at the bottom. Other options for different situations exist.

A reference for all theatrical fabrics, as well as fabrication, paint, and hardware, is Rosebrand at http://www.rosebrand.com/.

Scrims

Scrim is an open-weave fabric, most commonly used as a drop, that when front lit is opaque and that becomes transparent when an object behind it is lit. There are several types of scrim, but the most common is sharkstooth scrim, which comes in white, black, and light blue in widths from 11 feet to 39 feet.

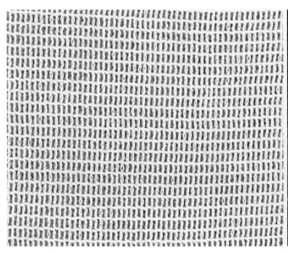

FIGURE 11.4   *Examples of scrim and scrim effects*

Scrim can be painted, usually in dyes or thinned paints to preserve its transparency as thick paint will clog the open weave. White scrim is most commonly used when painting is desired, but black scrim can be as well. It is harder to get lighter colors to read on black scrim than it is dark ones to read on white scrim.

Black scrims are very often hung DS of a cyc or painted drop to soften the look of it, and allow lighting to control its look with various effects. When this is done the scrim and drop or cyc must be separated with an electric between them.

Note: Any electric that is used to light a drop or cyc should usually be 3 to 4 feet DS of the drop or cyc.

Commonly a scrim should not be hung DS of another scrim because a usually unpleasant moiré effect can be created, a kind of visual interference created by the two open-weave patterns. If it is necessary to do this, the moiré effect can be diminished by specifying one of the drops to be made with the fabric running vertical instead of the common horizontal.

Again, Rosebrand is a good supplier and source of information.

Show Decks

Show decks are an additional floor added over the permanent stage floor to allow for the use of winched tracks to move scenic units and a variety of other effects that can be built into the floor like lighting and smoke. Generally, show decks are between 3 and 6 inches deep. It is also possible to lay a 3/4-inch ply floor with a 1/4-inch MDF layer on top of it, which together are thick enough to allow tracks to be cut and turn-around sheaves for drive cables to be set.

Show decks can be a substantial cost and take additional time at load-in, but can provide a lot of valuable effects. The main consideration for the designer in using tracks is that in most cases two tracks cannot cross each other. He also must take extra care in plotting the on- and offstage position of wagons because the tracks will lock in these choices and make them very difficult to change.

Wagons and Palettes

Wagons and palettes are moving platforms that most commonly carry furniture or scenery. Wagons are generally castered and from 3 to 8 inches high. Palettes are like low-profile wagons. They are generally smaller

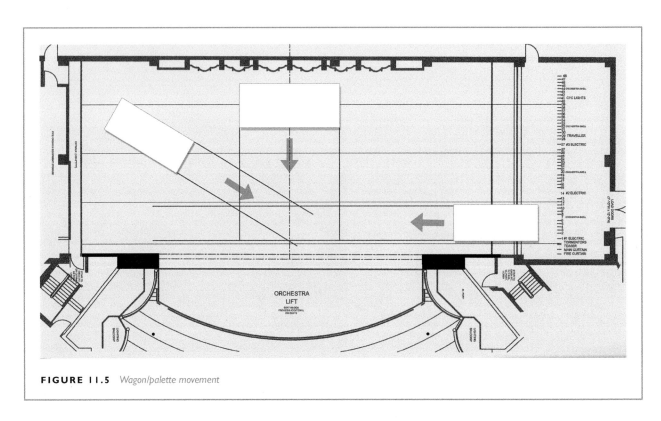

FIGURE 11.5 *Wagon/palette movement*

than wagons, carry furniture more commonly than scenery, and are on glides instead of casters.

A consideration in using wagons and palettes is that they be large enough to not create awkward staging that requires an actor to be stepping on and off the wagon or palette very often or two actors playing a moment with one on and one off the wagon in an awkward way.

In a common design using portals, wagon and palette movement is usually on and off stage through the In-One, In-Two, and so on, or US–DS, but if the masking elements are designed to work with it, wagons and palettes can come onstage at a variety of angles.

Revolves, Slipstages, Treadmills, and Jackknives

Other common ways to design scenery that moves are revolves, slipstages, jackknives, and treadmills.

A **revolve** is a turntable, ranging in size from small to full stage, which turns on a single, internal, usually centered pivot point. A revolve can sit on the stage floor, be built into a show deck, or be built into a larger wagon that can move on and offstage. This last option is by far the most complicated and expensive.

A revolve is commonly used to shift the position of scenery that is either permanently on it, or is shifted on and off it during the performance. Frequently, masking is designed as part of this scenery or to fly or track on and off to conceal or reveal different looks.

Revolves can also be used as a way of allowing actors to walk in space without their position changing.

Another revolve option is to design a ring around a revolve that can rotate with it or in the opposite direction (**Figure 11.6**).

A **slipstage** is a moving platform that is wide enough to completely cross the stage space and into the wing on one side. Scenery can be loaded onto the hidden side and the whole slipstage moved toward the opposite side bringing the scenery on. The now-hidden side can be loaded for the next shift back in the other direction. A slipstage only works if the stage has significant wing space. A slipstage can be surrounded by show deck to be relatively hidden.

A **treadmill** is in essence a belt built into a show deck fully across the stage that is motorized to move. Most often a treadmill is used to move actors, but small scenic elements or furniture can be moved as well. With sufficient wing space, a treadmill has the same effect as a slipstage, except it is continuous (a plus) and usually cannot shift large or heavy scenery (a minus).

A **jackknife** is a platform with an off-center pivot point that allows it to swing from an offstage position to an onstage one. This generally does not work well in a portal masking format. An option with slipstages is to design scenery or masking onto the back of them so their off position has a look or becomes its own masking.

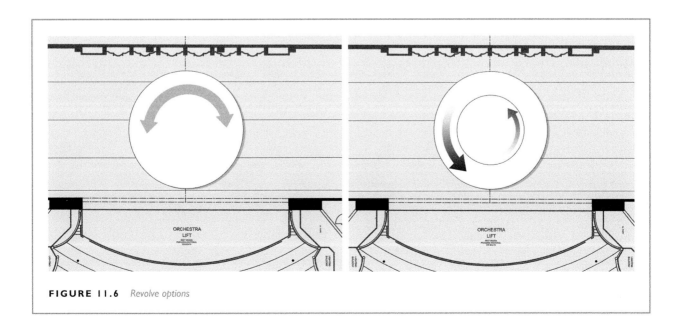

FIGURE 11.6 *Revolve options*

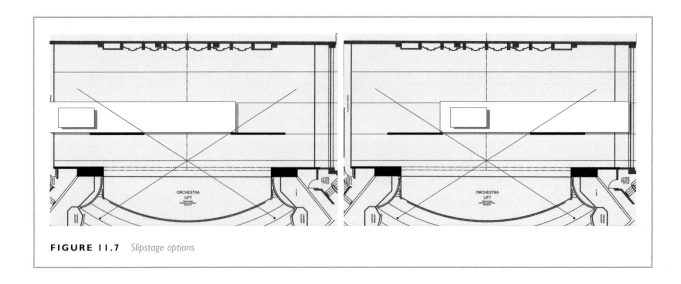

FIGURE 11.7 *Slipstage options*

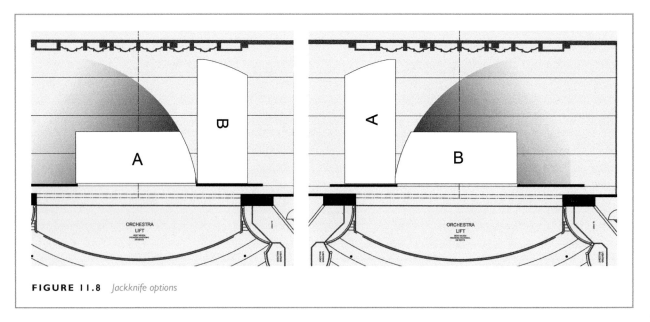

FIGURE 11.8 *Jackknife options*

Automation

Stage automation using hand or motorized winches, pneumatic cylinders, and a variety of other equipment make the movement of scenery exciting, and more efficient in terms of the number of crewpersons needed. The designer is best advised to design what he wants in terms of effect and then consult with the shop to determine what is required. One important consideration the designer should plan for early is to allow space on the groundplan for offstage winches, usually as much in-line with the desired motion as possible.

CASE STUDIES OF MOVING SCENERY

Following are several case studies of the design process of productions that involved changing scenery. Most, it should be noted, could be considered unit sets as not all elements of scenery change completely from set to set. Some change enough that this fact is hard to notice. The most important aspect of all of them, and the key to the successful design of a multiset production, is to make the design idea and the plan of how the show will move merge seamlessly.

The ideal synthesis is when the design idea and the functional design merge in an inseparable harmony.

An example of the unit set philosophy that involved less units and a different type of movement was *Farragut North* at the Contemporary American Theatre Festival.

Production: *Farragut North*

Farragut North is Beau Willimon's play of political corruption that was made into the movie *The Ides of March*. It is set in various locations in Iowa during a presidential primary. The locations include a campaign office, a hotel room, and an airport terminal among others.

Crucial to a successful production would be quick shifts between scenes. Study of the breakdown revealed that scenes such as the Hotel Room and Molly's Office required furniture, while the other locations did not or had minimal requirements. Work began with the groundplan (**Figure 11.9**). The ability to have the locations that required furniture always onstage but concealed in some way would be a good solution.

Thinking about the general look of elements that would be part of the permanent set led to looking at sets for political rallies and debates. A major theme in the play is the place of the media in political campaigns. A strong ultramarine blue, used in many TV news program sets was chosen as a principal color. It fit the political and media idea and would remain cold. Red would be used in the furniture and dressing of some of the individual sets as well as political posters.

A solution arrived at in working on the groundplan was to create wagons with off-center pivot points to swing, carrying the furniture pieces from a stored position to a more central prominent one. These wagons would have to have walls on the two adjacent sides that would hide the furniture in the stored position and be backing walls when it was in its playing position.

Two large tracked panels would have this same TV panel treatment but the panels were filled with blue scrim. They could play in various positions to vary the space. Shifts would be these panels changing position as the wagon pivoted. As an element that would add another layer to the shifts, a suspended upper panel with the same treatment had two flat-screen monitors in it, behind their blue scrim, that could flash a video montage of political coverage as the panel moved from SR to SL. In shifts when the SR wagon was moving, the panel would move to SL and vice versa when the SL wagon was used to balance the composition.

Rounding out the scenic elements was a tracking block of campaign posters, some furniture pieces that were moved on by crew and actors, and a flown airport gate information sign.

It was decided that to create a feeling of emptiness, the back wall of the stage would be lit in some moments and seen through the scrim panels. This allowed the loading door UC to be used for a final visual moment in which stage snow could fall US and video "snow" fill the video monitors as the main character appeared "left out in the cold" both politically and in the cold Iowa winter.

Themes

- Politics and media
- Shifting loyalties
- Iowa snow and TV "snow"

Elements Used

- TV blue—media panels
- Scene shifts that echoed the shifting loyalties
- Video snow and stage snow

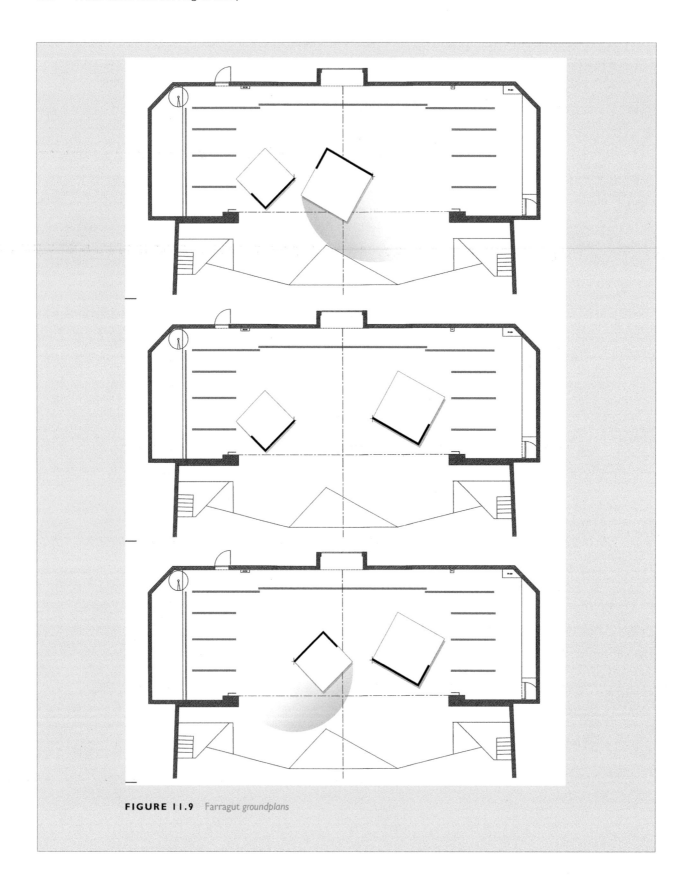

FIGURE 11.9 Farragut groundplans

Act One / Scene One:
The Bar of the Hotel Fort Des Moines

Act One / Scene Two:
A Small, Dingy Restaurant in East Des Moines

Act One / Scene Three:
Stephen's Hotel Room

Act One / Scene Four:
The Des Moines Airport

FIGURE 11.10   Farragut *storyboard Act 1*

Act Two / Scene One:
A Campaign Event in Cedar Rapids

Act Two / Scene Two:
Molly's Office at Campaign Headquarters

Act Two / Scene Three:
Paul's Hotel Room

Act Two / Scene Four:
The Small, Dingy Restaurant in East Des Moines

Act Two / Scene Five:
Stephen's Hotel Room

FARRAGUT NORTH by Beau Willimon   directed by Ed Herendeen   Frank Center
contemporaryamericantheaterfestival
AT SHEPHERD UNIVERSITY

FIGURE 11.11   Farragut *storyboard Act II*

FIGURE 11.12 *A Political Rally: The US scrim panels opened and the Poster unit on*

FIGURE 11.13 *The Hotel Room: The SL unit pivoted onstage. Some furniture shifted off it onto the stage floor to open the playable space up.*

FIGURE 11.14   *The Airport: Both pivoting units in offstage positions. The Flight Status Board flown in. The Scrim Panels open and the back wall lit.*

FIGURE 11.15   *Molly's Office: The SR pivoting unit onstage and the scrim panels open to show the poster unit.*

Production: *Good People*

This design for *Good People* by David Lindsay-Abaire was a co-production of the Fulton Theatre (Lancaster, PA) and the Walnut Street Theatre (Philadelphia, PA).

Good People is set in contemporary Boston with five locations. Three are in working class Southie and two are in upscale suburbs. It is a comedy about class in America today.

The multiple locations automatically require fast, fluid scene changes:

A1s1: Alley behind a Dollar Store, Southie
A1s2: Margie's Kitchen, Southie
A1s3: A Doctor's Office
A1s4: Bingo Night in a church basement, Southie
A2s1: Mike's House
A2s2: Bingo Night in a church basement, Southie

The play is realistic with the locations all needing realistic details. The stages are both large prosceniums. The initial problem was that the scale of the locations was much smaller than the theatre spaces, so there would need to be a designed element or elements that bridged this gap.

Work began on the groundplan. With the decision made that a turntable would be used to change sets, the diameter of the turntable had to be determined. With five locations, space would be at a premium, and working multiple locations on to a turntable also requires that access off and on to the individual sets would be around and through each other. The first turntable size considered was 36 feet as it fit both theatres' stage size well.

In the next round of work with the groundplan, the turntable was divided into sections, and access problems were worked on. It was necessary to create corridors between the areas for each location to allow actors to make entrances without seeing into another set as a door was opened, but this took so much space that the set spaces got cramped. The solution was to put only four locations on the turntable permanently and switch at intermission a set that only played in Act I with one that only played in Act II. It was decided that the Dollar Store location in Act I could play within the Mike's House location in Act II, if its furniture was removed.

A problem was discovered at this point in the process. The Walnut Street Theatre realized that they were using a revolve for a show before *Good People* and would not have time to strike it before *Good People* loaded in. They asked that this revolve be used for the show. This would mean the Fulton Theatre would have to build a revolve for its performances, but the revolve would not have to travel, saving money in transport and time at the Philadelphia load-in. The revolve at the Walnut was, however, only 28 feet in diameter. There was no point in discussion; it would have to be a 28-foot revolve that was used, but this was too small for the design as it had been conceived.

The change to a 28-foot diameter revolve led to a drastic reconsideration of the design. The new smaller space meant that the revolve would have to be divided into two parts instead of four by either a wall that sat on the revolve or a wall that flew in

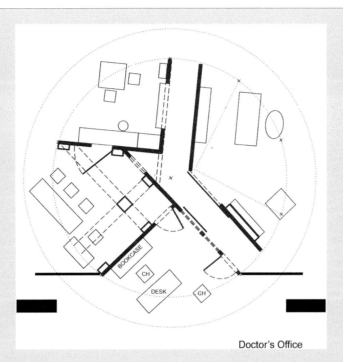

FIGURE 11.16 Good People *first turntable design: The Doctor's Office DS Note the access hallway SL. The return flats DSR and DSL were designed to fly when the revolve would spin. The dotted circle inside of the revolve's perimeter was the "clear" line for set pieces.*

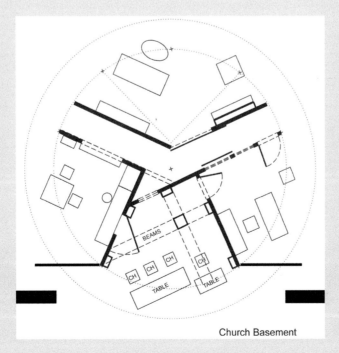

FIGURE 11.17 Good People *first turntable design: The Church Basement DS The dashed lines are overhead beams.*

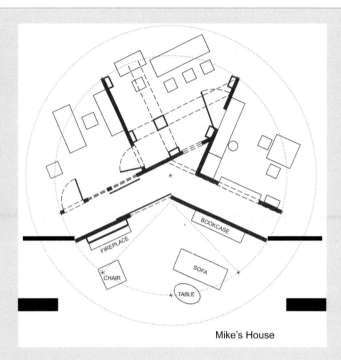

FIGURE 11.18 Good People *first turntable design: Mike's House,*
the biggest set, DS
The Dollar Store set was designed to fit within, and cover, this set.

FIGURE 11.19 Good People *first turntable design: Margie's Kitchen set DS*
Note the hallway access SR. The walls in these hallways, the backs of other sets,
would be finished and treated to be part of the onstage set.

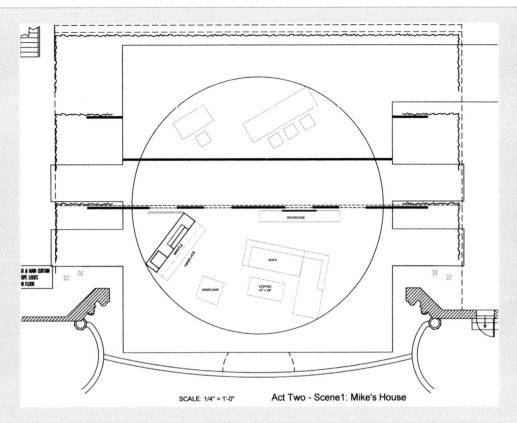

SCALE: 1/4" = 1'-0"   Act Two - Scene1: Mike's House

FIGURE 10.20   Good People *final turntable design*

and out. The space DS of this wall would be big enough for the furniture pieces that would be needed for each set, but would require that the walls of each individual set be very compressed and flat. This wouldn't look very good, and it would be difficult to support the walls.

If each location's walls were less complete, the surface of the revolve wall would have to be a major visual element of each set. What would this look be? The division of the locations into Southie and upscale suburbs suggested that no one look would work for both. If there were different treatments on either side of the revolve wall or two flying walls, this could work.

In a sketch of the earlier design, I had kept the walls of the Southie locations realistically low, and shown window blinds hung around and above them to fill the space. I liked the blinds idea. It came from an idea in the play, where the term *lace-curtain Irish* is explained as referring to Irish-Americans who have put on airs. The contemporary look of mini-blinds would be something of an "in joke" on this and also say something about the way the audience was looking into the lives of the characters. The color of them would be a good way to make the differences in the locations clear. Southie should be rougher, complicated, and textural. The suburbs should be simpler and elegant. I thought of putting an architectural image of Southie buildings on the blinds. This would clutter them up a bit and give some look of the real neighborhood. The suburbs could be simpler with no image and a more restrained color palette. This restraint on the suburb side begged for something more excessive on the Southie side, maybe a stronger color. Red seemed strong, passionate, and a contrast to the more monochromatic, elegant look on the other side.

The two walls of blinds, one red with a cityscape for Southie and one neutral and monochromatic for the suburbs, worked out to be on two adjacent linesets in good positions onstage. I placed the center point of the revolve evenly between them

I now had a revolve and two walls that could fly in and out in the center of it. What I did not have was a clue how the individual sets would work in this new design. If there were a lot of walls in the individual sets, a lot of space would be eaten

FIGURE 11.21   *The Dollar Store (model)*
The model includes the Southie blinds and a loading dock unit, the composition of which was cropped to suggest it was a part of a larger, more complete building.

up supporting them. Clearly each set should be kept very simple using only a few furniture pieces and as little other scenery as possible. But if there was not much scenery in the individual sets, how would entrances and exits be made?

An answer to this was found by looking back at the first abandoned turntable design. There I had spent a lot of time designing corridor spaces that would get an actor to where he could enter an individual set. I could solve the current problem similarly by putting doors in the big blinds walls. I would have to put another section of flying blinds US of the main one by about 4 feet that would act as a backing to these doors. They could not be practical doors, of course, as they were in a fly made of aluminum mini-blinds, but would be door-sized openings. In the groundplan I placed these backing walls without too much trouble.

Now I could work on the looks of the individual sets. The Alley behind the Dollar Store was unusual enough a location that it would need a set piece to make it clear where we were. I designed a unit that was a loading dock and industrial door that could be stenciled with the name "Dollar Store." I gave it a cropped feel so it didn't have to be any bigger than necessary. A couple of busted up chairs and a compactor completed this location (**Figure 11.21**).

The next set, Margie's Kitchen (**Figures 11.22** and **11.26**), needed a refrigerator and kitchen sink that I could make into one rolling unit. A kitchen table and chairs were easy enough to fit, but it seemed that this wasn't enough. The use of the door openings in the blinds walls had worked for the Dollar Store because the loading dock unit had been pretty substantial in size. In the kitchen, the space looked weak and empty. Also in the kitchen scene there are several bits of business that involve going off into another room. I added a flown wall to this set that would frame one to the doors in the blinds wall and make its use as the exit to another room in the house clearer. It also gave a surface to treat with wallpaper and prop dressing.

Each time I played with the elements in a specific set and the positions, in which they played on the groundplan, I had to rotate them to see how they fit in the US side of the turntable where they would be set before they rotated on. This was a frustrating process of little nips and tucks until things worked the way they should.

The Doctor's Office was the easiest set to make work because it had the least pieces, and the clean, monochromatic blinds looked just right as is (**Figure 11.23**).

FIGURE 11.22 *Margie's Kitchen (model)*
The refrigerator and counter/window unit are on the revolve. The door panel flew in and framed the opening in the blinds wall used for an exit.

The Church Basement set was my least favorite and the set I felt I never got right. It used brick columns with small high windows to try to show that it was in the basement and a basketball backboard to suggest that this was a multipurpose space in which Bingo was held some nights. I think I was just trying to do too much with it.

The last set, Mike's House (**Figure 11.25**), featured a very large fireplace unit, which it needed both for some prop business and to make it seem different and very upscale. This caused some problems because it, with the large sectional sofa, used a lot of floor space, and the space it took up on the US side of the revolve where it was preset was very tricky. The set prior to it was the Church Basement, and in that set none of the door openings in the blinds wall were used. The solution to the lack of space was to put a red blinds backing on Mike's bookcase and fireplace units that blocked openings in the red blinds wall in the Church Basement and gave the room that the Mike's pieces needed US (**Figure 11.27**).

The shifts were all á vista. Typically lights would fade as the blinds flew out holding on a character still onstage as the revolve moved them and the previous set off and the next set and its actors on. A shaft of light played across the blinds in their out position.

Design Process Recap

- A very technical show to figure out, where the solution to how the production would move was the biggest and first issue to solve.
- Making sure the technical solutions did not ruin the feel of the individual sets was an ongoing battle.
- A big part of the success of the look was the unusual use of the blinds as a scenic element, especially with the Southie painting done on them.

FIGURE 11.23 *Doctor's Office (model)*
This was the simplest set. Desk, chairs, and bookcase are on the revolve. The beige blinds had a simple window gobo effect painted on them to enliven the composition.

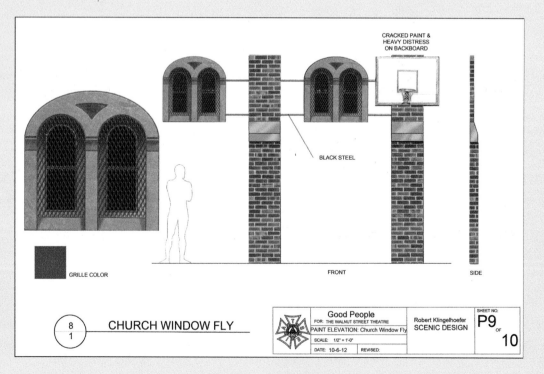

FIGURE 11.24 *Church Basement paint elevation*

FIGURE 11.25   *Mike's House (model)*
Fireplace unit and all furniture are on the revolve.

FIGURE 11.26   *Margie's Kitchen photo*

FIGURE 11.27 *Mike's House photo*

Production Credits

Good People, Fulton Theatre/Walnut Street Theatre, 2012
Director: Bernard Havard
Scenery: Robert Klingelhoefer
Lighting: Shon Causer
Costumes: Colleen Grady

Production: *Les Misérables*

This design for *Les Misérables* is essentially a large unit set with enough variations and individual set pieces that it seemed like a multiple set. It was conceived from the desire for cinematic movement between locations.

Cinematic movement is expected in the theatre today. The more scenes in the play, the more problematic long shifts become. The designer must plan for the movement of the scenery before he completes the individual sets themselves. In *Les Misérables* cinematic shifts were created simply by the number of moving pieces. In each shift so many elements moved at once that the audience felt like everything was changing, though in actuality many basic units stayed onstage.

Because all surfaces of the basic set would always be in view, they needed to be treated in a way that related to the bigger ideas in the play. In this case that was chosen to be the panorama of French history from immediately after the French

Revolution, through the rise and fall of Napoleon, to the restored monarchy of Louis-Philippe. The panels were treated with a cool rough texture and covered with torn and worn posters from several decades.

The design idea was that Jean Valjean is seeking redemption from his guilt and the never-ceasing pursuit by Javert. This was physicalized as an aperture high in the back wall through which a bit of sky and the idea of physical and psychological escape teased. In some scenes this space opened up only to be closed again in others. It could become barred in the prison, a stained glass window in the Bishop's house and the Judge's position in the trial. In the final moment a staircase connected it to the stage for the first time and allowed Valjean to ascend to heaven.

Design Ideas

- A human story played out against the panorama of history
- Valjean strives for escape and redemption, which are always denied or just out of reach

A pair of upper and lower panels tracked open and closed to reveal or conceal this circular aperture, which could itself fly in and out. Other flying pieces helped set various scenes. In addition, a flying bridge could be added to selected scenes. The degree of openness was generally used to match the emotional content of the scene with openness used in more promising moments and moments of fear or turmoil represented by more closed or obstructed looks.

Figure 11.28 is a model shot of the basic set, **Figure 11.29** is a diagram of the back wall showing some of its possible variations, and **Figure 11.30** is the paint elevation of the back wall panels showing its treatment.

Figures 11.31 through **11.36** show a series of other looks.

FIGURE 11.28 Les Mis *basic set*

This model shot shows the basic set with the lower panels closed, the upper panels open, and the oculus In. The side structures served as landing pads for the bridge unit. The floor shape was painted and there were grates DSR and DSL into the pit which were used in the sewer scene.

FIGURE 11.29 *Back wall diagram*

This diagram shows the main options made available for the play's 20 locations by designing a system of panels that could vary the look and use of the space. Note the platform US of the panels that let a guard in the prison scene or the Judge in the trial scene play elevated above actors on the floor. The lower panels got a lot of use in creating dramatic crowd entrances. "One More Day" began with most of the company US hidden by the panels. They were already marching DS when the panels opened.

FIGURE 11.30 *Les Mis back wall*

This is the paint elevation of the back wall showing the texture that was a combination of dimensional and painted effects. The posters were plotted and applied over the painted texture and then had some painting done over them to distress them.

FIGURE 11.31   Les Mis: *Prison scene*
The Prison scene made use of the US upper level, a platform permanently in place that the audience was only conscious of when it was used by actors, as in this scene when guards march back and forth across it.

FIGURE 11.32   Les Mis: *Bishop's House*
The Bishop's House added a flown piece of scenery that transformed the oculus into a church window.

FIGURE 11.33   Les Mis: The Bridge
The Bridge played alone, with the whole back US sky drop visible for Javert's suicide. This scene was staged so that the actor playing Javert moved as if to jump DS off the Bridge as a large piece of black China silk that had laid on the stage floor quickly flew up to cover him. This dramatic moment, accompanied by major movement in the lighting, gave the feeling of his falling toward the water and gave the actor time to exit off the Bridge.

FIGURE 11.34   Les Mis: Rue Plumet
This scene used the Bridge as an upper level and a rolling staircase to connect it to floor level. An architectural unit, with foliage and flowers, flew in. This was an optimistic moment, the home that Valjean had made for Cossette, and because of this showed a great deal of sky.

FIGURE 11.35   Les Mis: *The Barricades*
This scene added three rolling units that were composed of what appeared to be elements of a broken bridge and other architectural elements. A lot of sky was shown to create a sense of street between buildings US.

FIGURE 11.36   Les Mis: *The Barricades (production photo)*

Design Process Recap

- Designing a basic set capable of movements that would open and close the space created a core design that, with other flown and rolling pieces, could create very complex cinematic shifts
- This practical solution tied strongly to ideas of redemption, capture, and escape that are at the core of the story.

Production Credits

Les Misérables, Maine State Music Theatre, 2013
Director: Marc Robin
Set Design: Robert Klingelhoefer
Lighting Design: Jeff Koger
Costume Design: Kurt Alger

Production: *Ragtime*

As mentioned in Chapter 6, "The Designable Idea," a written statement for this production was: "*Ragtime* plays out across a broad American canvas as the dawning of a new century sees its own uncertain future." An American flag was superimposed on a dramatically lit cloud image that could suggest the sunrise or sunset of the America century (**Figure 11.37**).

This created a strong visual idea, but the next step needed to be a technical design that would solve how the production should move.

It seemed that the flag image would make a good In-One, an element that could reveal or conceal elements US of it. Perhaps that US space should be a cloudy sky without flag stripes so the flag would not always be such a dominant image. It would be nice, too, if there was a way for the flag In-One to be broken into several parts to allow some choices in how it could open or close. The natural way to break the flag was at a horizontal line where the stripes changed color. If this flag unit was built as two framed horizontal panels, they could be rigged to fly individually and rigged on a guide cable that would keep them in-line.

Exploring Possible Movement

Top left (**Figure 11.38**): Both flag panels in
Top center: Top flag panel out. Flown Bridge behind it.
Top right: Bottom flag panel flown up to cover Bridge.

FIGURE 11.37   Ragtime *paint elevation and cloud research image*

FIGURE 11.38 *Ragtime diagram*

Bottom left: Both flag panels out showing Bridge.
Bottom center: Bottom flag panel in, no Bridge.
Bottom right: Everything flown out.

The Bridge unit would allow actors to play at a height of 8 feet, either with the Bridge seen in front of the US sky drop or above the lower flag panel, which could also rise to hide it. This "shell game" approach would be used many times as it could reveal other scenery either above or below.

Two portals were designed. One, just DS of the flag panels, would extend the flag image. The other, all the way DS, would be iron truss that would echo other steel units including several rolling units to be used as ships, speaker's platforms, and many other things.

FIGURE 11.39 *Ragtime sketch of the opening look*

FIGURE 11.40   Ragtime *storyboard*
This was a very important production to storyboard to communicate to all involved the progression of one scene to the next and the use of a great number of set pieces.

FIGURE 11.41   Ragtime *photo*
This photo shows the House Unit US with Sarah upstairs and Coalhouse leaving.

FIGURE 11.42   Ragtime *sketch and photo*
This scene is the musical number "Buffalo Nickel Photoplay, Inc.," and shows the Atlantic City look with posters of Evelyn Nesbit and Houdini. The Houdini poster was plotted on paper and the magician had an entrance bursting through it.

FIGURE 11.43   Ragtime *sketch and photo*
Coalhouse's car shown in Henry Ford's factory in the sketch, and at the Emerald Isle Fire Company in the photo. Henry Ford stood on the bridge above the moving gears of his assembly line.

FIGURE 11.44   Ragtime *sketch and photo*
For the scene of Emma Goldman's Rally, one of the rolling steel units served as her speaker's platform.

FIGURE 11.45 Ragtime sketch and photo
For the musical number "President," the speakers were on the bridge and the lower flag panel was in.

FIGURE 11.46 Ragtime sketch
Sarah's funeral has been preset US of the lower flag panel during "President" and is revealed by it flying.

Design Process Recap

- A tight mechanical solution to how the production could move determined in conjunction with strong visual ideas.
- The "set as machine" idea tied in nicely with the industrial time period.

Production Credits

Ragtime, Fulton Theatre, 2008
Director: Rob McKercher
Scenery: Robert Klingelhoefer
Lighting: Bill Simmons
Costumes: Beth Dunkelberger

SUMMARY

- Designing moving scenery should put your focus on the importance of the movement more than the design of any individual set.

- Practical decisions and aesthetic decisions should be complementary, not separate.

NOTES

1. Arnold Aronson, *Looking Into the Abyss: Essays on Scenography* (Ann Arbor: University of Michigan Press, 2003), 188.
2. Aronson, *Looking Into the Abyss: Essays on Scenography*, 188.
3. Aronson, *Looking Into the Abyss: Essays on Scenography*, 191.
4. Aronson, *Looking Into the Abyss: Essays on Scenography*, 192.

CHAPTER 12

ON TO THE STAGE

However long you have had to work on your design, the time will come for it to move into the hands of others for construction and installation. Your responsibilities change in this next phase but do not stop.

THE FINAL PACKAGE

The amount of time you have to design a project will vary wildly from a few weeks in a last-minute situation, such as replacing another designer, to six to eight weeks in an academic calendar to six months or longer in a professional situation. Longer periods are possible in opera or on a new musical or other large project. However long the design period, it will end with the designer's preparation of a final package of materials to submit for approval.

This Package Will Usually Contain:

1. A color rendering or renderings of the scenery as it will look onstage and a white model (usually 1/4-inch scale) of the set or sets, *or* a full-color model (usually 1/2-scale)

2. A full set of designer drawings, including:

   a. Groundplan for a single or unit set or groundplans for each set if it is a multiple set. These should be named and/or numbered to correspond to the storyboard sketches.

   b. Section—for a multiple set production showing in and out trims for all flying scenery.

   c. Full elevations of every piece of scenery with individual views (plan, section, front elevation, and/ or side view as needed to explain the unit and appropriate details and notes for materials, molding, and construction methods.

3. Paint elevations, in 1/2 inch or 1 inch as appropriate, for all scenery. If digital, these may be submitted electronically but should be accompanied by a hard copy to serve as color reference (see Scenic Art section later in this chapter).

4. Prop sketches, notes, and/or research for most furniture and set props including vendor research and color swatches or samples as needed (see Props section in this chapter).

5. A Shift Plot if a multiple set production (see example in the next section).

6. An elements list (especially for a multiple set production) is a complete list with details as to size, position, or lineset number, and basic notes as to construction and materials (see example in the Elements List section).

7. A lineset schedule.

The Shift Plot

The Shift Plot is a document the scenic designer creates for several reasons. First, it is a way for him to check that the scenic units he has created will shift from scene to scene in the way he planned. All scenic moves, the panels opening and closing, flown units moving in and out, and furniture moves on the floor are listed individually in the order they need to occur to move from location to location.

The second thing the Shift Plot does is to serve as the first check of how many crewpersons will be needed to make each shift. The number of crew expected to be available has already been decided by the theatre's budgeting at this point, so the designer can use the Shift Plot to see how this works and whether crewpersons can perform two actions in a shift.

The third purpose of the Shift Plot is to give stage management an understanding of how the designer sees the production moving and the use of all scenic units.

Note: SB stands for Storyboard sketch number and Mini# stands for the number of the individual groundplan for this scene. The designer supplies a sketch for each scene in two forms. One is a complete storyboard of images that can be hung in the rehearsal hall, and the other is as individual sheets that the stage manager and/or director can have in their scripts. He also supplies individual groundplans, referred to as "minis", for each scene.

Example—Shift Plot

Les Misérables: MSMT Summer 2013

Director: Marc Robin
Designer: Robert Klingelhoefer

Act I

Preset

Prison Fly In
Upper Sliding Panels Closed
Lower Sliding Panels Closed
Oculus Fly In
Bridge In
Bishop Statue Set US

Shift

Open Upper Sliding Panels

Projection: 1815

1: Opening: Prison SB & Mini #1

Work Song

Shift

Close Upper Sliding Panels: 2 Deck
Prison Fly Out: 1 Rail
Bishop Fly In: 1 Rail
Freedom—Farmer, Innkeeper SB & Mini #2

Shift

Open Lower Sliding Panels (Partial): 2 Deck
Open Upper Sliding Panels: 2 Deck
The Bishop of Digne's House SB & Mini #3

Shift

Close Lower Sliding Panels: 2 Deck
Close Upper Sliding Panels: 2 Deck
Oculus Fly Out: 1 Rail
Strike Bishop Statue: 1 Deck
Bridge In: 1 Deck
Factory Fly In: 1 Rail

Projection: 1823

2: The Factory at Montreuil SB & Mini #4

Shift

Rolling Stairs On: 2 Deck
Open Lower Sliding Panels: 2 Deck
Factory Fly Out: 1 Rail
Red Light Fly In: 1 Rail

3: The Red Light District SB & Mini #5

Shift

    Red Light Fly Out: 1 Rail
    Rolling Stairs Off: 2 Deck
    Bridge Out: 1 Deck
    Oculus Fly In: 1 Rail
    The Runaway Cart SB & Mini #6

Shift

    Upper Sliding Panels Open: 2 Deck
    Lower Sliding Panels Close: 2 Deck

4: The Trial SB & Mini #7

Shift

    Oculus Fly Out: 1 Rail
    Bed On: 2 Deck

5: The Hospital SB & Mini #8

Shift

    Upper Sliding Panels Close: 2 Deck
    Furniture On: Actors
    Master of the House Fly In: 1 Rail

6: The Inn *Master of the House* SB & Mini #9

Shift

    Furniture Off: Actors
    Master of the House Fly Out: 1 Rail

Projection: 1833

    Upper Sliding Panels Open (Partial): 2 Deck
    Lower Sliding Panels Open (Partial): 2 Deck

7: The Streets of Paris—Ten Years Later SB & Mini #10

Shift

    Upper Sliding Panels Close: 2 Deck

    Lower Sliding Panels Close: 2 Deck
    Furniture On: Actors
    Oculus Fly In: 1 Rail
    ABC Fly In: 1 Fly
    Upper Sliding Panels Open: 2 Deck
    Lower Sliding Panels Open: 2 Deck

8: Café of the ABC Friends SB & Mini #11

Shift

    Furniture Off: Actors
    Oculus Fly Out: 1 Rail
    ABC Fly Out: 1 Rail
    Bridge In: 1 Deck
    Rue Plumet Fly In: 1 Rail
    Rolling Stairs On: 2 Deck

9: The Rue Plumet SB & Mini #12

10: The Attempted Robbery

Shift

    Bridge Out: 1 Deck
    Rue Plumet Fly Out: 1 Rail
    Rolling Stairs Off: 2 Deck

11: Act I Finale SB & Mini #13

Act II

Preset

    Upper Sliding Panels Open (Partial): 2 Deck
    Lower Sliding Panels Open (Partial) 2 Deck

1: A Street in Paris SB & Mini #14

    Lighting Shift Only

2: The Rue Plumet

    BARRICADE ASSEMBLED a vista: Cast and Crew
    Rolling Stairs On: 2 Deck
    Upper Sliding Panels Open: 2 Deck
    Lower Sliding Panels Open: 2 Deck
    Barricade Fly In: 1 Fly

3: At the Barricade SB & Mini #15

4: The Battle

Shift

>   Black Drop In: 1 Rail
>   Strike Barricades 1–3: Actors & Deck
>   Strike Rolling Stairs: 2 Deck
>   Barricade Fly Out : 1 Rail

5: The Sewer—Dog Eats Dog SB & Mini #16

>   Bridge In: 1 Deck
>   River Fly In: Rail

6: A Bridge Over the Seine SB & Mini #17

>   END SCENE: River Fly Out: 1 Rail

Shift

>   Upper Sliding Panels Close: 2 Deck
>   Lower Sliding Panels Close: 2 Deck
>   Set Wedding Tables: 2 Deck
>   Bridge Out : 1 Deck
>   Upper Sliding Panels Open: 2 Deck
>   Lower Sliding Panels Open: 2 Deck

7: The Wedding SB & Mini #18

Shift

>   Upper Sliding Panels Close: 2 Deck
>   Lower Sliding Panels Close: 2 Deck
>   Oculus Fly In: 1 Rail
>   Set Chair: Actors
>   Rolling Stairs On: 2 Deck

8: Valjean's Room SB & Mini #19

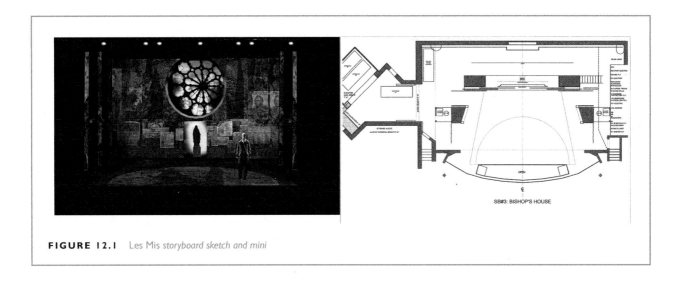

FIGURE 12.1 Les Mis *storyboard sketch and mini*

The Lineset Schedule

The Lineset Schedule is a list of the theatre's linesets and what is hung on them (example in **Figure 12.2**). It should list the name of the theatre, the name of the production, the names of the set and lighting designers, and the date. A revised date is also helpful so it is easy to determine whether the copy you have is the latest one.

After this information, list the linesets, giving their number, distance from plasterline, what is hung on each (scenery and electrics), and any notes or special instructions. A common way to list the linesets is to list the US most lineset first and then in descending order moving DS. This has the benefit of having them in the physical order they are in when looking at the stage from the house.

MAINE STATE MUSIC THEATRE 2014

LINESET SCHEDULE

Production: CHAMBERLAIN

Set Designer: Robert Klingelhoefer
Light Designer: Jeff Koger
Date: 5-2-2014

#	Distance from Plaster	Unit	Notes
US TRUSS	24'-11"	TREE DROP	
#24	22'-6"	BALL DROP	
#23	21'-7"	TRAIN DROP	
#22	19'-6"	BOWDOIN DROP	
#21	19'-0"		
#20	18'-5"	ELECTRIC	
#19	17'-11"	TRACKING PANELS	
#18	17'-4"	PORTAL	
#17	16'-8"	ELECTRIC	Brest US
#16	15'-11"		
#15	15'-2"	STUDY FLY	
#14	14'-8"	CHURCH PANEL	Off Center (see Plan)
#13	13'-11"		
#12	13'-4"	INAUGURATION FLY	
#10	12'-6"	ELECTRIC	
#9	11'-4"	TRACKING PANELS	
#8	10'-0'	PORTAL	
#7	9'-3"	BUNTING #2	
#6	8'-6"	ELECTRIC	Brest DS if necessary
#5	7'-9"		
#4	7'-3"	ELECTRIC	

FIGURE 12.2 *Lineset schedule*

FIGURE 12.3   The Neverending Story

The Elements List

The Elements List is a document the designer makes, usually to accompany the drawings sent to the scene shop, for the approval meeting. It is a list of all the scenic elements of the production with notes specifying the particulars of each unit. General dimensions, materials involved, and anything particular about the unit that might cause a question are included. It gives an overview of the set and can serve as a FAQ sheet.

Example

The Neverending Story

Childsplay—Tempe Arts Center
Robert Klingelhoefer, Designer
SET ELEMENT LIST 2–14–09
Basic Permanent Set

+8′-0″ Catwalk with SR, Center, & SL Sections

- US supports are black duv covered studwalls

- Sides include a black duv covered studwall and DS pipe legs

- Railing of 1 x 2 steel tube on pipe posts on offstage perimeter

- Ladder through 2′ sq. access hole from floor to 8′ level

SR Side Wall

- 3″ thick Wall with holes

- Large bottom-center hole is entrance

- Other, smaller holes may be used for effects

- All edges heavily rounded-over (2″)
- Mounts to SR Catwalk
- Lightly textured and painted; texture might allow fill between sections at install

USR Wall

- 3″ thick Wall with holes
- Large bottom-center hole is entrance
- Other, smaller holes may be used for effects
- All edges heavily rounded-over (2″)
- Mounts to US Catwalk, but stands-off 4–6″ to allow Circular Sliding Panel to operate behind it
- Lightly textured and painted; texture might allow fill between sections at install

Center Sliding Panel

- 11′ diameter Panel slides from behind USR Wall to cover Center
- All edges heavily rounded-over
- Might rig to "track" on face of catwalk

USL Wall

- 3″ thick Wall with holes
- Large bottom-center hole is entrance
- Other, smaller holes may be used for effects
- All edges heavily rounded-over (2″)
- Mounts to US Catwalk, but stands-off 4–6″ to allow match USR Wall
- Lightly textured and painted; texture might allow fill between sections at install

SL Side Wall

- 3″ thick Wall with holes
- Large bottom-center hole is entrance

- Other, smaller holes may be used for effects
- All edges heavily rounded-over (2″)
- Mounts to SL Catwalk
- Lightly textured and painted; texture might allow fill between sections at install

Closet Dressing/Projector Unit

- 8′ wide x 18″ deep castered "box" that contains Janitor's closet dressing (metal shelf unit with supplies, mop & bucket, etc.)
- Projector on other side is used for Magic Mirror gate effect
- Unit Revolves for projector use

US Grid Unit

- Hung Unit of open 3″ wide strips in false-perspective

Masonite Floor

- Covers area defined by catwalk structure and continues it DS onto apron
- Painted with false-perspective grid

Scenic Units

DS Street Panels (2)

- Soft (or lightly framed?) Panels 10′ wide x 24′ tall

Mid-Stage Street Panels (2)

- Soft (or lightly framed?) Panels 9′ wide x 24′ tall

US Street Panels (2)

- Soft (or lightly framed?) Panels 12′ wide x 24′ tall

Mid-Stage Center Street Panel

- Soft Drop 20′ wide x 24′ tall

Bookseller Panel

- Soft (or lightly framed?) Panel 10' wide x 24' tall

- Includes 18' high stack of fake books. Can be 3/4 depth and mount to panel

School Panel

- Soft (or lightly framed?) Panel 6' wide x 24' tall

Bookseller Desk

- Rolling desk that appears to be made entirely of fake books

Magnolia Pavilion Fly

- 2D Cut Profile with some applied detail

China Silk for Swamp of Sadness

- Dyed/painted

Morla Turtle Shell

- Rolling Unit

- Puppets will supply Head and coordinate Dressing/ Painting

Engywook's Observatory Unit

- Rolling Unit with wacky Telescope

Riddle Gate Unit

- Flown Unit of two vertical boxed flats and track

- Carved 2" foam on flats

- Flats fly in together and separate to 6' apart

- Electrics will wire eye effects

- No-Key Gate Unit flies in with this unit behind one section and is removed by actor

No-Key Gate Unit

- Small metal gate hinged in frame on low-profile base

- Flies in behind one post of Riddle Gate Unit and is removed by actor

- Actor crawls through Gate so it must be stable

Magic Mirror Gate Unit

- Flown Unit of 8' diameter RP material in a 2D Cut Profile Moon Gate with some applied detail

Uyulala Unit

- Flown Unit

- Cut Profile Arches with some applied detail

- Built in sections and rigged to two linesets to controlled-collapse

Wind Giant Silk

- Fly of vertical white China Silk strips

- Rigged to trip-drop into view and later release to drop onstage

Empress's Shell Bed

- Rolling Unit with applied detail and bed dressing.

COST-OUT

When the final package is turned over to the theatre company's production manager (PM), a cost-out process will begin. The PM or technical director will go over the drawings and determine the cost of materials for each unit. They will also estimate the shop hours it will take to build each unit. Their work will determine whether the design can be built for the money and in the number of man hours budgeted for it. This takes place prior to the approval meeting so any problems can be discussed then.

Generally, cost-out sheets are prepared for each unit of scenery to make it easy to see where the largest costs are and what can be cut to bring the budget in-line.

APPROVAL MEETING

At some point shortly before the shop is scheduled to begin construction, a final approval meeting is usually held at the theatre or the producing theatre's offices. In attendance will be the producer or artistic director and managing director of the theatre company, the director, the set designer, the theatre's production manager and/or technical director, the propmaster and the charge scenic artist. The designer will be asked to explain the design and walk the group through any scene changes, effects, or other variations. The shop and prop and paint departments will have looked at the package of materials the designer sent and will report any budget or production concerns. This meeting is for the producing theatre as a group, to discuss the feasibility of the design, both artistically and economically. The designer should be prepared to consider the problems that may be presented and offer any quick suggestions he has. Prior to this meeting it is helpful to think through potential problems in all departments and plan solutions. In many cases, the designer may have had conversations with the shop about the design and be aware of their concerns. This gives him the advantage of a little preplanning. This meeting may be the designer's only personal contact with the producer or artistic director, and he will want to be seen as organized, concerned with making this production the best it can be, and open to suggestions and concerns.

THE SHOP

One of the great pleasures of being a scenic designer is working with all the talented and creative people who will have a part in building, painting, propping, and installing your work. No one stays in the theatre long without a great love of the work, and this is very true of all these artisans.

It is very important in the scenic designer's training that he acquire a solid basic expertise in all areas of stagecraft. The designer does not need to be the final authority on the best methods and materials to build a particular scenic element, but he should have a firm grasp of a good way to build it. This will allow him to provide information to the shop that will be helpful to them, not impractical ideas that will take a great deal of time to figure out how to create, and will get you more quickly

and efficiently to what you designed. Structural design is very complex and is not expected of you, but the designer who presents drawings for scenery that is wildly unpractical should expect the extra work on the shop's part figuring things out to have an effect on the time and money the build will take.

Your set will be built by either a professional independent scene shop or the shop of the producing organization. There are many similarities of the two but also some stark contrasts.

If your set is to be built by an independent commercial shop, it may go through the bid process. When it is time to submit your drawings, you will be asked to send them to generally at least three different shops. You may have been asked to suggest a shop, if there is one you have worked with before. The shops who receive the drawings will prepare bids for the producer or producing organization of how much they will charge to build, paint, and install the set. Generally, the lowest bid will win the contract.

Considerations for the Designer in Working with a Commercial Shop

- It is very important in working with both types of shops, that your drawings and specifications be complete. They should include all elements you need the shop to provide. But in working with a commercial shop, this is even more important. The commercial shop's bid will be based on what is on the drawings. If something is changed or added after the bid is accepted, it will cause the commercial shop problems in manpower and space, the cost of which will greatly inflate the amount they will charge for these adds or changes.

- Review the bids carefully. If a particular item, a particular scenic unit seems unusually high or low in cost compared to the other bids, it may be a red flag that the shop either doesn't understand something about that unit, is unfamiliar with materials or techniques concerned, or, conversely, has expertise or equipment that make the construction of that unit easier for them.

- If you have concerns or questions about a bid, ask the shop or relay your concerns to the producer or production manager.

If your set will be built by the theatre's shop, while your set may be the only project that this shop has to deal with for the build period, as opposed to the several projects a commercial shop may be juggling at any given time, they will still have their own concerns. Generally, a commercial shop will have a large amount of space to build and paint scenery because of the number and diversity of projects they do. The scene shop of a theatre company may have space concerns about the size of the drops they can paint or their ability to do a trial set-up of the set in the shop. They also may not have expertise or experience in some construction techniques.

Considerations for the Designer in Working with a Theatre's Shop

• Ask questions early about the shop's concerns with any particular technique or material. Be prepared to make substitutions or suggestions to deal with these concerns.

• Ask about the shop's staffing and whether overhire can be brought in if necessary in a particular area.

Depending on your own schedule, your home city, and the location of the shop or theatre, it may be difficult to visit the shop during the construction period, but it is very desirable to see the construction and painting in process, before you see it finished in the theatre. To accomplish this, bring up in your contract talks that you would like the contract to include transportation costs for a shop visit. Stress that you believe this to be money well spent versus expensive problems later. If a shop visit proves impossible, ask the shop to send you process photos at certain intervals of the build, especially requesting photos of units that you have particular concerns about. The painting is usually a special area of concern as it will not be possible to do much more than touch-up painting in the theatre.

SCENIC ART

The painting of your scenery, because it is the final finish of the scenic units the audience sees, is of particular concern to the designer. Most designers probably consider themselves more painters than carpenters, as the painting of renderings and models is more a part of their own work. While the communication of your design to those who will execute it is important in all areas, in the area of

scenic art it becomes especially critical and presents some problems.

The head scenic artist is called the scenic charge artist in a shop with multiple scenic artists. The charge artist will communicate with the designer, plan the schedule and manpower for their department, and order materials.

The difference in scale between a 1"–1'-0" paint elevation and the actual full-scale scenery is 1:12. Techniques in painting scenery that are effective at real scale are almost impossible to accurately convey at 1/2-inch or 1-foot scale. This mandates a special level of communication between the designer and the scenic artist. Again, the designer should have a high level of understanding of the basic techniques involved in scenic art so he has a language of painting terms with which to talk to the charge artist.

Painting is most often planned in a series of steps, from preparing the scenery to be painted, to laying in background colors and textures, and advancing to more detailed painting in the foreground and then steps that will give finish the look and/or protect the scenery. The designer should be able to think in these steps to talk in detail about how the painting will be done.

An understanding of the look and uses of painting techniques such as wet-blend, scumble, dry brush, sponge, spray, and spatter will be critical as well. These are texture-creating techniques that the scenic artists will use to bridge the scale gap between paint elevation and actual scenery. They will be important in the conversation between designer and painter to bridge the communication gap in a hard-to-articulate area.

Paint elevations are required for all pieces of scenery and are generally done in 1/2-inch or 1-inch scale. They should be as close as possible to what you want the final scenery to look like. Notes on the paint elevation should call attention to techniques that may be difficult to see or finishes like high gloss or satin that the elevation may not show. Digital techniques narrow the gap between what the designer shows in his renderings and models and what he gives the painters in that they allow the same images to be adapted for use in all forms. Some scenic artists feel uncomfortable with digital elevations as opposed to those the designer paints in traditional media, but this is changing as digital elevations are becoming more widespread. The designer should be aware that what may be easy to create in Photoshop may be far more difficult and expensive to create in scene painting. The scenic artist should

FIGURE 12.4   *Paint elevation*

realize that with greater accuracy in what the designer provides in the elevation come greater expectations that the painting looks exactly like that elevation. Though it is still very expensive, large-scale digital printing is often a good choice for very labor-intensive scenic work. The inclusion of smaller scale plotted images within the use of traditional painting is quite common, but requires that the different looks of digital and hand-painted elements be blended in some way.

Nothing is a replacement for a trusting relationship between a designer and a scenic artist who have worked together before. As already noted, if the designer can make a visit to the shop about the time some of the major painting is done, he can express his opinions of how it looks and what might be tweaked to improve anything needed. The most common shop visit request is for a final paint technique such as a light spray or wash to be added to take down the crispness of the painting.

PROPS

Stage properties is a very diverse area that encompasses everything from silverware to upholstery and from chandeliers to fake food.

If the producing organization is a theatre company, the propmaster and his crew will be full-time staff members. If a commercial scene shop is building the set, an independent prop shop or propmaster may be used. In any event the level of communication on the part of the designer is the same as in other areas, and the attention to detail should match the propmaster's own.

The information the designer provides to the prop department varies somewhat by project and designer but may include the following:

- **The Designer's Prop List.** This generally does not include hand props, information for which the

FIGURE 12.5   *Painting in the shop:* Good People, *Fulton Theatre, scenic artists—Peter Tupitza and Erica Harney*

propmaster gets from the script and meeting with stage management and the director. The designer's prop list includes all furniture, set dressing, upholstery and drapery fabric, and any big-ticket items that affect the look of the production. The designer should receive the hand prop list as well and discuss with the propmaster any items about which he has particular thoughts or concerns.

- **Research photos.** These may include both historical research and vendor research of purchasable items from online and print catalogs. In a period design, it is useful for the designer to provide images that give an overview of the period using items needed for the production.

- **Color swatches** or other color information that will establish the color palette of the production.

- **Fabric specifications.** Fabric is increasingly being bought online as fabric stores are only common in the largest cities that carry the types of fabrics used in drapery and upholstery in large enough quantities and color options to be useful in scenic design, where it is not unusual to need 50–100 yards of a fabric. The designer may do some online shopping himself and provide the propmaster with actual fabric specs. This can have a design advantage in that the designer finds his fabric color earlier and can incorporate the actual choice into the design. It is more common that the propmaster will shop the fabric in stores or online and provide the designer with swatches to approve.

- **Written notes** that explain details in certain props or anything the designer feels needs a little more explanation. It is good to communicate how the economic level of the location or the taste of a character should affect prop choices.

Example

Eclectic Society

Walnut Street Theatre
PROP NOTES

COMMON ROOM (Main Space)
NOTE: General feel should be classy, that the furniture and dressings exhibit wealth and taste but have been worn by
    several generations of fraternity brothers.

Sofa—deep red leather/could be button-tufted/classy, worn (see research)
Armchair—should match (or complement) Sofa
Coffee Table—largish, oval, wood
Rug (under above grouping) classy, warm, worn oriental

2 Small Armchairs (at extreme SR & SL)—matching/deep red leather.

Game Table—octagonal or round, 42″ diameter wooden. (See research.)
4 Chairs (with Game Table)—club chairs, relatively open
Rug (under above grouping)—classy, warm, worn oriental

Mail Table—approx. 4′-0″ x 18″, pier table/lyre base (?)
Mailboxes—approx. 24 cubbyholes (1 for ea. resident brother) not over 4–0″ wide/possibility for a place to post notices

Piano—spinet/must move during performance/brown wood, worn
Piano Bench—match piano

Phone Booth—wooden, 30″ x 30″ footprint. (See research.)

Bookcase Dressing (SL shop built bookcases)—leather bound books, small standing frames with photos of previous
    brothers, homecomings, football games, certificates

Window Curtains (SR & SL)—deep red color (matches sofa) subtle tone-on-tone fabric/lined/on rings on black rod. **(See
    Disarray Opportunity Note.)**

French Door Sheers—on Doors to Dining Room SL: Ivory sheer on café rods on offstage side of doors

Sconces—one pair US and DS of DR Window
    Single between Phone Booth and Coat Room
    One pair US and DS of DL Window

LIBRARY (US)
Sofa—match to Common Room sofa, deep red leather/faces US
Rug (under above)—classy, warm, worn oriental

Mantle Dressing—small standing frames of photos and certificates (in addition to the Douglas Cup)
Sconces—one pair above fireplace
Framed Portrait—of previous notable above fireplace

US Window Curtains—deep red color (match sofa) subtle tone-on-tone fabric / lined / on rings on black rod. **(See Disarray Opportunity Note.)**

STEPS/GALLERY
Framed Pictures—12 (twelve) 18″ x 24″ wooden frames (approx. 2″ frame width) of B&W photos of previous groups of brothers, over previous 50 years. Will attach to 1/4″ x 1/4″ steel tube run to wainscot to "float."

Fanlight Sheers (2)—ivory sheers on US side gathered to center
2 Busts on Brackets—centered on fanlight/Fake Door and Meeting Room Door/one should be Pericles, the other Socrates, Plato or similar.

Sconce—single US of Meeting Room Door

DINING ROOM (Off SL below)
Chairs/Sideboard—there is enough offstage space to dress this offstage room with a row of chairs against the wall and maybe a sideboard or serving piece
Framed Picture(s)—2–3 portraits of previous Fraternity notables
Sconce—single on US Wall

MEETING ROOM (Off SL above)
Chairs—4–6 wooden conference table chairs could be visible
Framed Pictures—2–3 portraits of previous Fraternity notables would "float" above US wainscot in the same way as those on Steps/Gallery

Disarray Opportunity Note: In the first three scenes, the room is in disarray because of the mock search for the missing charter. The script says:

At present, the room is in disarray. The paintings are down and lean against the wall. The carpets have been rolled up and pushed to the side. Curtains are askew, and books have been removed from the library shelves. The effect is not slovenliness but abandonment, as if the premises are being vacated and the contents removed.

Some easy choices would be:

- Carpets partially rolled up or folded back

- Furniture askew

- Books messed up on shelves and some on floor

- Curtains irregularly drawn

More challenging might be:

- A curtain rod might be off one bracket at an angle

- One or more of the "floating" pictures could be rigged to angle or remove if the steel tube support was not permanent

Good for:
Sofa (worn effect)
Armchair options
Game table options (could be green felt top)

BEST OVERALL
Good for:
Sofa
Armchair
Drapes
Sconces Good
   Lived-In
Panel & Wall
Mantle decor
Pictures

FIGURE 12.6   *Prop research*

Note on fabric selection: The general softness or stiffness of a fabric is referred to as its hand. A fabric's hand has a lot to do with how it will lay or drape. Learning about the hand of different fabric types will help the designer make sound choices, especially with online purchases where he may not actually touch the fabric until it is purchased and shipped. The high cost of fabric makes these blind selections even more stressful.

A good prop shop can be very helpful in making the look of the show rich and appropriate. If the designer supplies detailed information and has good conversations with the propmaster, the impact on the show's look can be profound.

LOAD-IN

About two weeks before the first scheduled public performance of the play, the set will be loaded in to the theatre and installed. This period of time can be longer in the complex load-in of a new musical and shorter if the production is simpler. The designer is generally contracted to be in attendance from load-in though the first public performance of the production. Depending on the designer's schedule during the build period and how far the theatre is from his home, this may be the first time he has seen the built and painted scenery. During load-in the designer should act as another pair of eyes on making sure the correct decisions are being made, and everything he planned is coming together.

TECH

The period of technical rehearsals is when all the elements of the production come together. It is both the most exciting and the most stressful part of the entire process. All your previous decisions show their strengths and weaknesses at this point. The designer's role in tech is to work with the director and stage manager to make all the aspects of his design work with the lighting and the costumes. It is not unusual for some things that were planned to not work out in the way they were imagined three to six months prior. Everyone involved needs to keep working to make the production as a whole be the best it can be. This can involve making cuts or changes that are very difficult and stressful.

Calm consideration and reasoned decisions for the greater good are required. Remember what is coming together now is your real design, not the rendering or model you did six weeks ago.

Through the tech rehearsal process the designer makes notes of things the shop, paint, and prop department have to do. Production meetings are held after all rehearsals for everyone involved to communicate what needs to be done and how the schedule will work.

In a multiple set production, the shifts are what will make or break the show, and these will require hours of time to get right. The effect of a few seconds' difference in the speed or the sequence of the order in which the pieces move makes all the difference in the final effect.

DRESS REHEARSALS AND OPENING NIGHT

The rehearsal process continues into dress rehearsal and finally opening night. Gradually the notes get fewer and fewer, and the designer has more free time on his hands. He is still obligated to attend rehearsals. Contractually the designer is usually required to stay through the first public performance of the play. This can sometimes be considered the first preview but is usually considered opening night. Many theatre companies will find the designer on opening night to hand him his final check, a great way to end the project.

SUMMARY

- It is easy to feel your work is done when your design is approved and being built, but there is still very important work to do.

- You must be involved with the details of the execution of your work to be sure it is done the way you want it to be. This is not from paranoia or lack of faith in the craftspeople executing it, but because you are the person who knows the most about your design, and that gives you unique insights into things that others might miss.

- Tech is perhaps the most creative part of the process. It is where you make sure the ideas from early in the process come true and where last-minute course corrections are possible.

CHAPTER 13

REALITIES OF THE PROFESSION

In this final chapter, it seems time to look at the profession that you have been training to enter, and offer what insight I can into its realities. Designing must be your passion to succeed in this industry. Newcomers are often counseled to not enter the field if there is *anything* else they could be happy doing, and this is good advice. But with your passion, hard work, a positive attitude, and no small amount of luck, you can find a place in the industry that can be very fulfilling.

TRAINING FOR THE PROFESSION

The typical first step on the academic path into the industry is to complete a four-year undergraduate program and graduate with a BFA, usually in Design and Technical Theatre with an emphasis or concentration in Scene Design. This book is primarily aimed at students in their sophomore or junior year of such a program.

In that time, the undergraduate designer will probably only have the opportunity to design on their university's mainstage once or twice, if at all. Summer work during these years is very important in developing skills and connections beyond what your university can provide and building a portfolio of work. A portfolio is who you are, shows what you can do, and is how the professional world will see you.

WEBSITES AND PORTFOLIOS

From the sophomore year in your BFA program, onward, for the rest of your career, it is extremely important that you keep a portfolio of your work up to date and ready to show. Today the best advice is to create a professional website that is an online portfolio of your work. This allows you to refer potential employers to your website immediately, before you can meet them in person.

Your website should be:

- **Clear and attractive,** showing your work in a classy, professional manner.

- **Free from cute, personal touches.** Do not use background music or distracting effects like crawling text, excessive pop-ups, and distracting colors or patterns.

- **Focused on the work.** Make sure the focus of the website is on the work, not the design of the site. Avoid site-building software that locks you into a lot of templates. Keep it simple.

- **Easy to navigate.** Make sure it is easy for the visitor to get around your website. Plan the way in which they go from a home page to a portfolio index to an individual project and back to the index for more.

It is also important to have a way to present your portfolio in a one-on-one meeting. This can usually be done on a laptop or iPad in digital form, either presenting from your website or from a PowerPoint that you have made. As much as digital means are the standard today, it is worth having a paper-based portfolio, as well, for situations in which electronic media is not an option.

In developing your website, you will have designed a graphic look that can easily carry over into your other forms. Creating a PowerPoint is very easy. Your backgrounds and text styles can match your website. For your paper-based portfolio, make pages in Photoshop that combine images, text, and background, and print them. An 11″ x 17″ presentation book is a good, easily portable size to consider.

Portfolio and Web Design

As already noted, the focus of your portfolio and website should be on the work. This sounds simple, but it is amazing how many students fall into the trap of making fussy designs or using distracting colors.

The test for viewing your portfolio is that when you click on a new page or turn a new paper page, your eyes go **immediately** to one dominant image on the page. Usually, if this is the first page devoted to a specific project, it should be the best photo of that project.

There are several factors to consider in how to achieve this:

- **Size:** This image should be the biggest one on the page.

- **Position:** Its position should be strong and the same as the other "best" photos on other pages. You can reverse this position on some pages to create variety, but training your viewer's eye to look to a certain spot on the page is a good idea.

- **Control Emphasis:** Make sure this photo pops out from the background.

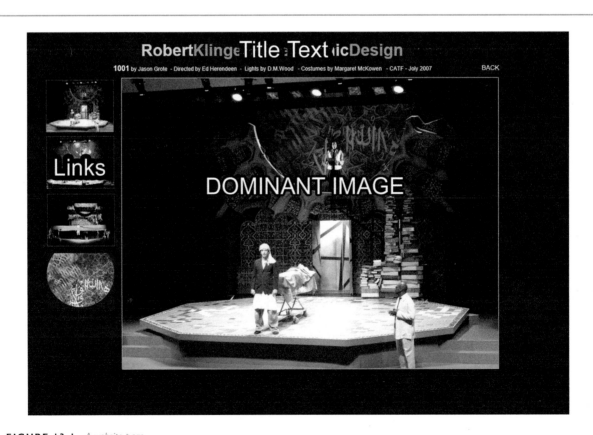

FIGURE 13.1   *A website page*
Note the position of the dominant image, with the title text above it. The links to other pages of this project are the thumbnails at left.

In planning your background, there are several considerations:

• Your background should not be too bright or too colorful. On no account should it be a bold pattern or image

• Consider a dark neutral color. Black can be OK, but remember theatre photographs often have dark backgrounds and you don't want the border areas of your photos to disappear. It will make the bright areas appear to float and this can seem odd. A dark color can work, but remember that your work will have sets in many colors and you don't want any of your designs to clash with their background color. Dark gray is a good way to go, creating no color clashes. It is dark but not too dark. If you want to go with black, consider putting a thin white or gray line around each photo. This can be done in Photoshop by clicking "Blending Options" > "Stroke" and adjusting the color and size of the line.

• While you don't want too much going on in your background, a very restrained texture can look good, like a subtle fabric texture. Choose something that has a connection to the theatre, not fieldstone or brick.

If the big **"go-to"** photo is the first thing you want your viewer to look at, the second is the title information text block. This will immediately explain what this project is.

This text box should contain:

• The title of the play. This should be the biggest and clearest text on the page

• The director, lighting designer, costume designer, and video or projection designer, if there is one. This is done to acknowledge your collaborators on this project *and* drop names. The theatre is a very small world, and if the person looking at your work knows someone you have worked with, good things may happen.

• The theatre where you did the show.

• The year you did the show. Adding the month is optional. No one cares about the day.

• It is important that this text block is in the same position every time too.

• Round out the page with one or two smaller images.

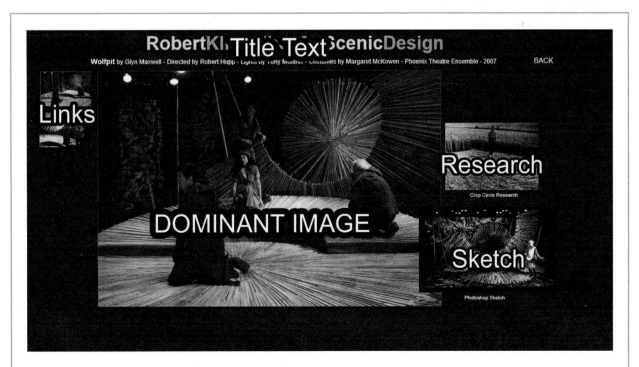

FIGURE 3.2 *A website page*
Note the research image and sketch in a subordinate position to the dominant image at right.

As a set designer you will be showing production photographs, photographs of your models, and scans of renderings and sketches. Most important are production photographs because they show how your finished work looks onstage, but if on a particular show your model shot is better than the production shot, use it for the "go-to" shot. While production photos are the best to show, overall, it is also important to show examples of the sketches, renderings, and models that got you there.

The **"money shot"** is when you have a beautiful production shot and show prominently beside it a photo of your model or rendering that very closely matches it. This demonstrates what you can do like nothing else. Another thing to consider showing is any particularly interesting research images that can demonstrate where your inspiration came from and what you did with it.

There are no rules about how many photos to use of a particular project except that you should not show so many that it seems like you are padding the project with duplications or images that are not good quality. You do not want your viewer to get bored. If it is a big project with lots of cool stuff, show it.

These guidelines apply to websites and paper portfolios, but each of these has a few rules of its own.

While working on your website, when you have a page or two made, preview them. Most site builder software offers a preview function. Check the size of your page. You want each page of your site to come up on most monitors as a full page with nothing off the screen or breaking the screen edges.

Monitors come in different sizes and can be set to different resolutions. You will not know what sizes all the monitors that your site will be viewed on will be, but 1366 × 768 is a fairly standard resolution. What you want is for your pages to look composed for most monitors when that page is opened. If there is more page out of frame, some of your work may not be seen. You will at least have to include a "scroll down" message on your page. It is better to add multiple pages per project than to make your visitor scroll down.

Navigation

Look at a lot of professional designers' websites and pay attention to which ones navigate easily and which do not. Keep what you choose simple. A row of thumbnail photos

in a band, either up and down on the left side of the screen or horizontally across the top or bottom of the screen that link to other pages, is best.

Make This Part of Your Template, the Same on All Your Pages

This will cover navigating to multiple pages of one project. To navigate to other projects or sections of your website you will need another way. A common choice is to include at the top of each page a few text links (**Figure 13.3**) that can take you back to a "Home" page, from which you can go to other sections of the site, or to a "Portfolio" page (**Figure 13.4**) that you would go back to after each project. The choices are up to you, but creating a navigation plan in outline form early on in the creation of your site will save you time later in the process.

Order of Projects

There are no hard and fast rules here. One suggestion is that you start your portfolio with your second best project and end it with your best one. This makes a big impression when you start and then leaves your viewer with an even better one when they finish. Given that what you feel is your best work may not be what your viewer thinks makes too much worry about this a moot point. You don't want to go in chronological order because that will have no correlation to how the quality or type of show is figured into the order.

Start with what you think is good and then find an order you like that has enough variety to stay interesting without creating too many shocking changes.

Having friends critique your site as you create it is really the best way to get feedback on what is working and what is not.

Upkeep

Your website and portfolio will require diligence to keep them current. Get in the habit of adding a project to your website and portfolio soon after the production opens. This will also serve as a time for a last critique of that project: what you learned and what you could have done better. Periodic redesign to keep the site in step with its contents and just to make it more interesting and fun for yourself is not a bad thing.

FIGURE 13.3   *Website navigation: The menu page*

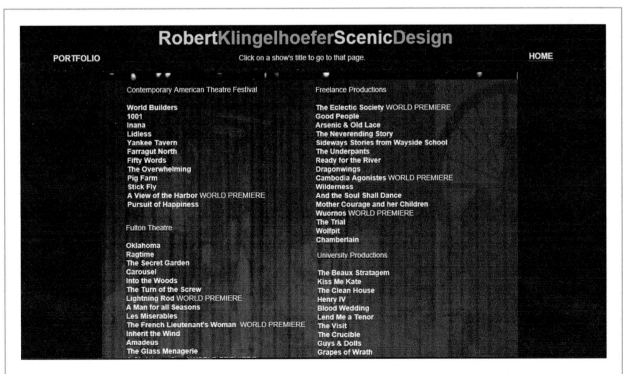

FIGURE 13.4   *Website navigation: The portfolio menu*

GRAD SCHOOL

You have finished your four years in an undergraduate program and now have to make some big decisions. That you went to college and got a bachelor's degree is a major accomplishment, and you should be proud, but the transition from high school to college is a pretty clear path. Your next decisions and the next few years of your career may be more difficult.

The next typical step in academia is to do a three-year master's program. This choice should be considered, first, as an issue of temperament. Are you ready to go right into grad school or would it benefit you to work for some period of time and then decide whether to go? What work would you do? No one leaves their undergraduate program, BFA in hand, and begins designing at the best professional theatres. You can try to put together a career designing in small theatres but will likely need to support yourself doing something else. That can be working in a theatre in another capacity, like in the prop department or as a scenic artist or stage carpenter. Assess your theatrical skills with the advice of your professors and decide what your most immediately marketable skills are. It will be important in this time to "keep your eyes on the prize" and try to get small design jobs that will keep you focused on your goal of working as a designer.

Consider that working for some period of time may be good for you emotionally in that it will give you a while to work and think before you take the next step. Grad school will be very intense and will only do what it is designed to do for you if you are ready. Grad school should be a time to develop toward a mastery of your skills and to begin to develop yourself as an artist. If you are not ready to do that, it will be a waste of time.

Should everyone go to grad school? No, of course not. Some choose to work for a while and then happily continue past the point where they feel the need to go to grad school. For the majority, however, it is probably a good choice. Grad school will develop your artistic skills, challenge your passion, and begin to network you in the industry. Attending a top grad school is a testament to your abilities that will be recognized as you move into the professional world and can be very helpful in getting started in developing a high level career. The reputation of the Yale School of Drama, for instance, and the level of the professional training it provides is without question,

especially in scene design. Ming Cho Lee is a legendary teacher, and the most important American designer of our time. Successful graduates of Yale's program enter the profession with strong advantages both in their training and in networking with student directors who are also moving into the profession.

Consider that all grad schools are different. Some, like Yale, are the highest quality training and the best networking, but these benefits can come at the price of a higher stress level. If you don't want to go that route, pick a school whose design professors you like personally and whose work you like. You will have three rigorous years working with these people, so choose carefully. They and the university as an institution should have professional connections to help you be ready to enter the profession when you get your MFA.

While these things that a good grad program will get you are important, the theatre is, thankfully, very forgiving of individual paths. Try to listen to your heart and the advice of professors and professionals who know you, and do what seems best.

One more consideration about grad school is that to teach at the university level it is generally required that you have an MFA. Academia is considered by many to be a safer career path than to work professionally, because it is a regular paycheck. One interpretation of these facts would seem to make a case for finishing your BFA, going immediately to grad school, and three years later, MFA in hand go for a steady teaching job. Here, I'm afraid, I have strong opinions. Scene design is an art and a craft. It is not an academic discipline. It is not like history, in which, to teach a freshman class is to lecture on dates, places, and historical figures. The difference is, I believe, that you must practice your art before you can teach it. While a few years between your BFA and your MFA may have enabled you to design a few shows professionally, you do a disservice to your future students, to yourself and to the profession to teach right out of grad school.

ASSISTING VERSUS DESIGNING

As you begin to look for work as a designer, with or without grad school, there are basically two career paths to choose from. It is possible to combine them, but most young designers usually end up mostly in one or the other.

The first path is to seek work as an assistant to an established designer. This works best in New York, but needs to be in a city with enough work that at least a few professional designers keep busy there and hire assistants. You will be hired if your skillset includes strengths that a certain designer requires, like drafting or model making. Every working designer is different in what they, personally, like to do, or choose to do, and what skills they want assistants to do for them. They are looking for assistants who can draft or build models at a very high professional level. The work their assistants do for them will be regarded as their own, so there is a lot of pressure that it be excellent.

Advancement in this path involves working successfully for your designer until they feel comfortable suggesting you for design assignments that they are offered but cannot, or choose not, to do.

This path has the advantages that you will learn a lot from the designer who employs you, make connections in the industry, and when you begin to get offers of your own, they may be at bigger and better theatres than would hire you without the pedigree of having worked with an established designer. This may happen quickly or take quite a while.

The other path involves beginning to design at whatever level of theatre will hire you. Generally, this will be, at first, smaller theatre companies with small budgets. Summer stock is not what it used to be but still offers start-up design opportunities. Basically in this option, you hang on, designing more and more in bigger and better theatres as you build your career.

This option has the advantage that you will begin designing your own work earlier, but it may be a long road until you get to more choice projects.

Again, an issue to think about here is your temperament. Will you be happy doing your own work in smaller theatres or working in a bigger pool but not designing for yourself for a while?

ACADEMIA, TV, AND FILM

The primary fields that relate to the theatre, and can offer other employment options are teaching and work in TV and film. Teaching can be very satisfying, especially if you begin it at the right time. One trap that many young designers fall into is that they take a teaching position at a small college in which they are a one-man band: the set designer, the technical director, the lighting and the sound designer. It is obviously very hard to be good at all these

areas, and the production process when one person is trying to do it all leads to a very high burnout rate.

Skills in Theatre Design translate very well into work in TV and film where salaries and budgets may be much higher. Making some forays into these areas is best taken into account in your choice of a grad school and who you choose to assist.

GETTING JOBS

It is often said that it's who you know in the theatre that gets you jobs, and there is a lot of truth to this. As previously stated, it is usually a director whom you have worked with or who has seen your work who will get you a design by asking the theatre to hire you. It may be someone else at the theatre, the artistic director or production manager, but it will likely be someone you know.

This "someone you know" will not be responsible for your success, however; your talent and hard work will. You must be ready, with all your skills polished, when that personal connection comes up.

Constantly trying to get better must be your life's goal. Take every design as a way to learn more and do better.

USA829

United Scenic Artists, Local 829, is the professional union of scenic, lighting, costume, and projection designers as well as scenic artists and computer artists. It is an autonomous local within IATSE, the International Alliance of Theatrical Stage Employees, Moving Picture Technicians, Artists and Allied Crafts of the United States, Its Territories and Canada.

Why Join

Membership is a milestone in a designer's career, demonstrating to the world that he is an acknowledged professional in the field. Membership is by examination, a rigorous process that ensures that those who achieve it are experienced practitioners of their art. Membership offers many advantages.

- Membership is a validation of your abilities that is recognized throughout the industry.

- As a member, work you do for major theatre companies will be covered by a collective bargaining agreement.

- If it is covered, you will have a union contract in place for that job that will offer protections, including minimum fees, working conditions, and terms of future use for your designs.

- If the job is for a smaller company that is not covered by a collective bargaining agreement, you are encouraged to sign an individual project agreement with the producing organization that will spell out many of the same terms and conditions.

- If either type of contract is signed, the employer will make a pension and welfare payment with the contract of 15 percent of the total fee to the union. This establishes a pension for you upon retirement and, with qualifying minimums, provides you with health and life insurance. As a self-employed contractor this may be your best option for having insurance.

- You are free at any time to do any work you choose, not covered by a collective bargaining agreement, unlike some unions in which you are only allowed to work under a union contract.

Making the step to join USA829 is a milestone, but when to join is a consideration.

When to Join

Generally, you should wait to join the union until you have some significant professional work under your belt. The examination process (see the next section) involves a portfolio review, and the work you show should be polished and professional. Also, if you are working only for small companies that you know will not sign an individual project agreement, then you will not be able to get the full advantages of membership. As soon as you are at a level where these conditions are not an issue, however, joining USA829 is a solid step in advancing your career.

How to Join

Go to USA829.org and click on the "Membership" tab. Information there will cover the Examination process.

NEW YORK, NEW YORK

Joining the union is a big step and one that will help move your career along. You will get instant respect in the profession when you are a USA829 member. Another milestone to consider is whether or when you will go to New York or one of the other major U.S. cities where you can do work at a higher level. The advantages to being in one of these cities—and New York is still the pinnacle of the profession, though this has lessened a bit in the last few decades—are that you will be in a market that offers a much greater number of possible places to work, and more of these theatres are known throughout the profession than are most theatres in smaller cities.

New York is the gold standard. Even work at smaller theatres in New York is instant attention and respect everywhere else. Your work will ultimately be what gets you jobs, but being a New York designer doesn't hurt. In my time there, the 1980s and early '90s, a New York address and a 212 area code was money in the bank, especially impressive outside New York. This is still true.

Chicago is another good choice, as are Boston, San Francisco, Seattle, Philadelphia, and Washington D.C. There is good theatre in Los Angeles, but not as much, and it is eclipsed by the film and television industries.

It can be good for you to test your mettle by working in a major market. Again trust your temperament. If the idea of living in a big city is not for you, don't do it, but you will have lessened the possibilities for your career growth and you might regret it later on. If you're going to do it, do it while you're young.

BUSINESS RESPONSIBILITY

If you have not yet joined the union, it is advisable to create your own contract to spell out the terms with which you will work on a project. Theatres will have their own contracts that they will offer you, but these, even from the nicest companies, may be more about protecting themselves than protecting you. Take some responsibility for the business of your art, and you will be happier and more ready to do the work after some basics get covered.

Designers are infamous for caring much more for their art than for the business part of the job, but you can do both.

Go to the union website (https://www.usa829.org/Portals/0/Documents/Contracts/UPAs/2015-2017-New-

LA-Address/SDA_Theatre_Agreement_2015-2017_C. pdf) and download the "Standard Designer's Agreement— Theatre 2015–2017" and read it. This document contains language that covers a wide range of situations in the field that you should know. It is the document to which union contracts of different types refer.

If you don't see most of these things in contracts you are offered, set up a meeting with the managing director or business manager of the theatre and talk about these issues. Explain to them, nicely, that there are some things you would like addressed in your contract for clarity and the protection of both yourself and them.

Good Contracts Make Good Business Partners

The first section of the "Standard Designer's Agreement—Theatre 2015–2017" outlines some basics of what the designer should expect from the producer, and vice versa.

The Designer will provide visual presentations, specifications, selections, and/or approvals, and consultation customary for the execution of designs. The details of these responsibilities will be spelled out later.

The Producer will provide, on a timely basis, all necessary theater dimensions, production schedules, and/or other information required by the Designer to fulfill his/her obligations to the Production.

The Producer will tell the Designer about pre-production conferences connected with the Production, and the Designer will, at the request of the Producer, attend such conferences in so far as his commitments permit.

The Designer will be responsible for the completion and delivery to the Producer of all designs and design specifications. A reasonable design period of not less than four (4) weeks is necessary prior to submission of the design for bid or beginning construction.

The Designer shall not be required to perform the work of the production staff.

Producers of small projects when you're starting out may assume you will be doing the painting, prop work, or even some construction. This should be made clear immediately.

The Producer agrees to engage adequate quality personnel for the proper realization and installation of the designs for the Production. Unless otherwise agreed to you will not be expected to perform functions other than designing the set.

Duties of the Designer

A. The Scenic Designer shall design the setting and render the following services, if required, and agrees:

1. *To complete sketches or sketch model(s) of the settings as necessary.*
2. *To supply working drawings, specifications for construction and color schemes or sketches as needed by the date specified in the contract Rider.*
3. *To design, select, or approve properties required for the production, including draperies and furniture.*
4. *To supply specifications for competitive bids for scenery or property suppliers mutually satisfactory to the Producer and the Scenic Designer.*
5. *To attend appropriate rehearsals of the Production and to coordinate the scenic rehearsals when needed.*
6. *To design and/or coordinate special scenic effects for the production, including but not limited to slides and projections.*

This contract should, of course, include **the Fee** and how and when it will be paid. It is customary to break the fee into thirds with 1/3 paid on contract signing, 1/3 paid when all drawings and specifications are due, and 1/3 on opening.

Additional Work

1. For any substantial changes or additions to scenery, costumes and/or projections during the construction period, requested by and/or approved by Producer, the Producer and Designer shall agree upon additional compensation to be negotiated in good faith.

This means that if during the production process the producer wants to change a lot of things in the set or add a lot of new scenery that was not previously a part of the deal, he must pay you more for this new work.

After the show opens, if the producer wants you to change your work, he has to pay you. The 829 contract makes this into a paid by day rate. This can help clarify what you're being asked to do because you and the producer will have to meet, discuss the new work, and agree how many days of work it is for you. This is the number of days you will be paid for.

Next, is a big one, because having this clear and agreed to at the beginning of the job will prevent this area of constant struggle and miscommunication:

Reimbursable Expenses

A. The Producer shall reimburse the Designer for expenses incurred in the creation of the design for the Production including, but not limited to, the following: art and drafting materials, supplies for model building, meals while in transit at the request of Producer, research materials, telephone, fax, postage, shipping, and copying.

Reimbursable Expenses do NOT include, nor shall the Designer be responsible to pay for, any materials necessary for the implementation of the design nor that are included in the Production's production budget (such as lumber, equipment rentals, costume materials or projection content).

B. The Producer agrees to make funds or forms of credit available, in advance, for production related expenditures.

The Producer shall notify the Designer prior to the commencement of work if they are tax exempt and if so, Designer shall use best effort to use a legally executed Tax Exempt Form as provided by the Producer.

All cash expenditures will be accounted for to the Producer in the form of receipts or other proofs of purchase, submitted to the Producer no later than thirty (30) days after the official opening of the production. Producer shall reimburse the Designer for receipted expenses within fourteen (14) business days of submission.

A rider to your contract should set a limit on how much the producer will reimburse you so both sides understand it. This will let you know how much money you can get for the model you are about to build, or you may make it clear to the producer that you do not intend to build a model for this show because it will be too expensive.

Your contract should cover what happens in the future to your design:

All uses of the design, subsequent to the initial Production as detailed in the Cover Sheet shall be according to the terms of the Subsequent Use Addendum of this Agreement.

The designer shall be offered the first opportunity to render Design Services for any future production, remounting or revival of the Production, produced, co-produced, leased, licensed or assigned by the Producer or its licensee(s) subject to the then current United Scenic Artists rates and conditions.

Subsequent use covers a number of situations concerning the future of your design after opening night.

Co-productions require an adjustment to the fee because you are deigning to satisfy two theatre companies and two theatre spaces, and this will be more work. A common amount for this is to add 50 percent of what the fee would have been at a single theatre.

Tours also need to reflect the additional work in your compensation.

Property rights and subsequent use are important as well. Property rights clarify who really owns what. Typical is that the theatre owns the scenery but the designer owns the design. What if the producer sells the scenery after the production closes, which he has the right to do—does he owe you? This should be discussed ahead of time. If the scenery is going to be used for stock pieces or for parts in a new design, he will not. Because you own the rights to the design, if the subsequent use involves another theatre using the set you designed to do the play you designed it for, you get paid.

Postponement and abandonment covers the usually pretty rare situation of what will happen if the producer at some point during the process decides to not open the production. Where you are in your process will determine how much of your fee still applies.

Billing is how and where your name will appear in programs, posters, and advertising for the production. This can seem a small matter when you're excited to begin work but can piss you off later when you feel ignored or left out.

Generally, look to negotiate **most-favored-nation status** on many of these issues, which means if the lighting designer gets the use of a car out of town or the costume designer gets an addition to her reimbursable amount, you do too. If anybody gets something, everybody gets it. This can remove stress and hurt feelings and make it easier for everyone to get along.

Safety liability and insurance is a big issue that may never cause you problems but is worth having in every contract you sign in case it should be needed. Basically this uses language that states you as the designer are responsible "for visual specifications only," and if the producer or his agents, the shop that is building your set, deem anything to be unsafe, you will make changes to correct it. This protects you from any responsibility if there should be an accident and someone is hurt by the scenery. It puts the responsibility on those building the scenery to decide what is safe and what is not and to be responsible for calling attention to it. If a safety issue is brought up, you must act quickly to make it right but will then not be liable.

Travel, housing, and per diem is another category that is often the source of much stress and confusion and is best dealt with in the contract early on.

The Producer agrees to provide, when the Designer(s) and/or Assistants are required to travel away from their point of residence for work on the Production:

A. *Economy class transportation on a first class carrier. If the Designer elects to use his/her own motor transportation, he/she shall be reimbursed for his/her expenses up to but not to exceed the cost of transportation as set forth above.*

B. *Transportation costs to and from both, his/her home and the Theatre, and the airport,* *terminal, or depot, whichever is applicable, by the least expensive reasonable means of transportation.*

C. *Safe and secure single occupancy, clean and sanitary hotel accommodations with private bath.*

D. *Per Diem meal allowance as listed in the applicable Rate Sheet.*

E. *If a Designer agrees to remain in residence at a Not-for-Profit Theatre for an extended period, the Per Diem may be negotiated at the IRS meal allowance rate for the year in which the travel occurs.*

A FINAL THOUGHT

The theatre is a very curious business. On the one hand, it is an art form centuries old with all the gravitas that brings. On the other hand, it is a very mom-and-pop business, small, personal, and idiosyncratic. Please realize that, if you have made it your life's work, you are part of something important. You are part of a select, yet very diverse, group of people who get to practice a very special craft and art. You and your collaborators—and included here is everyone from the director, the other designers, all the craftspeople and technicians, to the performers who will complete the work—take very base materials, and like the alchemists of old, use them to create something that will draw audiences to sit in a darkened room and experience magic.

Not a bad way to spend your time.

INDEX

Note: Figures and tables are denoted with *italicized* page numbers.

professional realities 269–79; assistant designer
positions as 274–5; billing as 278; business
responsibility and contracts as 276–9;
fees and expenses as 277–9; getting jobs
as 275; grad school considerations for
274; liability insurance as 279; New York

and other major market work as 276;
portfolios and websites as 269–72, *270–1*,
273; property rights as 278; teaching/
academia opportunities as 274, *275*;
television and film opportunities as 275;
training and education as 1–2, 269, 274;
USA829 membership as 275–6
projects: The Designable Idea 106; Model
Play 138; The Project Play 52; Project Play
Complete 162; Research a Designer 30–1;
Researching the Project Play 85–6; Sketch
and Plan 31, *32*; Space for the Project Play
139–40; Stage Pictures 52; Text 64–5
property rights 278
proportion: door 198, *200*; models reflecting
178; refining, in design 150, *150*; window
199, *201*
props: color swatches for 264; designer's prop
list of 263–4; fabric specifications for 264,
267; furniture as (see furniture/furniture
blocks); research on 264, 267; sketches of
253; staging with 253, 263–6, *267*; written
notes on 264–6
proscenium stage: groundplan of 188; 17th
and 18th century rise of 10; single set
productions on 191; as theatrical space
109, 118, *119*, 120–1, 127, 129, 131–2,
131–2, *133–7*, *133–8*

Ragtime 88, *88*, 166, 246–50, *246–51*
raked floors 197, *198*
reading lists 30, 64, 85
Ready for the River 181, *181*
realism: Brechtian 19; selective 142, *143*;
simplified 28; as style 54
recycling styles and themes 23
Reinhart, Max 13
renderings: as artwork of communication
166–77, *167–76*, 253, 272; darkness
conveyed in 167, *168–71*, 169; digital
rendering techniques 169, 172–4, *172–6*;
final package including 253; portfolio
and website including 272; resources
and materials for 174, 177; traditional
rendering techniques 166–7, *167*, *168*
research 67–86; accuracy of information from
77; acquisitive 71–3, *71–3*; combining key
images from 77; designable idea based on
91, 93, *94–5*, *95*, *98*; digital tools for *68*, 77,
84–5; on economic style 70; on historical
period of setting 67–75, *69–75*, 76, 91; on
location 76, 91; making connections from 79,
98; nonspecific 76; on other productions 76;
photographic 70, 264; on play and playwright
76; pre-photographic 68–9; production bible
of 77; production case studies reflecting
77–84, *78–84*; on props 264, 267; quantity
and depth of 76–7; research agenda for 77;
research file compiled from 84–5; topics to
research 76–7
reversal of design 148, *148*

revolve, for moving scenery 225, *225*, 232,
233–5, 235–7
Riders to the Sea 146
The Ring Cycle 23, *23*, 24, 24–5
rocking chairs, meaning associated with 90
rocking horses, meaning associated with 90
Romeo and Juliet 60, *61*, *142*
Rosebrand 223
Rosenthal, Todd 29
Royal Shakespeare Company 20

scenic design: artwork of communication for
163–89, 253, 269–72, *270–1*, *273*;
contemporary 5, 18–33; craft and art of 1,
3–8; designable idea for 59, 87–106; design
aspects of 3–5, 141–62, 219–20, *270–1*,
270–2; director-designer collaboration on
21, 23–4, 35–52; history of 9–18, 28–9;
introduction to 1–2; moving scenery in
151, 219–51 (see also hanging or flying
scenery); productions using (see productions;
productions, specific); professional realities
for designer 1–2, 269–79; projects
practicing (see projects); reading lists on
30, 64, 85; research informing 67–86, 91,
93, *94–5*, 95, 98, 264, 267; for single set
productions 127–32, 191–218; space in
4–5, 20, 107–40; staging of 17, 253–68;
text as basis for 4, 36–7, 53–65, 74, 91;
training and education in 1–2, 269, 274
scenography 21
scrims 223, *223–4*
script see text
The Secret Garden 119
section, drafting of 188–9, 253
selection: design strategy of 142, *143–5*, *144*;
minimalism as 142, *144*, *144–5*; selective
realism as 142, *143*
shift plot 253–6, *256*
Shklovsky, Victor 19
shop: commercial 261; cost-out process for
260; designer drawings provided to 188,
253, 261–2; designer working with 261–2;
scenic art production in 262–3, *264*;
theatre's 262
show decks 224
shutters and French doors, meaning
associated with 90
sightlines: digital renderings checking 173, *174*;
groundplan checking 188; section checking
188–9; space considerations of 118, 120,
122, 123–7, *124–6*, 134, *134–5*
Simonson, Lee *18*
simplification: modern stage design use of 13,
17; simplified realism 28
single set productions 191–218; box sets for
191, *192*; breaklines in 203, *203*; ceilings
for 193, *194–5*; doors for 197–9, *199–200*;
edge options for 191, *193*; floors for
193, 196–7, *196–8*; interior elements
of 191–206, *192–206*; molding for 199,